Sunset
Complete
Home Storage

By the Editors of Sunset Books and Sunset Magazine

Outdoor tools and equipment queue up neatly along this boldly striped garage wall (Garage, Attic & Basement Storage, page 13).

LANE PUBLISHING CO. • Menlo Park, California

Cover: Here are ways to gain the most from tight spaces throughout the house. *Top:* Careful closet planning creates storage for two wardrobes in one short wall (*Bedroom & Bath Storage,* page 34). *Lower left:* Hardworking unit houses dishes, flatware, linens, and wine, along with small buffet (*Kitchen Storage,* page 57). *Lower right:* Mini-loft holds bulky items above car hood in otherwise wasted space (*Garage, Attic & Basement Storage,* page 33). Cover design: Naganuma Design & Direction.

Editor, Sunset Books:
    Elizabeth L. Hogan

Fifth printing February 1989

Your complete storage handbook...

Most of us appreciate, and live more comfortably with, orderly surroundings. Yet, as families grow, possessions accumulate, and storage space shrinks proportionately, it becomes a challenge—sometimes a perplexing one—to keep things in the tidy, good order we'd like.

For their ingenuity in meeting this challenge, the three *Sunset* titles that make up this anthology have each met with widespread, grateful readership. Now, this complete, three-in-one handbook presents hundreds of answers to storage riddles throughout the home. For every household item that you may need to keep in good order, from boats to baby powder, canned goods to cancelled checks, you'll find ideas that are simple, practical, flexible—and good-looking, as well.

Contents

KITCHEN STORAGE

Hundreds of ideas for food and wine storage, cabinets and pantries, work centers and islands, home offices and hobby areas. Dozens of kitchen storage aids to buy or build—shelves, drawer dividers, utility carts, wall grids, spice racks, and more. Reference list of cabinet and storage manufacturers.

BEDROOM & BATH STORAGE

Innovative ways to maximize storage space in bedrooms, bathrooms, and closets. Ideas for utilizing underbed space, making bedrooms double as hobby or work areas, organizing closets and dressing areas, choosing the right bathroom cabinetry, storing personal-grooming appliances. Do-it-yourself projects. Unusual new storage products.

GARAGE, ATTIC & BASEMENT STORAGE

Practical and creative ideas for storing specific items such as sports equipment, seasonal clothing, books and documents, luggage, and more. Tips for organizing workshop tools, garden gear, recyclables. How to improve attic access, reduce moisture buildup and temperature fluctuations in the basement, utilize overhead space in the garage.

Sunset

Ideas for
Kitchen
Storage

Ideas & Projects

By the Editors
of Sunset Books
and
Sunset Magazine

LANE PUBLISHING CO. ● Menlo Park, California

We thank . . .

. . . the many architects, designers, and homeowners whose ideas have come together in this book. A special acknowledgment is due Allmilmö Cabinets by Plus Kitchens, and Dada North American, Inc. To Kathryn L. Arthurs and Hilary Hannon go our thanks for their work in assembling the color section.

Editor, Sunset Books:
  Elizabeth L. Hogan

Seventh printing March 1989

Cover: Open Shelves, Hang-ups, and Built-ins

Cooking utensils, measuring cups, and mixer attachments queue up along a strip of stainless steel hooks (made by a fabricator of store display racks). Handsome beech counter below features a built-in unit to power a number of attachments, including this juicer. Open shelves above hold stacks of dishes and a set of custom-made acrylic canisters; tabs on canisters pull to dispense staples. Architect: David Stovell. Photographed by Nikolay Zurek. Cover design by Zan Fox.

Book Editors:
Maureen Williams Zimmerman
Helen Sweetland

Staff Researcher: **Donice G. Evans**

Contributing Editor: **Marian May**

Design: **Roger Flanagan**

Illustrations: **Joe Seney**

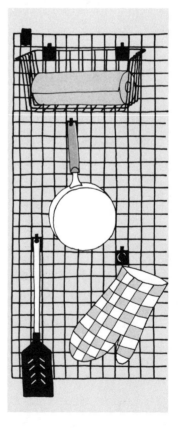

Contents

INTRODUCTION

Maximum use calls for maximum access

"I need more storage space!" is a familiar and frequent wail from the kitchen, usually as something new, like a food processor or casserole dish, is being crammed into an already bulging cupboard.

Generally, it's not just a matter of too little space. Somehow, you always make room—stacking, pushing aside, shoving into an inaccessible corner—with the result that the new utensil or appliance, or whatever it displaced, is rarely dug out and used.

Maximum use calls for maximum access. Since this principle is basic to serious kitchen storage planning, this book focuses on ideas for *active* storage, the placement of things you use regularly.

Guidelines for good storage

Whether you're trying to increase the storage in your kitchen in the simplest and least expensive way possible, or designing the ultimate in storage for a brand-new kitchen, these guidelines can help you through the project.

First, determine your needs and priorities. If you love to bake, you'll need more than average space for utensils, special baking pans, and perhaps a heavy-duty mixer. If your specialty is stir-fried dishes, you'll want a place for sharp knives (see pages 52–53), a wok, and a cutting board next to the cooktop. Whatever your interests, put yourself in the middle of your kitchen and mentally put away all the equipment you use most often; you'll then have an individualized storage plan that meets your needs.

The second step is to choose the right kind of storage for your needs. Though built-in cabinets (pages 8–15) and shelves (pages 32–39) carry the main burden of storage in most kitchens, you don't necessarily have to rip out the old cabinets and install new ones. Instead, consider the exciting variety of auxiliary storage units you see pictured throughout this book. Stacking bins are inexpensive, handy containers for cleaning equipment, produce, even toys. Handsome hooks and hang-

At the root of modern kitchen storage: the Hoosier cabinet

Many of our modern ideas about kitchen storage and food preparation centers aren't new at all; in fact, they can be traced back to those big, boxy cabinets that revolutionized American kitchens—the Hoosiers. Manufactured from the late 1800s until World War II, these hold-it-all cabinets were the first mass-produced, popular kitchen aids to combine a food preparation area and a multitude of storage compartments in one compact unit. Early ads for the Hoosier cabinets claimed that they reduced kitchen work by half—and many housewives would probably have agreed.

Every cubic inch of the Hoosier was put to good use. There were lots of drawers for spices, silverware, knives, and mixing spoons. Some models were also available with sugar and cornmeal bins, a tin-lined bread drawer, and a built-in flour bin and sifter—welcome luxuries in the days when the family bread supply was baked at home.

The two big doors in the base of the Hoosier opened to reveal pot storage on shelves only half the depth of the cabinet. This allowed ample room on the inside of the doors for racks of pot lids and cooky sheets, a convenience now being designed into many contemporary cabinets.

Overhead were cabinets, sometimes behind frosted glass, for china and crystal treasures. Everyday dishes were stacked conveniently in the wide opening that was often closed off with a roll-up tambour door.

Tying the Hoosier all together was a recessed porcelain-enameled work counter that was pulled out whenever extra table space was needed—at jelly-making time, at Thanksgiving for wrestling the turkey, or for afternoon lemonade and homework.

When modern kitchens with built-in cabinets became the rule instead of the exception, the Hoosier, having loaned out all its ideas for compact storage and work space, was relegated to the garage.

But the disappearance of the Hoosier cabinet was merely temporary. Today, these handsome almost-antiques are being incorporated into some contemporary kitchens. Look for them in antique stores—if you're not lucky enough to have one hidden away in your basement or garage.

ers can hold aprons and dishtowels, as well as pots and pans. And lazy Susans can bring to life the lost space in the back of a corner cabinet.

Finally, how do you obtain the units you've selected? At one extreme, this step can mean the considerable expense of having new built-in cabinetry custom created by a cabinetmaker; at the other, it involves no more than buying or building some simple hanging devices, racks, drawer organizers, or shelves. A quick walk through your local hardware store or kitchen cabinet showroom will turn up lots of ideas; a more concentrated survey of what's on the market can start with brochures from the major manufacturers (see pages 78–79).

Guidelines for maximum access

Following some simple guidelines will maximize space and accessibility in your kitchen, no matter what kind of storage structures you have.

• Store frequently used items between knee and eye level.

• Store items where you use them most. If you use an item in several locations, store it at the first or last place you use it (for example, dinnerware can be stored near the dinner table or next to the dishwasher). If it's an inexpensive item, consider buying several and storing one in each place you use it.

• Items used together should be stored together. It doesn't make any sense to keep your electric hand mixer in a wall cabinet on one side of the kitchen and the beaters in a drawer on the other side.

• Design cabinets and shelves to the cook's height and reach (keeping in mind that any substantial departure from the norm could be a factor if you decide to sell the house). In an existing kitchen that can't be adjusted, add a roll-around work table that's the right height; use a sturdy step stool to reach high wall cabinets.

• Don't stack items on top of one another. That way you won't have to move several items you don't need before you reach the one you do need.

• Arrange canned and packaged goods in a single row on a door rack or on shallow shelves. With single-row storage you won't have to shove cans aside to find the one you want.

• Use inexpensive storage aids such as door racks, turntables, drawer dividers, and roll-out shelves to customize existing cabinets.

• Review your storage situation from time to time. If you haven't used an item in ages, consider moving it out of the kitchen or giving it away. Reserve precious kitchen storage space for items you use regularly.

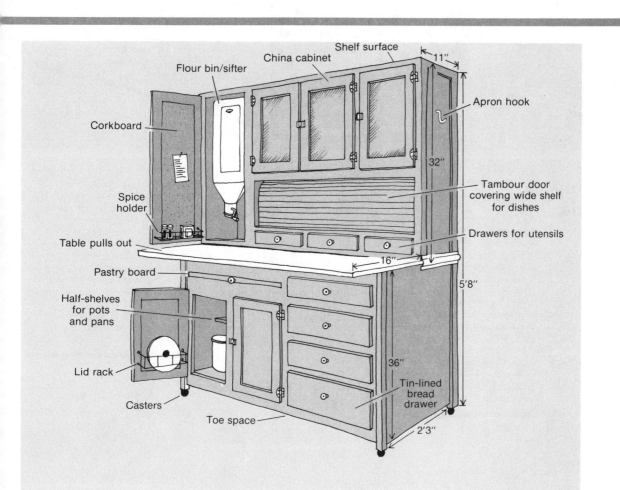

INTRODUCTION
Consider the tasks at hand

Imagine it's time to add the crucial ingredient to the dish you're cooking. You must keep stirring, but what you need is on the other side of the room. If you often find yourself doing unplanned reaching and stretching exercises in your kitchen, it may be time to rearrange your storage.

Most kitchen activities take place within the triangle formed by the three major kitchen appliances—the refrigerator, the range, and the sink. Think of each point

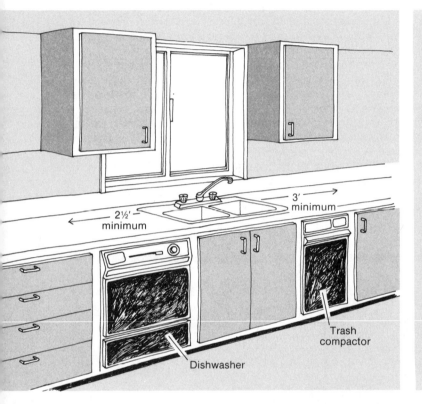

Sink Center Besides the obvious—a sink—this center may include a dishwasher, garbage disposer, and trash compactor, as well as cabinets and drawers. In this area, food is rinsed and trimmed, wastes and recyclables are disposed of, dishes are washed and stored.

Provide storage space for chopping board, food preparation utensils, wastebasket, and dishwashing and cleaning supplies. Stow dishes and glassware as close as possible to dishwasher for easy unloading. Underneath sink is a convenient spot for storing paper bags.

Cooking Center Range—or cooktop with separate oven—is focus of cooking center, which can also include a microwave or convection oven and several electric cooking appliances.

In base cabinets, store pots and pans, cooky sheets, roasting racks, and muffin tins. Fill drawers with spoons and spatulas and other cooking utensils. You'll also want to keep potholders and condiments within easy reach.

of the triangle as a separate and distinct center; then plan storage appropriate to each. If you have some extra space, include a food preparation center, as well.

Above all, keep an open mind when you're planning your work centers. If space is at a premium in your kitchen, combine some of the centers; but if space is not a problem, you may want to develop additional work centers—an office center, play center, dining center, or beverage center, for example—to fit your own needs.

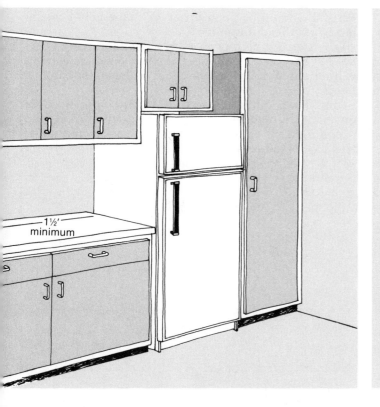

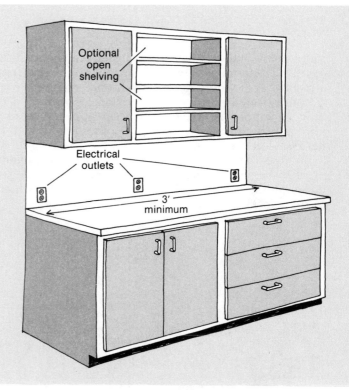

Refrigerator Center

Often, this center consists of not only a refrigerator and several cabinets, but also a floor-to-ceiling pantry or broom closet wedged between refrigerator and adjacent wall. If you store nonperishable food items near refrigerator, putting groceries away is a snap. Tuck plastic wrap, foil, plastic bags, and freezer containers in a nearby drawer or cabinet.

In hard-to-reach cabinet above refrigerator, keep extra rolls of paper towels or infrequently used items such as picnic supplies and party goods.

Preparation Center

If you have extra room in your kitchen, design a food preparation center with storage for small appliances—food processor, toaster, mixer, can opener, for example. Locating center near refrigerator and/or sink simplifies mixing and serving chores. Keep cook books and recipe boxes close by. With canisters, mixing bowls, and small utensils in cabinets and drawers, you'll waste little motion preparing meals.

CABINETS
Setting the storage style

More than anything else in the kitchen, cabinets set the style and determine how the room looks—ranging from a mellow spot where family and friends congregate, to a sophisticated European-style kitchen with a slick modern emphasis. Often, the total appearance of a kitchen can be suggested simply by the style, finish, or hardware of the cabinet doors.

Style must also relate to function, because cabinets need to be workhorses, able to conceal behind closed doors literally hundreds of items you'll want on hand in the kitchen.

If you're not planning to install new cabinets, you can update the looks of your old ones—and sometimes get more work out of them, too—simply by replacing or redecorating the cabinet doors or changing simple accessories such as door pulls.

• Remove old doors and drawer fronts; build new ones from lengths of ¾-inch oak or oak plywood panels.

• Attach a decorative grid of half-rounds. Or remove old moldings, then sand and repaint or restain the cabinets for an uncluttered look.

• Leaving the framework as is, paint the doors a fresh new color.

• Install sliding or push-up doors, especially convenient in overhead locations.

• When there's no room for a cabinet door, hang venetian blinds, canvas curtains that slide on rings along a wall-mounted dowel supported in midspan, or bamboo blinds.

• Round, smoothly sanded holes in the corner of a door are a substitute for door pulls. A decorative wood strip extending a bit below the bottom of each wall cabinet door also eliminates the need for pulls.

• Cover just the cabinet doors with wallpaper, or go all out and cover everything—walls, ceiling, even the refrigerator. (Covering an entire room with small-print wallpaper will make the room look larger.)

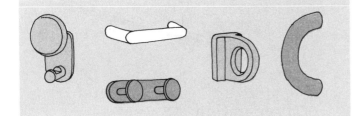

▲
DOUBLE-USE KNOBS

These cabinet knobs and handles can accommodate potholders and towels.

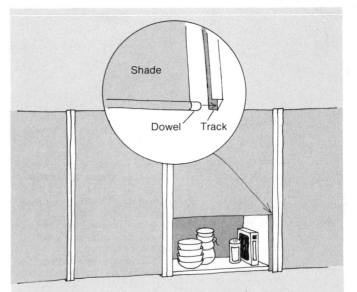

**SHADES ENCLOSE ▶
CABINETS**

Bright fabric, canvas, or heavy plastic shades replace cabinet doors. Dowels in bottom hems run in tracks along cabinet sides. Pulls can be added.

◄ BEFORE: DARK AND DULL WITH STANDARDIZED STORAGE

Small, drab kitchen is overwhelmed by heavy, dark cabinetry. In spite of window at left, room is dark and faintly oppressive. Wall and base cabinets have typical stationary shelves.

◄ AFTER: BRIGHT AND INVITING WITH SPECIALIZED STORAGE

Though no walls were moved, kitchen appears larger. Mirror replaces window, and newly symmetrical room has focal point: glass-doored display cabinet at end. Office at opposite end of kitchen is completely integrated into cabinet design and is better suited to owner's needs than additional food or utensil storage. Several base cabinets feature pull-out wire shelves. Architect: Gilbert Oliver.

CABINETS

Distinctive designs for a unique kitchen look

Cabinets are the basic elements both in your kitchen storage scheme and your kitchen decor. If you have a new kitchen on the drawing board you'll want to give a lot of thought to cabinet placement, style, and interior elements.

In placing the cabinets, work to achieve the most effective floor plan and work-center arrangement (see pages 6–7). Then let your imagination take over. Manufacturers can supply you with their latest cabinet designs (see pages 78–79), or you can work with an architect, designer, or cabinetmaker to create your own. For ideas and inspiration, examine the many cabinet variations that appear throughout this book.

Cabinets are usually designated as base or wall units, but some extend from the floor to the ceiling. Depths can vary. Ends of peninsulas and corners take special thought, as do islands of cabinetry. If you prefer windows to wall cabinets, substitute low shelves or a separate pantry (see pages 42–47) for traditional wall cabinets.

Experiment with style and color. Cabinet doors can hinge open, slide, or roll; they may or may not have a visible framework; they can overlap the framing or fit flush; they can have molding or be unadorned. Pulls range from the invisible to the highly ornamental. Paint, stain, wallpaper, fabric, glass, tile, plastic, wood, and metal—all are suitable for cabinets. Your choices of color, pattern, and texture are boundless.

Cabinets: custom or prefab?

Cabinets are probably the most costly items in your kitchen, especially if you order them custom built. Custom cabinets can easily skyrocket to more than twice the price of prefabricated units.

Of course, custom cabinets offer the greatest flexibility, since they're designed and built to fill specific needs and spaces. To reduce costs, use custom cabinets only where there are unusual structural problems. Instead of having dividers built into these units, install inexpensive plastic trays and sliding shelves.

Fortunately, a wealth of ready-made, standard-sized units is available in wood, metal, plastic laminate, or a combination of materials. The best cabinets have easy-gliding drawers and adjustable shelves; many have swing-out corner storage units, pull-up shelves, and divided tray storage.

Other ready-to-go possibilities range from skinny pull-out cupboards for canned goods to tall cabinets with louvered doors that conceal an entire laundry area. It's even possible to find one large cabinetry unit with cooktop, refrigerator, and fold-down table.

Fairly new on the prefabricated market are the elegantly modern units imported from Europe. One firm offers more than 40 door styles and colors. Outfitted with vinyl-coated-wire baskets that glide out smoothly, these miracle storage pieces have a place for everything. As costly as many custom cabinets, the units are generally ordered through an architect or designer. Be prepared to wait as long as 6 months for delivery.

▲
OPEN TO VIEW: CHEERFUL RED CABINETS

Glossy, tomato-tone wall and base cabinets brighten a house that has generous expanses of white wall. Loft kitchen is open on one side to floors above and below.
Architect: Willard Martin of Martin/Soderstrom/Matteson.

◄ **LOUVERS FOR TEXTURE, VENTILATION**

Louvered cabinet doors of light-colored wood provide airy effect, especially when combined with overhead plant mezzanine. Louvered doors are especially good for ventilation in hot weather; circulating air keeps packaged food fresh. Architect: James Oliver.

▲ **COMBINING CABINET STYLES**

Elegant smoked glass coexists well with sophisticated ridged plastic laminate. Each cabinet serves a different purpose: behind glass, display pieces attract admiration; plastic laminate doors conceal more utilitarian kitchen gear. Design: Plus Kitchens.

Also available is a new, durable wood cabinet that snaps securely together without nails or glue—a boon to the barely handy man or woman. Referred to as the 10-minute cabinet, it requires no special tools.

Buying stock sizes

Stock cabinets come in standardized sizes. Before you place your order, plan and measure very carefully. It's often wise to ask the supplier to check your measurements.

To minimize costs, use the widest cabinets available that will fit into the space. One wide unit will cost considerably less than several narrow ones.

	BASE CABINETS	WALL CABINETS
Depth	24"	12" to 15"
Height	34½" (allows for 1½" countertop). Standard finished height is 36".	12" to 36" (15", 18", 30" are most used)
Width	9" to 60". From 9" to 36", increments are 3"; above 36", increments are 6".	

CABINETS

Corners call for access ideas

▲ CORNER SPACE CAPTURED WITH DOORS ON THE DIAGONAL

Angling doors diagonally across this corner opened up space that's often lost. Appliances and other kitchen gear rest on triangular shelves.
Architect: William B. Remick.

◄ FLOOR-TO-CEILING LAZY SUSAN

Taking a good idea to its logical conclusion, corner lazy Susan measures 12 feet from top to bottom. Three sections, reached through separate doors, turn independently of each other. Each ¾-inch plywood tray measures 36 inches in diameter and has an aluminum lip. Middle section stores most-used equipment, bottom section is for less-used items, and top—reached via ladder—is for kitchen gear that's seldom used.
Architect: William B. Remick.

Small muffin tins and cake pans have been known to disappear forever into the far reaches of base cabinet corners. If your shelves extend into an unreachable corner, you can either position a ready-made lazy Susan in the corner or store only objects large enough to grab at one end and pull out.

But when you're remodeling cabinets or installing new ones, you can solve the corner problem. If your difficult corner is on an interior wall, open the other side and you'll have built-in shelves or a cabinet for the adjoining room, too. Utilize a corner on an outside wall to hold a wastebasket or recycling bins—they can be concealed behind a kitchen cabinet door, yet be accessible from outdoors.

More corner ideas: Design new cabinets to turn the corner on the diagonal (see photographs on page 12). Eliminate the vertical center post in the corner cabinet for easier access to what's inside. Use double doors that swing outward from the corner intersection or a double-hinged door that folds out of the way. Turntables attached to a door, built into the cabinet, or designed to pull out from the corner increase access.

▲
BASE CABINET ROUNDABOUT

Typically difficult cabinet corner received special treatment: L-shaped door opens both sides of corner, and built-in lazy Susan matches cabinets. Extra-high edges on shelves prevent spills. Architect: Ron Yeo.

◄ **CORNER EXPANSION CREATES PANTRY**

Instead of ending kitchen with a blank wall, or two difficult cabinet corners, owners created a walk-in pantry closet. Three walls of pantry provide storage. Appliance "garage" at end of sink counter is recessed into pantry space; appliances slide out onto kitchen counter when needed, disappear later behind tambour door.

CABINETS

Pull-outs to fill almost any need

Those narrow spaces between cabinets or next to appliances cry out for specialized pull-out storage. Cans lined up one deep, flat pans and cooky sheets, pot lids, rows of packaged food, bottles and cans of spices—all are popular items to store in pull-outs.

Ranging from knife racks a few inches square to floor-to-ceiling pantries, pull-outs glide in and out on strong slides or casters.

Adding specialized pull-out storage is easiest when you're installing new cabinetry or drastically modifying old. A number of stock cabinet lines feature pull-outs; you can also have them custom-built.

More pull-out (and drawer) ideas are on pages 50–51.

▲ BAKING CENTER IN CUSTOM UNITS

Pull-out at left has two coated-wire baskets and a deep bottom bin. Solid front panel blends with the rest of cabinetry. Baking center also includes auxiliary sink and a trio of drawers for staples. Architect: Gilbert Oliver.

◄ TALL PANTRY PULLS OUT

Gliding smoothly on heavy-duty hardware, one of a pair of birch and alder pull-out pantries plays its part right in middle of kitchen, not off in the wings where most pantries are located. Architect: Michael D. Moyer of The Architectural Design Group.

◄ RANGE-SIDE ACCESSIBILITY

Scaled-down version of tall pantry shown at left, this base cabinet component puts spices and condiments within easy reach of cook. Narrow cabinet with vertical dividers on other side of range provides balance.

▲ SIDE-BY-SIDE PULL-OUT VARIATIONS

One of these pull-outs has two levels: top is a coated-wire rack sized for spices; below are generous compartments for bottles of oil, vinegar, and seasonings. Just to the right, three wire baskets for produce pull out smoothly like drawers; closed, cabinet door conceals them.

◄ BETWEEN REFRIGERATOR AND SINK

Below counter level, strategically located pull-out combines dishtowel rack with miscellaneous storage. High sides around base prevent even tall boxes from toppling. Shallow shelves above counter store glasses and mugs. Architect: Paden Prichard.

WORK CENTERS

Put pots and pans near burners and oven

Whether you need a family-size stockpot to simmer soup or a tiny pan to melt butter, you'll want to have your pots and pans within easy reach of the cooktop and oven.

Many people prefer to store cookware in drawers (in fact, some ranges come with a pot-and-pan drawer). But strong drawers with sturdy slides are essential—cookware is heavy.

Pot racks hung within an arm's reach of the cook (see pages 70–73) are a decorative option, especially if your favorite pots are made from gleaming copper or colorful enamel.

For right-at-hand storage of the cookware you use most often, consider open shelves; they're more convenient for stacking pots and pans than conventional cabinets.

▲
CUBES ON BOTH SIDES

Flanked by green cubes, range is surrounded by storage. Two-compartment modules (made of inexpensive particle board) stand side by side to form each large cube. Chopping-block tops are heat-resistant, and also handy for quick slicing. Small utensils dangle from wood strip nailed to wall behind range.

**SLIDING SHELVES ▶
UNDER COOKTOP**

Pots and pans can't be much closer than this to where they'll be used. Sliding shelves disappear behind harmonizing cabinet doors.
Architect: William Zimmerman.

◀ COOKWARE LINES UP INSIDE SHALLOW CABINET

Squeezed into an oddly shaped kitchen, extra-shallow cabinet keeps pots and pans within easy reach of range and forms one leg of L-shaped cooking center. Counter over cabinet serves as small-scale bar, convenient to living room just beyond doorway.
Architect: Mark Pechenik.

◀ VISIBLE STORAGE SURROUNDS COOKTOP

Vertical divider dowels and six coated-wire bins share underburner space with two very large drawers. Casseroles and soufflé dishes fit snugly in bins; coated wire lets chef spot a needed piece quickly.
Architect: Gilbert Oliver.

WORK CENTERS

Wrap storage around the refrigerator

Containing crisp greens for salads, nutritious dairy products, chilled beverages, fresh fruit and vegetables, and frozen food of all kinds, the refrigerator is the focus for meal preparation. It makes sense to concentrate storage around it.

Refrigerators are large vertical design elements. To give the refrigerator a more built-in, cohesive appearance, put tall cabinets or a refrigerator-height series of shelves next to it.

Incorporate varied storage into the framework around the refrigerator, but leave some counter space nearby to set down grocery bags. A counter or the top of an island directly across from the refrigerator works very well; just allow room for the refrigerator door(s) to swing open.

**REFRIGERATOR FACES ▶
INTO KITCHEN,
SHELVES FACE OUT**

Relatively simple piece of cabinet construction converted this refrigerator from a freestanding appliance to a refrigerator-plus-glass-storage cabinet; in top cabinet, vertical dividers hold hard-to-store flat items. Shelves for glasses and mugs are quite shallow—about 6 inches deep—and are hidden behind tall doors.

A PLACE FOR EVERYTHING

Whether it's wine bottles, cooky sheets, or a jar of peanut butter, it fits into this compartmented cabinetry around refrigerator. Cabinets are same depth as refrigerator; when doors are shut, they're flush with refrigerator doors. Architect: John Brenneis of The Bumgardner Architects.

FREESTANDING STORAGE STRUCTURE

Freestanding unit not only camouflages back of refrigerator, but also provides attractive storage on top. Table functions as kitchen eating and sitting spot and as a place to put bags of groceries. Additional storage is tucked in underneath table. Architect: Wendell Lovett.

ISLANDS

For an oasis of storage, discover the kitchen island

If you have floor space, you can expand your kitchen storage with an island. Pack it with shelves, drawers, bins, and cabinets; extend it out with an eating counter; or let it serve as home for a sink or cooktop. Some islands are tiny, with just enough tiled surface for a hot-from-the-oven casserole. Others are very big, the capacious centers for kitchen activities.

Allow plenty of open space between an island and adjacent surfaces—4 feet of clear space is about right.

MULTIFUNCTION ISLAND ▶

As extra work surface and part-time serving counter, this island would be valuable enough. But there's more: it deflects kitchen kibitzers from work triangle and stores kitchen equipment underneath. Doors on both ends of island open for access to shelves; drawers pull out from far end.
Designers: Don and Roberta Vandervort.

◀ CENTRAL ISLAND OFFERS SPECIALIZED STORAGE

Cheerful yellow plastic laminate wraps top of this large kitchen island. Holding a huge assortment of spices, flavorings, and other cooking essentials are three shallow, island-long shelves. Cooktop with barbecue unit is located above shelves; on other side of island, sink has its own cabinet storage underneath. Architect: John Galbraith.

◀ COOKING ISLAND IS KITCHEN FOCUS

Shelves along outside of island-with-a-cooktop display casseroles and pots and pans. Cookware is conveniently close to burners.
Architect: Bernard Judge.

ISLANDS

Movable islands go where they're needed

From simple serving carts to practically permanent islands of formidable dimensions, roll-arounds add flexibility to a kitchen storage plan.

Some movable islands are so well disguised that you'd never know they move: casters can be hidden for a built-in look, and the island's design can duplicate the kitchen's built-in cabinetry. You can wheel one of these islands next to a counter or appliance or even a permanent island, for extra work surface—varying your kitchen's floor plan as needed.

Small serving carts may be designed to slide into a "garage" under a counter, freeing floor space completely. Serving carts can increase your available counter space and offer a classic way to transport food and dishes from kitchen to dining room and back again.

ISLAND IS PART-TIME KITCHEN BONUS . . .

Right where it's needed for chopping or mixing chores, hexagonal island sits in center of kitchen. Under tiled top is extra cabinet space; side towel bars double as handles when island is moved. In dining area, serving counter ends on the diagonal, with glassware storage below. Wood grille panel is opened to connect kitchen with rest of house.
Architect: William Patrick.

. . . PART-TIME ▶ BUFFET COUNTER

A quick rearranging and serving counter is one island longer and party-ready. Tiled tops match, as does cabinetry. Grille panel is closed to screen view of kitchen.
Architect: William Patrick.

Look beneath lavish array of
gleaming cookware and see an
island that is basically a butcher
block table fitted with casters.
Modified to include a lift-out
metal bin with cover, sliding
tray, wire basket, and even
towel pegs, island moves from
one kitchen work center to
another.
Architect: Peter W. Behn.

▲
**ROLL-AROUND
MULTIPURPOSE CART**

For flower arranging—or any
other purpose—this cart rolls
out to become a work island.
Shelves and drawers provide
storage. When bouquets are in
vases, tuck cart into its home
underneath counter.
Design: Plus Kitchens.

APPLIANCES
Housing the handy portables

**MIXER STAYS ON ▶
SWING-UP SHELF**

Heavy mixer stays put on shelf that swings up almost to counter level. When not in use, shelf (still horizontal) swings down into cabinet. In right foreground, knife holder is attached to inside of cabinet door.
Architects: Buff & Hensman.
Interior designer: Regina Mirman.

**ELEGANT WOODWORK
SHELTERS APPLIANCES**

Used instead of wall cabinets, counter-level storage compartments preserve windows and add look of fine furniture to working kitchen. With doors closed, all you see is beautiful koa wood (inlaid dark strips are East Indian rosewood). Pivoting on side screws and washers, cabinet doors tip back into interior, out of the way. Architects: Larson, Lagerquist, and Morris.

▼

Sometimes, small appliance storage involves no more than pushing a blender into a corner. But with the proliferation of kitchen appliances, counters can be overrun in no time with toasters, coffee makers, can openers, juicers, blenders, and food processors. Less-used small appliances—waffle irons, slow-cookers, and pasta makers, for example—may not be out on the counter, but they still need to be easy to reach.

Where do you keep all these marvelous machines— out in the open on shelves? Behind closed doors? Tucked away in high storage?

For answers, consider small cabinets, deep drawers, spin-out shelves, and built-in compartments. All help keep equipment at hand but out of sight. With special hardware, small appliances can glide out, pop up, or swivel out and back in again.

A long parking strip at the back of a counter can provide space for all the gadgets and appliances you use daily; a row of electrical outlets adds to the convenience. You can even close in the space between wall cabinets and countertop with doors that pull down, slide across, push up, fold, or open on simple hinges.

Or consider hiding small appliances behind shutters or screens: in a country kitchen, a row of low shutters with fabric inserts; in a more formal kitchen, a small but beautiful folding Oriental screen.

UNITS POWER MULTIPLE APPLIANCES ▶

Available in several styles, power units are space savers.
A) Power pack is mounted flush with counter surface. Tray under counter pulls out and holds a food processor, blender, mixer, and bowls in specially molded compartments. Blades, disks, and beaters are stored in rack on inside of door.
B) Even less apparent is undercounter drawer that stores not only equipment, but also power head. Deep drawer is mounted on metal drawer slides. Power is supplied through a short length of shielded flexible cable entering from back of drawer.

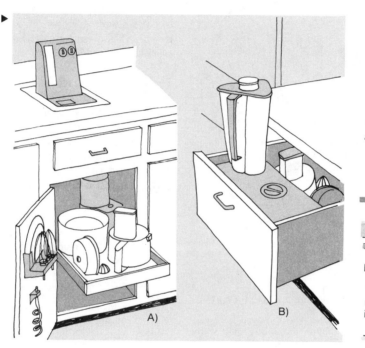

A)

B)

TAMBOUR DOOR COMPARTMENTS

Nearly every small appliance you own can be kept out of sight in these 12-inch-deep countertop compartments. Tambour door panels work like a roll-top desk. Thin fir slats on linen backing slide up and down in grooves cut into sides of 16-inch-high compartments. Architects: Zinkhan-Tobey.

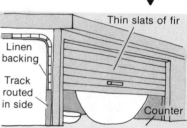

▼

Thin slats of fir

Linen backing

Track routed in side

Counter

TAILORED FOR TOASTERS ▶

Easily accessible, toaster oven on countertop has its own convenient electrical outlet. Pull-out unit over cutting board sits ready and waiting for freshly sliced bread or muffins, glides back in when not in use. For perfect compatibility, locate bread drawer under a toaster's tip-out compartment.

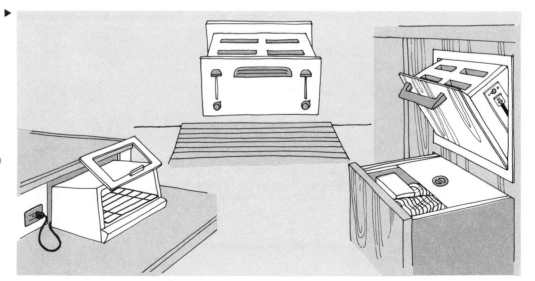

APPLIANCES

Making space for the not-so-portables

A serious consideration facing the buyer of a microwave oven, convection oven, or other heavy appliance is where to put it so it won't gobble up much-needed counter space. If you're rebuilding or remodeling a kitchen, you can design built-in spaces for large pieces—oven, meat slicer, electric mixer—that are too heavy and unwieldy to carry from cabinet to counter.

In existing kitchens, install slide-out trays or special lift-up devices, or park heavy appliances on a utility cart and roll them to a convenient spot.

Because microwave ovens are heavy and need a lot of space, most owners prefer to have them built into a wall or cabinet. Before building a niche for a microwave, note its dimensions and weight. Most microwaves are between 17 and 20 inches deep, so placement in a standard 24-inch-deep base cabinet is simple. On the other hand, placing a unit above the counter is more difficult because wall cabinets are usually only 12 to 15 inches deep. Make sure the cabinet is sturdy enough to support the oven's weight.

Additionally, all microwave ovens require from ¾ to 1½ inches of space on all sides to draw in and exhaust air. Read the installation instructions carefully for exact specifications. The microwave models designed to fit into wall cabinetry directly over a cooktop include an exhaust fan and light.

Smaller and more portable than microwave ovens, convection ovens are usually not built in permanently. Put them on a counter or on a cart.

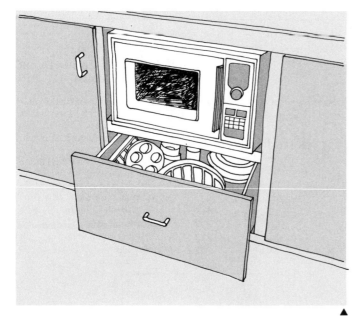

▲
REBUILD A BASE CABINET

Door was removed from base cabinet and strong shelf added for oven; deep drawer fits underneath.

OVEN ENCLOSURE ▶
ON OUTSIDE WALL

Inside, microwave front is flush with kitchen wall; outside, enclosure matches house exterior. Both heavy box enclosure and electrical conduit leading to it are waterproof. Architects: Zinkhan-Tobey.

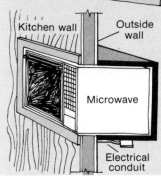

RECESSED MICROWAVE ▶

Partially recessed into a wall, microwave oven sits underneath wall cabinet. Space between bottom of oven and counter below can accommodate an extra cabinet. Oven extends to back of generous wall framing, allowing front of oven to fit flush with cabinets. Architects: Singleton-Pollock and Associates.

◀ **USE AND STORE APPLIANCES IN PREPARATION CENTER**

Food preparation center includes metal-lined bin for staples, spice shelves, and back-of-the-counter storage for large mixer and electric pasta maker. Folding doors are optional.

◀ **CUT CORNER OF ROOMY CABINET**

Keep your appliances, large and small, in one capacious cabinet. Cut off corner of an ordinary base cabinet, exposing wide shelf space for easy access. Two doors conceal array. (Countertop will have to be refinished.)

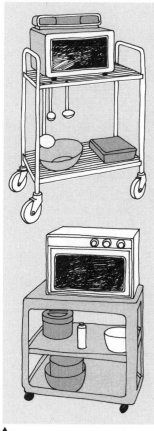

▲ **PUT AN APPLIANCE ON A UTILITY CART**

Both in style and size, sleek convection or microwave oven fits well on either of these high-tech utility carts. Shelf space on carts is added bonus.

CLEANUP
Around the kitchen sink

Is the counter around your kitchen sink or the cabinet under it a jumbled catchall for sponges, dishcloths, scouring pads, dishwashing detergent, and cleanser? Do you have to pull out several items before you spot the one you're hunting for?

Here are some pointers to help you organize your around-the-kitchen-sink storage:

• Keep the counters around your sink as clear as possible so they'll be free for preparing food and stacking dishes.

• Hang dishtowels and dishcloths inside the undersink cabinet on a slide-out bar or swing-out rack.

• Hang your dish drainer under the sink on two hooks attached to the inside of the cabinet; lean the drainer tray against the cabinet wall.

• Attach a paper towel holder to the inside of the undersink cabinet door.

• Keep cleaning equipment and supplies off the cabinet floor; put them in racks, on shelves, or in plastic stacking bins.

• Measure the plumbing and the available space under your sink before buying or building storage items.

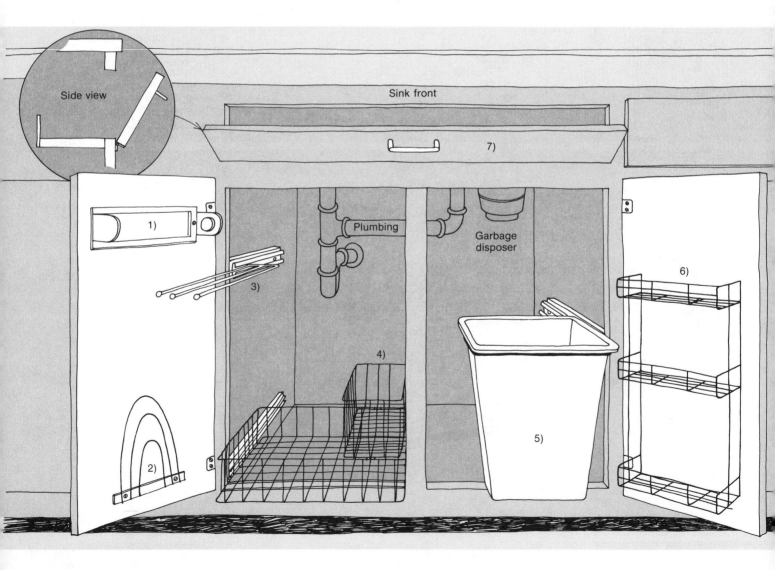

Side view

Sink front

7)

1)

3)

Plumbing

Garbage disposer

6)

4)

2)

5)

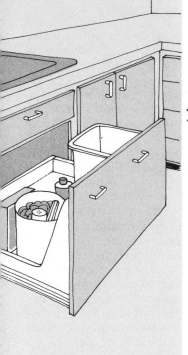

◀ STORAGE DRAWER BEHIND MOCK CABINET DOORS

Mock doors under kitchen sink are actually the front panel of a huge, undersink storage drawer that pulls out on metal slides. Drawer bottom and sides are ½-inch plywood cut to fit undersink space. Allow space in back and on each side for mounting heavy-duty, full-extension drawer slides (follow manufacturer's instructions). Existing doors or a panel custom cut to match kitchen cabinets are glued and screwed to side pieces and drawer bottom. Cutaway sides let in air and light and increase accessibility.

▲
BUILT-IN UNIT FOR UNDERSINK CABINET

Built-in shelf with vertical dividers below can be custom fitted for your needs. To design this simple unit, place sheet of paper on cabinet floor and position on paper all cleaning supplies regularly stored under sink; determine divider widths and shelf height. Construct unit from wood, using plan as a construction guide. Consider installing a sliding shelf for wastebasket.

◀ UNDERSINK STORAGE ACCESSORIES

These storage accessories fit inside undersink cabinet and keep sinkside equipment organized. Some of these accessories are easy and inexpensive to construct; others can be purchased at hardware stores or kitchen cabinet showrooms.

1) Metal or plastic paper-towel dispenser is mounted to inside of cabinet door.

2) Wire or plastic rack on door holds bags.

3) Metal rack for towels slides out on track mounted to side of cabinet.

4) Sliding rack for cleaning supplies is made from vinyl-coated wire; clip-on basket can be moved to fit around plumbing.

5) Pull-out metal rack for wastebasket glides out on side-mounted track.

6) Door-mounted rack with three shelves is available in vinyl-coated wire, plastic, or metal; or construct your own from wood.

7) Long, shallow shelf behind false front of sink organizes brushes, scrubbers, and sponges.

▲
CONTAINERS ELIMINATE ▶ UNDERSINK CLUTTER

Plastic dishpan and stacking bins can help you organize undersink clutter. Plastic caddy keeps cleaning supplies neat and portable.

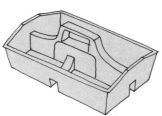

CLEANUP
Taking care of trash and recyclables

Efficient and orderly ways of dealing with kitchen wastes can put an end to messy, overflowing wastebaskets, unpleasant trash odors, and some of the drudgery of garbage duty.

Place your kitchen wastebasket in an accessible spot near where trash is generated. Once you locate all the waste production points in your kitchen, such as the can opener, food preparation counter, or chopping block, you may find, as many people do, that the best place for the wastebasket is under or near the kitchen sink.

Always line your wastebasket with a heavy-duty grocery bag or plastic liner. Your wastebasket will stay cleaner, and your trash will be more likely to make it outside to the garbage can in one uneventful trip.

Not all kitchen waste ends up in the wastebasket. Much will go down your sink's garbage disposer. Some kitchens are equipped with trash compactors that can compress what would fill three to four 20-gallon garbage cans into one odorless, leakproof, disposable bag.

If you're a gardener, you may want to keep organic kitchen wastes in a separate container to add to a compost pile. And if you have room in your kitchen, you can put recyclables in separate receptacles to save sorting time later on. Aluminum and tin cans (flattened), glass bottles and jars, newspapers, and paper bags are all recyclable.

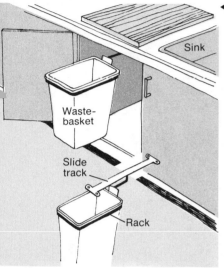

◀ PULL-OUT WASTEBASKET

Wastebasket slips into metal ring holder that pulls out on slide track fastened inside undersink cabinet. In extended position, wastebasket can be lifted out of holder for emptying; it slides into cabinet when not in use.

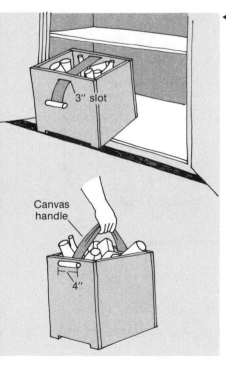

◀ PORTABLE BOX FOR RECYCLABLES

Portable plywood box keeps bottles, cans, and papers handy but out of the way. Store box in a base cabinet or on a shelf, or in a convenient spot near kitchen door. When box is full, lift it by the handle and load it into your car for a trip to the recycling center.

Make box from ¾-inch plywood to fit your own specifications. Cut narrow 3-inch slots in opposite sides about 1½ inches from top for handle; make handle from heavy-duty canvas, allowing an extra 4 inches for slack. Feed handle through slots and attach ends securely with heavy-duty staples to stops made from 4-inch lengths of dowel 1 inch in diameter. Sand and finish.

▲ WIRE RACK FOR UNDERSINK DOOR

Use inside of undersink cabinet door to mount waste rack made of vinyl-coated wire. Plastic liner or small wastebasket can be used in rack.

TIP-OUT WASTE BIN

You can deposit and unload waste easily with a tip-out waste bin. When opened, full storage space is exposed so it's easy to reach to bottom. Unit can also be fitted with a wastebasket.

For bin to tip forward, back must be lower than front (see illustration). Build sides, bottom, and back from ½-inch plywood; match front to kitchen cabinetry.

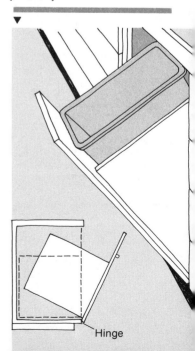

◄ DUAL-DUTY DRAWER

Underneath the kitchen sink isn't the only place to put a wastebasket. Here, a pull-out for wastes and recyclables is located directly below cutting board so food scraps can easily be swept off into it. Height of drawer saves bending.

Drawer can be fitted with two plastic wastebaskets: one for wastes and one for recyclables. Grocery bags can be stored in any remaining space in back of drawer.

Sides, back, and bottom of drawer are built from ½-inch plywood; front matches kitchen cabinetry. Drawer pulls out smoothly on metal slides.

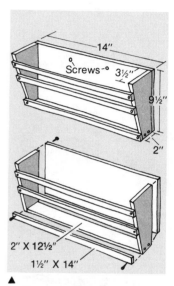

▲ GROCERY-BAG RACK

Attached to inside of a cabinet door, rack provides organized storage for grocery bags.

To make rack, cut two 9½-inch-long end pieces from a 1 by 4 board. Taper them so they are 3½ inches wide at top and 2 inches wide at bottom. Cut three 1½ by 14-inch front slats and a 2 by 12½-inch bottom piece from ½-inch plywood. Cut a 9½ by 14-inch back from ¼-inch plywood or hardboard.

Glue and screw side pieces and bottom to back, and slats to side pieces. Sand and finish; attach to inside of cabinet door with screws.

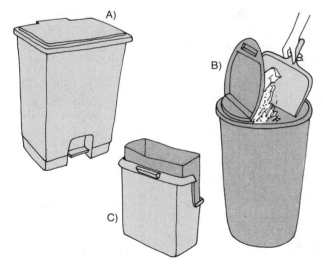

◄ THREE WASTEBASKET DESIGNS

When plumbing in undersink cabinet interferes with placement of wastebasket, look for a specially designed one; or opt for a covered container you can keep out on kitchen floor.

A) Step on the pedal of this wastebasket and lid springs up.

B) Here, lid locks open and leaves your hands free.

C) Cutaway wastebasket fits under plumbing in kitchen sink cabinet. Use grocery bag for liner.

SHELVES

Open or closed storage?

Chances are, a look into a professional kitchen in a restaurant or hotel will reveal the whole *batterie de cuisine* positioned for convenience on open shelves. Pots line up in graduated sizes; spices, knives, and mixing bowls are only a reach away, as carefully organized as the instruments in an operating room. The cooks can find what they need easily and can tell at a glance what needs to be reordered.

In home kitchens, too, the trend toward open shelving is growing, partly because we are all becoming more aware of food and its preparation, whether it's how to put a food processor to ultimate use or how to spin out ribbons of tender pasta.

Many people feel increasing pride in keeping all the implements of good cooking right out on display, with bright labels, packages, and pans adding color to the open shelves. "Now this is a *cook's* kitchen" is what you hear when someone sees all the utensils, crockery, cans, and bottles stored in plain sight. The whole room has become sort of an extended pantry with the cook's personal tastes in food and equipment on view. In short, it's a kitchen of character.

The practical side of shelving

Other practical reasons explain the popularity of open storage. Shelves are less expensive than traditional cabinets and drawers, and are easy to install. They can be permanent, built-in units constructed integrally with a new kitchen, or they can be made simply with boards and brackets or even with prefinished, precut kits that come complete with hardware for hanging.

Not only are shelves less expensive than cabinets, but they're also often portable (a boon to renters) and can be rearranged easily. You can usually adjust the height of shelves to accommodate large items or seasonal storage.

In addition to wood, shelf materials include metal, heavy plastic, glass, particle board protected with polyurethane and outlined with wood strips to prevent chipping, and sturdy vinyl-coated wire. Edging strips can

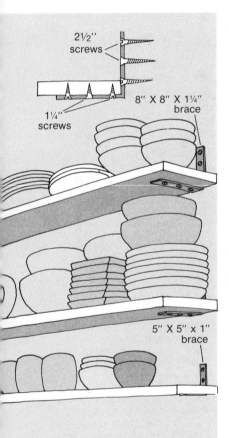

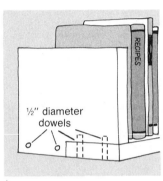

▲
SPILLPROOF END PIECES

Simple end piece secures items on open shelf. Cut end piece in L-shaped lap to fit a corresponding cut in shelf. Four dowels, each ½ inch in diameter, are glued in—two into end and two from underneath.
Architect: Donald Erdman.

▲
USE L-SHAPED BRACES FOR SUPPORT

Open shelves rest on L-shaped corner braces (angle irons). Fasten braces to wall studs with 2½-inch-long screws, then fasten shelves to horizontal part of braces with 1¼-inch screws. Wide shelves are 2 by 10s attached to 8 by 8 by 1¼-inch braces; narrow shelf is 2 by 6 held by 5 by 5 by 1-inch braces.

CONSIDER INDUSTRIAL ▶ SHELVING

Freestanding or anchored to a wall, industrial shelving is hard-working and indestructible. Made of metal and sometimes available in bright colors, high-tech shelves can solve many kitchen storage problems. Team these units with coated-wire or plastic baskets and stacking bins, or see-through plastic or glass storage containers.

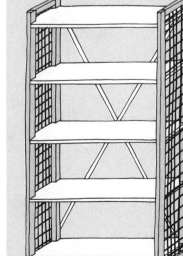

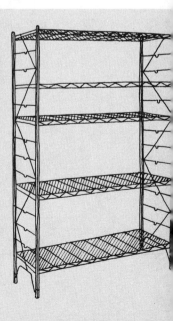

conceal undershelf lights. Shelves can be suspended from the ceiling, supported on a counter, screwed directly into a wall, or supported by metal tracks and brackets, braces, dowels, or clips; or they can be part of freestanding units.

But is it for me?

The opened-up kitchen clearly is not for everyone. Dust on dishes not often used, general disarray, and a daily confrontation with tomato soup cans are simply not tolerable to everyone.

Closed cabinets, on the other hand, conceal everything. Dishes, food, and ordinary clutter can be cleared off the open counters, leaving the traditional neat and orderly kitchen cherished by many cooks.

If you're ready to trade in your traditional closed cabinets but are unsure about that out-in-the-open living, one solution is to build shelves like conventional cabinets—but leave off the doors. Later, if you decide you want a closed-up kitchen, simply add doors. Or consider a combination of cabinets constructed with doors (to hide the real embarrassments) and without.

**ABOVE-THE-SINK
OPEN SHELVES**

Casseroles and cook books, coffee makers and canisters—all of these kitchen items and more are accommodated on open shelves. Boxlike shelves match wood countertop, contrast pleasantly with white cabinets and walls.
Architects: Richard Strauss and Kathleen H. Strauss.

▼

SHELVES

Open shelves in the kitchen— easy to see, easy to reach

NO TRADITIONAL WALL CABINETS HERE

Handsome, natural-wood kitchen employs open shelves instead of traditional wall cabinets. Middle and bottom shelves hold everyday dishes, glasses, spices, condiments, and brightly packaged foods; deeper top shelves accommodate large items, such as platters and a clam steamer. Heavy wooden brackets support shelves. Design: Margy Newman.

▼

Depending on your kitchen's floor plan, you can locate open shelves almost anywhere. Often they're hung against a wall, alternating with or replacing the cabinets; but they can also be suspended from the ceiling, built into an island, or tucked in between wall studs.

Shelf style is up to you. From the multitude of choices, consider shelves with lips to keep breakable glassware and ceramics from sliding off, or very shallow shelves to store spices or teacups one deep in space that otherwise might not be used. Whatever shelf style you choose, make sure the shelf material is easy to clean.

Throughout this book you'll notice many different shelves—and any number of places to put them. For more ideas, refer to the *Sunset* books *Bookshelves & Cabinets* and *Wall Systems & Shelving.*

**OPEN CABINET HANGS ▶
OVER KITCHEN ISLAND**

Striking oval cabinet suspended from ceiling above cooking/dining island is accessible from every side. Concealed at bottom of cabinet are cooktop light and exhaust fan. Coordinating open cabinets against wall take place of traditional closed wall cabinets. Shelves in these units adjust to hold everything from coffee mugs to a tall ceramic pitcher.
Architect: Robert C. Peterson.

▲
**CURVED DESIGN MAKES
CORNER MORE ACCESSIBLE**

These double-curve, open cabinets are attractive alternative to both conventional cabinets and conventional shelving—and their design makes corner space much more accessible. Compartments keep good-looking kitchen articles on display and handy for frequent use.
Design: Plus Kitchens.

**◀ IF YOUR DISHES ARE
TOO PRETTY TO HIDE . . .**

Why hide a favorite pottery collection behind cabinet doors? All you need are stained wooden shelves and an expanse of wall to create a stunning kitchen display area like this one.
Architect: Bill Kirsch.

SHELVES

Shelves in unexpected places

Adding a shelf or two to your kitchen may seem like a relatively small step to take in improving your storage, but it can make a big difference in saving you time and motion.

Focus on the work centers (see pages 6–7): tuck shelves above the cooktop, ovens, refrigerator, or sink; cover the side of an appliance with a series of shallow shelves. Shelves against a window can mask a less-than-perfect view; light, in turn, enhances the objects on the shelves. Stack up shelves in a corner where walls would otherwise be bare.

Scrutinize available walls for shelf possibilities, but make sure that cabinet doors will swing freely after shelves are installed.

▲
STRIKING SOLUTION FOR A TIGHT CORNER

Where no space exists for a traditional wall cabinet, open shelves just fit between window and doorway. Enclosed in a wooden frame, unit is not only handy but also very attractive. Exterior is painted blue to match kitchen cabinets; bright white interior provides sharp, clean contrast. Metal tracks and clips make top shelf adjustable. Cabinet designers: Woodward Dike and L. W. Grady. Interior designer: Phyllis Rowen of Rowen and Mentzer.

CREATE A SPARKLING ▶ WINDOW DISPLAY

Tempered glass window shelves display flowers, plants, potted herbs, and bric-a-brac. Especially suitable when your view is less than picturesque, shelves can be adjusted to any height by moving metal support brackets along tracks on sides of window frames.

SPICE SHELF ▶ UNDER CABINET

This handy spice shelf—actually an extension of handsome oak cabinets above—stretches 8 feet, the full length of cooktop counter. Stored one-deep, spices are easy to see and reach. Architects: Wagstaff & McDonald.

◀ SHELVING UNIT OVER PASS-THROUGH

Located over pass-through between food preparation and dining areas, wooden shelving unit makes storage space accessible from both sides. Unit is screwed securely to ceiling beams and has wooden slats on the bottom for hanging stemmed glassware. Architect: John O'Brien of O'Brien & Associates.

SHELVES

Supplement counter space with accessible shelves

In many kitchens, the backs of the counters fill rapidly with assorted jars, small appliances, cook books, and fruit bowls, encroaching on precious food-preparation space.

But where is there another place as convenient as the countertop for the assorted paraphernalia? A shelf or two close to counter height can do the trick.

**CORNER LEDGE ▶
IS CUSTOM-MADE
FOR COFFEE MAKER**

Previously unused corner is now permanent home for automatic drip coffee maker, thanks to handy ledge built on the diagonal. Above it, oak cabinet with glass-paneled doors is also on the diagonal to make corner more accessible and allow space behind it for coffee maker's wiring and plumbing.
Architect: Richard Hahn.

**ELIMINATE ▶
COUNTER CLUTTER**

Shelf units on countertops actually create more space for food preparation because they hold kitchen gear that would otherwise clutter counters. Extra height of shelves helps to divide kitchen and living area on far side, yet room retains feeling of openness.
Architect: Richard Sygar.

**◄ HANDY SHELF
DISPLAYS COOK BOOKS,
BRIGHTENS COUNTER SPACE**

Cook books and metal canisters
are off counters and out of the
way, but still within easy reach
on this handy shelf. Fixtures
mounted to underside of shelf
light baking counter below.
Architects: Fisher-Friedman
Associates.

**▲
ADD INTEREST—
AND STORAGE SPACE**

You can maximize your work
space by displaying decorative
items on eye-catching staggered
shelves rather than on kitchen
counters. Shelves are made
from plastic laminate edged
with wood.
Architects: Sortun-Vos.

**▲
RECESSED MINI-SHELVES
DESIGNED FOR SPICES**

Recessed shelves 3½ inches
deep keep spices within easy
reach of cook, yet off counter
work space.
Architect: Peter W. Behn.

PANTRIES

Fitting in a mini-pantry

The pantry in grandma's house was stocked with enough food to last for weeks on end. But with the scarcity of extra space in today's homes, most of us don't have the luxury of a separate, built-in pantry.

It is possible, though, to tuck a small pantry ingeniously into your kitchen so you can buy in quantity when prices are low and cut down on your trips to the grocery store. Small pantries bring food storage out of standard cabinets and into specially designed compartments. In an effective pantry, food is easy to see and easy to reach.

PANTRY CABINET PUTS UNUSED CORNER TO WORK

Custom-built wooden mini-pantry fits into corner between sink and oven, a space that might otherwise be wasted. Shelves are shallow to provide visible and accessible single-row storage of canned goods and condiments—and to make room for extra storage on inside of each door. Pretty ceramics find a home on top of unit. Architect: Woodward Dike.

▼

◄ DOUBLE-DECKER PANTRY OVERHEAD

Plastic laminate doors of two-tiered overhead cabinets slide instead of opening out into head space. Upper level, 5 inches deeper than lower level, holds large pans. Doors of lower level add a cheerful splash of color to predominantly white kitchen.
Architect: Wendell Lovett.

◄ STEPS PROVIDE UP-FRONT STORAGE

Nothing gets lost in the back of these cabinets. In unit on left, spices line up on graduated storage steps, keeping entire inventory visible at a glance. One compartment in divided cabinet on right has three steps for jars and packages.

Paper towel holder under cabinet is out of sight, but towels are within easy reach.
Architect: Gilbert Oliver.

PANTRIES

If you have space to spare, plan a walk-in pantry

Whether it's a tiny closet or a real room, a walk-in pantry gives you a complete overview of your provisions and plenty of room to store them. If you're a canning or preserving buff, what could be more gratifying than surveying rows of colorful ready-for-the-winter fruits, pickles, jams, and jellies? Even supermarket packaging can be enjoyed as a display of eye-catching designs.

With a light inside the pantry you'll have a clear view of the line-ups of canned goods and paper products. A surface, such as a small table or handy ledge, is convenient for setting down bags and boxes of groceries as you restock the pantry.

NARROW ALCOVE CALLS ▶ FOR SHALLOW SHELVES

Painted with black semigloss, these long, wooden shelves transform a narrow alcove into a mouth-watering display of home-canned foods. Thanks to metal tracks and brackets, shelves can be adjusted to any height.
Architect: Michael D. Moyer of The Architectural Design Group.

WELL-PLACED APPLIANCE ▶ TURNS OPEN SHELVES INTO WALK-IN PANTRY

Refrigerator turns area of open shelves into pantry that's easily accessible, yet partially closed off from view. Shelves are lined with checkered, vinyl-coated shelf paper that's cheerful and easy to wipe clean.
Architects: Larson, Lagerquist, Morris.

JOINT VENTURE IN ▶ WINE AND FOOD STORAGE

Convenient walk-in pantry features wine "cellar" on far wall and a cooler to keep wines at proper temperature. Tripod holds uncorking device. Pantry shelves are fixed at various heights; stock pot and party-size coffee maker fit on counter. Ladder brings top shelves within reach.
Design: Gordon Grover.

◀ THIS ONE HAS IT ALL

Walk-in pantry has everything you could want in kitchen storage. Shelves on walls adjust (using metal tracks and clips) to accommodate kitchen equipment of all different heights; hooks hold baking molds and small cooking utensils. Packaged foods and canned goods fit in single rows on shallow door shelves. Especially convenient are counter for preparing food and storing appliances, undershelf baskets for fruits and vegetables, and storage place for stool.
Architects: Sortun-Vos.

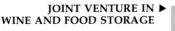

PANTRIES
Floor-to-ceiling storage

If there's no room in your kichen for a large walk-in pantry, what better place to store edibles and other kitchen essentials than in a floor-to-ceiling pantry near one or more of your work centers?

A pantry near your range or cooktop would make top-of-the-stove cooking a breeze; a tall cabinet near your oven could hold casserole and baking dishes (and the ingredients that go into them); and a pantry near the refrigerator would be a convenient spot for sleepy-heads to find breakfast foods such as cereals, bread, and jam. Whatever they store, floor-to-ceiling pantries maximize space, minimize steps, and look like a million!

WORK-CENTER STORAGE ▶

Built-in pantry in warm, dry spot next to oven keeps cereals, crackers, and other foods crisp. Sugar, cooking oil, condiments, and canned goods in pantry are only a reach away from food preparation counter. Architects: Richard Strauss and Kathleen H. Strauss.

RECESSED SHELVES ALLOW STORAGE ON DOOR

Both inside of door and bottom half of tall end-of-counter cabinet are lined with pegboard for hanging up baking and cooking paraphernalia. Top half of cabinet features recessed shelves for spices and condiments.
Architects: Buff & Hensman.
Interior designer: Regina Mirman.

SEEING DOUBLE

Attractive twin pantries with U-shaped shelves display tableware, crockery, baskets, cook books, spices, and brightly packaged foods behind sparkling glass-paned doors. Architect: Marshall Lewis.

PANTRIES

The larder—updated

The larder is an old-fashioned idea that's worth a second look. The handsome built-in storehouses featured here are great for cooks who like to stockpile canned and packaged foods when they're on special at the supermarket or who buy large quantities of their favorite fruits and vegetables at height-of-the-season prices.

If your larder is primarily for fresh produce, it's best to keep it cool and dark. Use wire shelves or vents to the outdoors (cover them with fine window-screen mesh) to keep air circulating, and avoid storing any bruised or damaged produce.

◄ FLEXIBLE CABINET STORES ASSORTMENT OF FOOD

Sparkling white double doors swing open to reveal a flexible food storage system. Tall bottles of soda and a big basket brimming with oranges fit in capacious drawers. Mounted on metal slides, drawers have so much room above them that they serve as pull-out shelves as well. There's even room in them for plastic stacking bins. Shelves above drawers adjust on metal tracks to accommodate jumbo-size food packages.
Architects: Fisher-Friedman Associates.

SHELVES GLIDE OUT ► FOR EASY ACCESS

Cabinet door next to top oven is actually front of four-shelf unit that pulls out on metal slides; bottom cabinet houses two handy slide-out shelves. Both units provide quick access to food and very visible storage.
Architect: Michael D. Moyer of The Architectural Design Group. Interior designer: Joan Simon.

EVEN DOORS ARE MINI-PANTRIES

Spacious yet compact pantry features U-shaped shelves that make sure nothing is ever out of sight and forgotten. Shelves adjust to accommodate everything from packages of nuts and cereals to small appliances. Even the double doors provide storage space; bottles and canned goods on door shelves fit one-deep, keeping labels visible. Trash compactor and water cooler occupy separate compartment. Cabinet designers: Woodward Dike and L. W. Grady. Interior designer: Phyllis Rowen of Rowen and Mentzer.

▼

A WHOLE WALL OF KITCHEN STORAGE

The beauty of these cabinets lies in their natural finish, clean lines, and almost unlimited storage capacity. Spacious shelves behind cabinet doors hold packaged food, canned goods, and dishes; vented tip-out bins are filled with fruits and vegetables; space between cabinets and ceiling stores large baskets and crockery.
Architect: Robert C. Peterson.

DRAWERS

Sizes, shapes, and styles for every kitchen need

Drawers are storage on the move—efficient containers that slide out to display their contents, then slide in again, out of the way. They can match or complement any kitchen decor and hold just about everything.

Custom drawers are expensive, but they do provide specially designed storage; they also carry through the style of the rest of the cabinetry. Much less costly are stock drawers, which are available in standard sizes at most building supply centers; these, too, can be custom fitted for particular uses (see pages 50–51).

Building your own drawers can be economical, but it's one of the most exacting of all cabinetry projects. Skill in woodworking is required for all but the simplest box design that merely pulls out from a shelf without slides or runners.

If you do decide to build your own, be sure to plan carefully, investigate all the available types and sizes of hardware, and keep in mind this rule of thumb: a drawer shouldn't be much deeper than 30 inches (the length of a long arm) or much wider than 3 feet (or it'll be awkward and heavy to open, even with sturdy handles on both sides).

◀ KICK-SPACE STORAGE

These prefabricated drawers fit under specially designed base cabinets to make good use of a space that's usually lost. Floor-level drawers provide children with easy access to toys and drawing supplies; or they might store picnic utensils, garden gloves, a supply of dishtowels, or any number of other things. Design: Plus Kitchens.

INTERIORS ARE ▶ SPECIALLY DESIGNED

Handy, custom-made food preparation island features butcher block counter and drawers with custom interiors. Slanted racks in shallow drawers keep entire inventory of spices visible; deep drawer holds several knife blocks. Design: Gordon Grover.

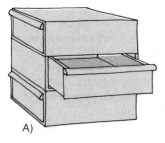

A)

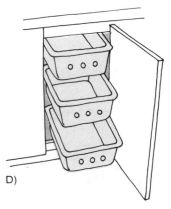

B)

C)

D)

VERSATILE READY-MADES EXPAND STORAGE

Ready-made plastic drawers expand storage space in a jiffy and bring a clean, bright new style to the kitchen.

A) Among the most versatile are freestanding stacking drawers that interlock. Made in individual units, they can be piled up so all drawers open in the same direction—or in different directions.

B) This special drawer unit screws in under a wall cabinet. Also available is a deeper version for one or two loaves of bread.

C) Space that's often wasted between shelves can be put to use with a neat stack of two slide-out drawers on their own supports. Widely available, they're sold in 12-inch and 16-inch widths.

D) Plastic trays, working like drawers, slide in and out on a rack that fits into a cabinet at least 15 inches wide.

OPENING DRAWERS WITHOUT HARDWARE

The high cost of good-looking hardware makes these drawer-opening ideas valuable. None uses hardware; all are easy to make.

A) Simplest pull is a hand hold. Half circles cut out of tops of drawer fronts provide firm openers.

B) Finger holes drilled in drawer fronts have rustic look. For finger comfort, round edges of holes with a beading bit in a router.

C) Hardwood caps fit over edge of plywood drawers. A cap or other pull attached to a drawer immediately under a counter should extend out 3½ inches; 2½ inches will do for pulls on lower drawers. All have finger grooves routed on undersides. Caps are first glued, then nailed.

D) Ribbons of maple decorate the plain fronts of plastic laminate drawers. Rout a finger recess on top and bottom of wood strips before screwing them into place.

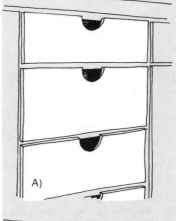

A)

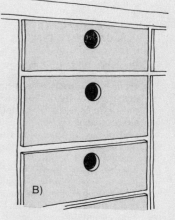

B)

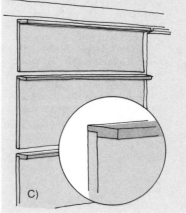

C)

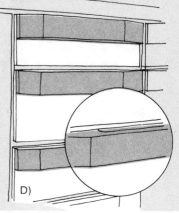

D)

DRAWERS

Dividers to organize drawers and tip-outs

Dividers in drawers are great organizers, creating distinct spaces that bring order out of chaos. With drawer dividers you can put your hands immediately on the items you need, as well as put them back more easily. Though you may already have drawer dividers for tidying silverware, consider using them for organizing baking and cooking utensils, pot tops, even food staples.

Many cabinet manufactures now offer drawers with dividers as part of their stock cabinetry. But using basic carpentry tools, you can customize your existing drawers with dividers; or you can purchase divided trays or baskets made of wood, plastic, vinyl-coated wire, and straw. Also available in many different sizes are interlocking plastic organizers you can make into whatever configuration you need in your drawer.

Simple cardboard or metal boxes can maintain order in your kitchen drawers. Even a shoe box can be a drawer organizer. Removable or portable drawer dividers are easy to clean and relocate.

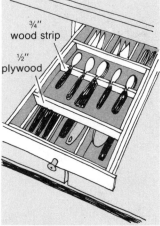

▲
CUSTOM COMPARTMENTS FOR BAKING UTENSILS

Spatulas, measuring spoons, beaters, cooky cutters, and other baking tools stay in tiptop order in this divided drawer.

Cut liner pieces for all four sides of drawer from ½-inch plywood. Cut grooves in front and back liner pieces to accommodate lengthwise dividers made from ½-inch plywood. Cut grooves in side liner pieces and in lengthwise dividers for ¼-inch hardboard crosswise dividers.

Place liner pieces against sides of drawer and slide lengthwise and crosswise dividers into place; glue if desired. Sand and finish.

▲
SPLIT LEVEL SILVERWARE DRAWER

Resting on plywood side pieces, silverware tray on top lifts out or slides so utensils underneath can be reached.

From ½-inch plywood, cut four liner pieces to fit inside drawer, allowing room for 1½-inch-deep tray to sit on top. Cut grooves in front and back liner pieces for ¼-inch dividers. Glue liner pieces to drawer. Cut dividers to fit into grooves. Sand and finish.

To construct lift-out tray, cut a bottom piece (wide enough to rest on liners) from ¼-inch plywood. From ½-inch plywood, cut four side pieces 1¼ inches deep. Assemble tray with glue and nails. Cut wood strip from ¾-inch plywood and make grooves that will hold silverware as shown. Sand and finish.

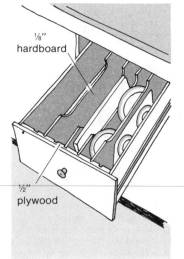

▲
VERTICAL DIVIDERS

Dividers in a deep drawer provide practical storage for hard-to-store shallow items—small baking pans, muffin tins, pot tops, and trays. Dividers can be removed for occasional cleaning and adjusted to accommodate larger items.

Cut an equal number of corresponding ⅛-inch grooves in two ½-inch plywood pieces. (Cut more grooves than needed so dividers can be adjusted.) Glue pieces inside drawer. Make dividers from ⅛-inch hardboard. Cut away top edge of each divider (see illustration). Sand and finish. Rub a bar of soap on ends of dividers so they'll slide more easily into grooves.

▲
EASY-TO-MAKE SILVERWARE TRAY

Here's a removable insert to keep everything in its place in your silverware drawer. Constructed from ½-inch plywood and ¼-inch hardboard, tray calls for only very basic carpentry skills.

Cut four side pieces from ½-inch plywood. Drill holes in two end pieces to serve as handles. Glue and nail pieces together. Cut bottom from ½-inch plywood, and glue and nail to side pieces. Cut dividers from ¼-inch hardboard; glue and nail into position (drill pilot holes for nails). Sand and finish.

◄ **DIVIDED TIP-OUT BIN**

Handy dispenser for staples such as flour, sugar, and rice opens at an angle so you can easily reach to the bottom. Potatoes and onions can also be stored in such a bin if there are holes for ventilation.

Make bin from ¾-inch plywood. Inside can be lined with metal or covered with plastic laminate. Attach bin to cabinet with piano hinge along bottom. Attach metal drawer stop or chain to top edge at back to keep bin from opening too far.

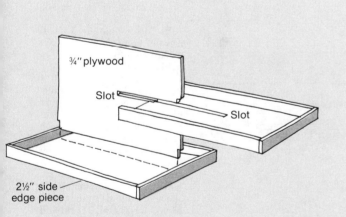

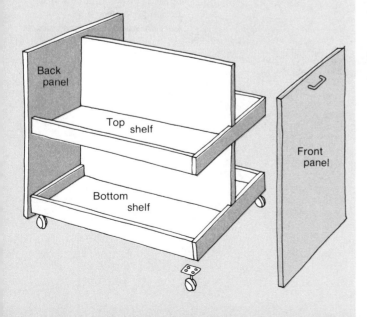

◄ **TWO-LEVEL UNIT ON CASTERS**

Kitchen paraphernalia can be kept within easy reach in this four-compartment storage unit that slides under a counter when not in use.

Construct it from ¾-inch plywood; use glue and nails to join pieces.

Cut vertical divider as shown in illustration, adding ¾-inch-wide slot for top shelf. Cut bottom shelf piece and attach 2½-inch-high edge pieces. Attach divider to bottom shelf.

Cut top shelf with ¾-inch-wide slot halfway through board. Attach 2½-inch-high edge pieces to front and sides of top shelf. Slide top shelf slot into slot in vertical divider as shown; glue and nail into place. Attach front and back panels with screws. Sand and finish; mount on casters.

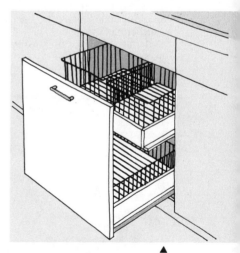

▲ **COATED-WIRE BINS**

Removable bins in pull-out keep fresh vegetables separate and provide optimal ventilation. Here, bottom bin is attached to drawer front; top bin operates on its own slides.

RACKS AND HOLDERS
. . . for knives

Knife storage requires some special thought. First, there's safety to consider. Throwing knives into a general utensil drawer can easily result in nicked fingers. Second, knives stay sharper when they don't bounce around in drawers or on countertops.

A simple knife rack answers both concerns; so does a specially designed cutlery drawer—and both are great organizers. Some of the attractive and functional knife racks shown here are available in department, cookware, and cutlery stores; others are easy do-it-yourself projects.

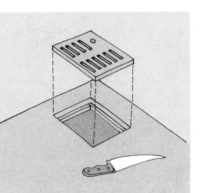

▲ KNIFE SLOTS IN BUTCHER BLOCK

You can store your knives right where you'll use them most if you incorporate knife slots into a butcher block table or countertop. Simply drop knives into slots, and your entire cutlery collection is at your fingertips.

▲ REMOVABLE SLOTTED RACK

Custom-made slotted rack fits flush with cutting board but can be removed easily. For safety, use ¼-inch plywood to cordon off area inside cabinet where blades will hang down.

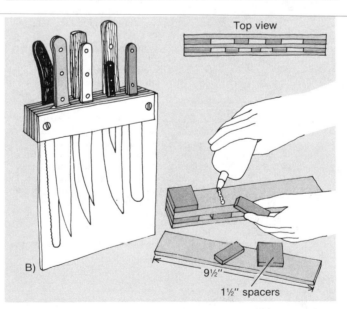

A)

Wood screws   12" or more   1½"   1½"

Top view

9½"

1½" spacers

B)

◄ HANGING KNIFE RACKS

Hanging racks are convenient for knife storage and easy to make. Attach them to a wall, cabinet, or edge of a butcher block table using 3-inch-long screws. Panel of clear plexiglass can be added to front of either rack to shield knife blades.

A) Assemble this rack from a 1½ by 12-inch (or longer) hardwood strip and two 1½-inch wood pieces. Using glue, attach small pieces to ends of hardwood strip and clamp. Sand and finish with polyurethane sealer. Attach plexiglass, if desired.

B) This hanging rack has two rows of knife slots; it's constructed from 4 feet of hardwood flooring that is 2 inches wide and ⁵⁄₁₆ inch thick. Cut flooring into three 9½-inch pieces, four 1½-inch pieces, and five ¾-inch spacers. Glue a 1½-inch piece to each end of one long piece, then add three spacers. Glue another long piece on top, and add two remaining 1½-inch pieces to ends; attach two remaining spacers. Glue third long piece on top, and clamp. Sand and finish with polyurethane sealer. Attach plexiglass, if desired.

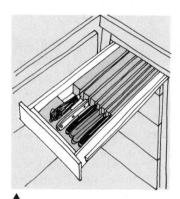

▲ CUSTOMIZING YOUR CUTLERY DRAWER

Cutlery drawer keeps knives handy, organized, and stationary. Some cabinet manufacturers offer special cutlery drawers, but you can make such a drawer yourself quite easily.

Cut wood the same width and half the length of inside of drawer. Make a series of grooves for knife blades in board. Glue to bottom of drawer; add thin piece of wood where knife handles rest. Sand and finish.

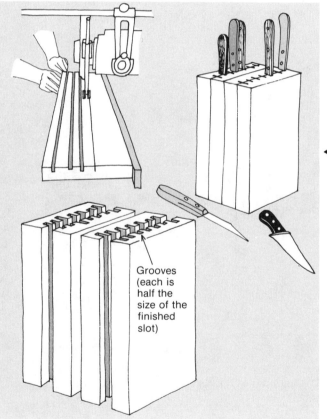

Grooves (each is half the size of the finished slot)

▲ KNIFE ORGANIZER FOR DRAWER

Simple grooved strip works well in kitchen drawer. Cut 2-inch wood strip the width of your drawer. Along strip make grooves for knife blades. Glue strip to drawer bottom, and glue thin piece of wood where knife handles will rest.

◄ MAGNETIC-STRIP KNIFE RACK

Like magic, magnetic-strip rack attracts steel knives and holds them securely in place. Available at department, cookware, and cutlery stores, rack is a solid wood piece with inlaid magnetic strips. Attach to wall or outside of cabinet using a screw at each end. You can also place magnetic-strip rack in a drawer.

◄ MAKE YOUR OWN KNIFE BLOCK

Sturdy block keeps your entire cutlery collection organized— and portable. Use a 4-foot length of 2 by 8 of any clear wood.

Cut grooves down entire length of board. Number, width, and depth of grooves depend on size and number of knives you're storing. (Here, seven grooves form 14 slots; remember that finished slots will measure twice the depth of grooves.)

Cut board into four equal lengths. With grooves aligned, glue pieces together to form two rows of slots, and clamp. Sand and finish.

RACKS AND HOLDERS
. . . for herbs and spices

Hardly a kitchen is without a healthy collection of jars, tins, shakers, and boxes of spices and herbs. Arranging them is a challenge: on the one hand, there's a wide range of sizes and shapes to contend with; on the other hand, many containers look exactly alike except for the name. How can you store spices and herbs so they're close to where you use them—usually the cooktop or food preparation center—and so you're able to find the one you need without a long search?

Here's an illustrated assortment of spice racks, many making use of often-overlooked storage space. Whichever arrangement you choose, be sure to display spices so they can be recognized at a glance. Then you'll be able to avoid sprinkling in cayenne pepper when you wanted cinnamon; you also won't have to dig through your entire collection for the one container you need. If your spice containers have a habit of walking away from their allotted places, you may want to label the shelf edge or the spot directly behind each container with the name of the spice stored there.

Generally, spice and herb containers should be stored away from direct heat, moisture, and light. Keep the tops tightly closed between uses to prevent loss of flavor.

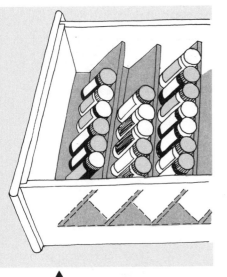

▲ ANGLED DIVIDERS INSIDE A DRAWER

You'll have little problem finding the spice you need in this custom-fitted spice drawer with angled dividers.

From ¼-inch plywood, cut four dividers, each the width of drawer and 4 inches high. Cut four triangular wood supports the width of drawer (see illustration). Sand and finish, then glue pieces into drawer.

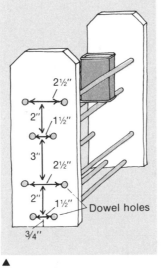

▲ TWO-TIERED SPICE RACK

This rack can be placed on a countertop or mounted on a wall. It holds jars and large tins upright, small tins at an angle. You can expand or alter rack to meet your own specifications.

Cut two 11-inch-long pieces from a 1 by 4. Cut eight 14-inch lengths from ⁵⁄₁₆-inch dowels. Drill holes for dowels in end pieces (see illustration for positioning holes). Glue dowels in holes. Sand and finish.

◄ SPACE FOR SPICES BETWEEN THE STUDS

When there's no place left in your kitchen to organize spices, don't panic. The 3½-inch-deep by about 14½-inch-wide cavities (those not jammed with pipes, vents, or wiring) inside your walls are ripe for exploration. These cavities lie between vertical 2 by 4 studs that frame walls. Because they're out of sight, they're often overlooked.

Cut a hole in wall between two studs; then build a unit to fit opening. Use ½-inch plywood for top, bottom, sides, and shelves; use ¼-inch plywood for back. Dowels hold spices in place. Sand and finish; then slip unit into wall and attach securely. Nail 1 by 3-inch trim around outside edges.

◄ BACKSPLASH SPICE SHELVES

Decorative and problem-solving, these shelves utilize space between countertop and wall cabinets. Assemble open-shelf spice unit from 1 by 6s or 1 by 4s butt jointed, glued, and nailed together. Add a ¼-inch plywood back, and screw unit to wall studs. Sand shelves and finish them to match cabinets.

TWO-SIDED SPICE RACK SWINGS OUT

Spices line up one-deep on each side of this sturdy holder; rack swings out from wall cabinet on piano hinge attached to side of cabinet. Shallow enough (5 inches deep) to permit storage behind, rack is tapered in back so it can swing clear of adjacent items.

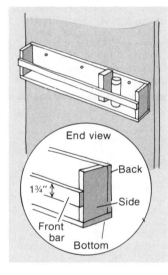

◄ DOOR-MOUNTED RACK

Tap storage potential of cabinet doors by attaching a simple wire, metal, or wood rack to inside.

To build a wood rack to your own specifications, cut back, bottom, and sides from 2¼-inch lattice; cut front piece from 1¾-inch lattice. Rack should be 2 inches shorter than width of cabinet opening. Glue and nail rack together; sand and finish. Attach rack to door using screws long enough to hold rack but short enough not to pierce door front.

Lazy Susan spice tray

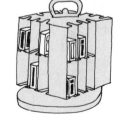

Revolving spice cube

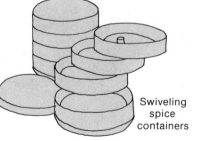

Swiveling spice containers

◄ COUNTERTOP SPICE ORGANIZERS

Keep an organizer near cooktop or food preparation area for quick access to seasonings you use most often. Easily cleaned plastic organizers like the ones shown here can be found in department, cookware, and hardware stores.

RACKS AND HOLDERS

. . . for wine

◀ STACKED TILES OR TUBES

Handsome terra cotta drain tiles about 1 foot long and 4 inches in diameter make cool, dark holders for wine. Build them in as part of kitchen construction (as shown in illustration) or simply stack them in an existing cabinet or rack.

Mailing tubes fitted snugly on cabinet shelf provide quick, inexpensive, and portable wine storage. Heavyweight tubes about 4 inches in diameter can be stacked two or three rows high.

4" diameter

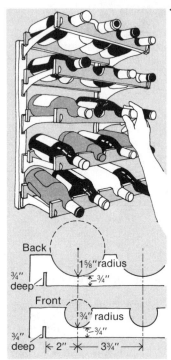

Back

1⅝" radius

¾" deep

¾"

Front

1¾" radius

¾" deep

¾"

2"

3¾"

◀ BRACKETS SUPPORT BOTTLE HOLDERS

Readily available bookshelf tracks and brackets form sturdy skeleton of wall-mounted bottle rack that's especially suited to narrow space.

Plan rack so you can mount tracks directly to wall studs (usually about 16 inches apart); use long wood screws for maximum strength.

Front and back wooden holders are 1 by 2s; oiled walnut is a good choice if rack is to be on display. Small and large cutouts cradle bottles.

Placement of 10-inch brackets depends on size of bottles. Good spacing for easy removal of standard-size bottles is 3½ inches between top of one holder and bottom of holder above it. Caution: Make sure brackets are fitted securely into slots in tracks.

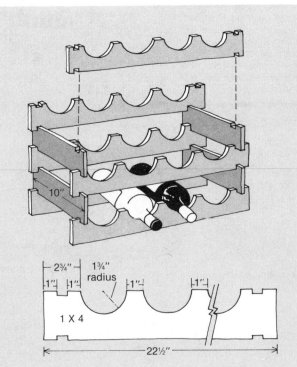

10"

2¾"

1¾" radius

1"

1"

1"

1"

1 X 4

22½"

◀ STACKING RACKS

Add sections to wine storage unit as needed.

Cut half circles in pine 1 by 4s as shown; sand. Cut cross-lap notches ⅜ inch deep and ¾ inch wide on upper and lower edges of boards. On both edges of 10-inch connectors, cut slightly undersized notches, then sand until they fit tightly with matching notches; assemble and stack.

These racks are designed for shelves about 23 inches across but can be built wider or narrower—just increase or decrease number of half circles for bottles and 1-inch spaces in between.

Few homes have a cool underground vault where wine bottles can repose in a carefully controlled atmosphere. But wine can be kept quite nicely in the kitchen—if you plan your wine storage area carefully.

Above all, a steady temperature is important. Wine cannot tolerate radical shifts between warm and cold, but it will keep satisfactorily at any relatively even temperature between 45° and 75°F/7° and 24°C. Never place a wine rack next to an oven or a drafty doorway. Instead, choose a dark, quiet place close to the floor, away from sunlight and the vibrations of machinery and slamming doors. It's also important to store bottles on their sides; if corks dry out and shrink, air can seep in and spoil the contents.

Whether you're thinking in terms of an entire room designed especially for your wine collection, or merely a small unit to fit inside a kitchen cupboard or on an open pantry shelf, there's a wealth of stacking racks, storage boxes, and folding racks to buy or build.

If you are (or would like to be) a serious collector of wines, you might consider relocating your brooms and converting the closet to a wine "cellar." With careful planning, a small closet can hold several hundred bottles of various sizes. To circulate air and maintain a constant, ideal temperature (around 60°F/16°C), a refrigeration unit with a fan can be installed in the ceiling.

On the other hand, if storing jug wines is your only problem, you're in luck. Usually meant to be used soon after purchase, jug wines can be placed in an upright position nearly anywhere that's cool.

More ideas for storing wine in or near the kitchen are pictured on pages 19 and 43.

◄ LENGTHS OF PIPE INSIDE CABINET

Custom storage unit features wine cabinet, shelves for dishes, and built-in hot tray for buffet serving. Wine bottles rest in glued-together 6-inch lengths of PVC pipe. Larger bottles slide into compartment underneath. Architect: Gilbert Oliver.

DINING AREAS
Creating an eat-in kitchen

If you don't have a large eat-in kitchen but would like to set up a special area where your family can have breakfast and lunch (or dinner on the run), look to your kitchen island, base cabinets, or other storage units. Tuck a few stools around a cooking island and it becomes a short-order lunch counter; establish a separate dining area using a storage-shelf room divider; create a ceramic-tile snack bar at the end of a kitchen counter; or add a tabletop to convert a corner base cabinet into a breakfast nook.

Use the cabinets and drawers under, over, and around your new eating area to store glasses, plates, silverware, and the small appliances you like to have nearby at mealtimes—a toaster or coffee maker, for instance.

▲
**CORNER TABLE
WITH STORAGE
ABOVE AND BELOW**

Built around brick chimney, corner table seats three for breakfast. Storage pedestal supplements glass-doored cabinets full of dishes. Architects: Sortun-Vos.

**SHELVES NEXT TO ▶
BREAKFAST TABLE**

Attractive shelves, crammed with cook books, food magazines, and kitchen-related miscellany, separate breakfast table from rest of kitchen. On kitchen side of divider is cooktop with pot and pan storage beneath. Through doorway at far end of kitchen is separate dining room. Architect: William Zimmerman.

◀DROP-LEAF COOKING ISLAND

With cooktop in center of cooking/eating island, food won't get cold in this kitchen. Drop leaves on two ends extend work surface, and stools can slide underneath on three sides. Overhead unit houses stereo speakers, plant lights, and illumination for cooktop. Architect: John Brenneis of The Bumgardner Architects.

◀CABINETS FRAME KITCHEN DOORWAY

Just behind counter extension, series of green-painted cabinets extends around doorway. Side cabinets are convenient for storing everyday things; overhead ones are for less-in-demand items. Cabinets with white louvered doors add even more storage space along display wall.

DINING AREAS

The pass-through connection

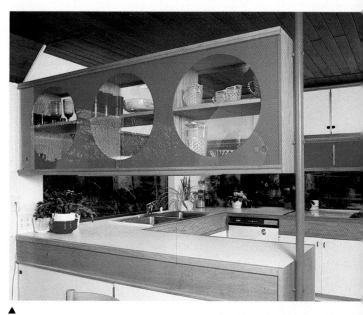

You use dishes, silverware, and glasses in the breakfast area or dining room, but wash them in the kitchen. Where's the best place to store these things, and how can you most conveniently move them from one room to the other?

A pass-through is the answer to both questions. You expect it to provide the convenience of handing food and dishes directly into the eating area. But taken a step further, a pass-through can offer a world of storage.

At its simplest, a pass-through is just an opening in a wall or divider. A counter on either the cooking side or the eating side (or both) increases a pass-through's practicality.

You can fit in shelves, cabinets, and hooks below, above, or on the sides of a pass-through. Storage you can reach into from both the kitchen and the eating area is a great way to save steps. In deep pass-through dividers, install sliding shelves or drawers that pull out from two sides to make the storage more accessible.

▲ **SEE-THROUGH CABINET ABOVE OPEN COUNTER**

Circles cut in orange plastic laminate behind sliding plexiglass panels show off dishes; shelves are open on kitchen side. Cabinet doors underneath also slide, eliminating problem of clearance.
Architect: Wendell Lovett.

◀ **STORAGE PASS-THROUGH SERVES EATING AREA**

This handsome pass-through links enclosed patio and kitchen. Glassware is displayed behind small-paned cabinet doors overhead; drawers and cabinets fill undercounter space. Auxiliary sink serves dining area.
Architect: Woodward Dike.
Interior designers: Phyllis Rowen, Suzanne Bryson.
Cabinet designer: L. W. Grady.

TWO-WAY CHINA CABINET ▶

Doors and drawers of this pass-through can be opened from both sides. Replacing a solid wall, pass-through made both kitchen and dining area seem larger. Rooms are brighter, since glass cabinet doors and pass-through let light pass between areas.
Architect: Robert Arrigoni of Backen Arrigoni & Ross, Inc.

COUNTERTOP COMPARTMENTS

Big enough to hold a favorite set of dishes, these sliding-door compartments are accessible from dining room on far side of pass-through as well as from kitchen. And no counter space is lost: tops of compartments form a shelf.
Architects: Buff & Hensman. Interior designer: Regina Mirman.

▼

◀ SLINGS FOR SILVERWARE

Threaded around narrow blocks of wood, very fine plastic window-screen mesh forms pouches for silverware. Seamed to leave long edges finished and smooth, then seamed again to flatten, mesh's double thickness provides strength. Cloth can be substituted for mesh.

TABLEWARE AND LINENS

Keeping treasures on display— or hidden away

Displaying beautiful dishes, glassware, and silver is half the fun of having them. Open shelves or a glass-doored china cabinet let you admire your treasures between meals—and when it's time to use them, you can run an instant inventory of table-setting possibilities.

Table linens—less likely to be on display—are most convenient if they're stored near the table. Everyday placemats and napkins can be kept in a handy drawer or on an open shelf; tablecloths can be hung from dowels that swing out, glide out, or are stacked across a

◄ ANTIQUE AUGMENTS BUILT-IN STORAGE

A world of dining storage is offered here. Dishes and table linens fill antique china cabinet at left; casseroles, baskets, groceries, and more dishes occupy shelves behind tall, narrow doors. Shallow cupboards are recessed into dining area wall. Interior designer: Joan Simon.

shallow cabinet. If there's no space to hang your table-cloths, you can keep wrinkles to a minimum by rolling them around large mailing tubes and giving the rolls plenty of room in a drawer.

You may want to add some secure storage for especially valuable items such as silver. One idea for this is a compartment behind a false kick-space panel (see page 76). Wherever you put silver, enclose it in layers of flannel or special tarnish-retardant cloth to block air flow and cut down on the need for polishing.

**CUSTOM CUPBOARDS
FIT DINING NEEDS**

Everything from table leaves to coffee cups is kept in floor-to-ceiling cupboards along wall separating dining room from kitchen. Table leaves fit between blocks of wood nailed to top and bottom of tallest cupboard compartment. Extra folding chairs, also divided by blocks of wood, stand in compartment sized for them. Shelves fill in remaining cupboard space. Design: Pennington & Pennington.

◄ **SHALLOW DRAWERS
FOR TABLE LINENS**

Stack of shallow drawers is concealed behind a cabinet door until it's time to set the table. Low shelf fronts make placemats highly visible and act as pulls when selection is made. Architect: Bo-Ivar Nyquist.

▲
**BASKETS OF COATED WIRE
IN TWO-WAY CABINET**

Easily visible through coated wire, dishes can be removed from both sides of two-way cabinet. Placemats and napkins lie flat in adjacent drawers. Cabinet is well located, standing between informal eating area and formal dining room, with kitchen to one side.
Architect: Gilbert Oliver.
Interior designer: Nancy Brown, ASID.

TABLEWARE AND LINENS

Keeping dinner table items in the kitchen

In more and more homes, the "good" china and table linens are finding their way into the kitchen. One reason for this is today's more casual lifestyle: the kitchen is often the setting for family dining—and sometimes even for entertaining. Another reason is that many newer homes have small dining areas instead of formal dining rooms, and there's simply no space in them for storage.

Luckily, the kitchen is full of possibilities for storing and displaying tableware and linens. Just use your imagination! Keep a service for twelve on sliding shelves in a versatile base unit that doubles as a buffet; conceal a half-dozen tablecloths behind a movable cabinet that looks built-in; or turn traditional wall cabinets into a stunning display of china and glassware by substituting glass-paned doors for solid ones.

**◄ COUNTER BUFFET FOR ►
KITCHEN ENTERTAINING**

Base unit below windows runs full length of kitchen. Strong sliding shelves hold heavy plates, yet glide out smoothly. Closed, cabinets have a handsome, tailored look. With buffet set up, dried flower arrangement separates serving area from cooking area. Architect: Woodward Dike.

**NEXT-TO-THE-DOOR ►
DISH STORAGE**

Proximity to dining room was a priority here, so tableware is stationed near doorway. Small-paned glass cabinet doors show off china, silver, and crystal on tempered glass shelves. Backs of cabinets are simply the kitchen walls (note vertical groove pattern) painted white. Designer: L. W. Grady.

MOVABLE CABINET CONCEALS LINENS

Cabinet with microwave oven on top just *looks* built-in. Moved away, cabinet reveals table linens hanging—wrinkle free—from smoothly finished boards. Spice rack pulls out sideways so it's accessible even when microwave cabinet is in place. Auxiliary sink and warming oven share stationary cabinet at right. Architect: Jane Hastings of The Hastings Group.

WORK AREAS/OFFICES

Make space for hobbies and other activities

All kinds of activities go on in the kitchen besides cooking: flower arranging, sewing, ironing, appointment making, gift wrapping, and art projects are just a few of them. If you want to keep your papier-mâché away from your boeuf bourguignon, plan a kitchen hobby area with plenty of appropriate storage.

Consider adding an auxiliary sink if you do lots of flower arranging or other projects requiring water. Put the sink and accompanying storage (drawers for scissors and deep shelves for vases, perhaps) outside the kitchen work triangle.

**WELL-CONCEALED ▶
KITCHEN LAUNDRY**

Sophisticated European fir
cabinetry with black plastic
laminate counters hides a pull-
out ironing board and, in tall
cabinet next to board, a washer
and dryer.
Architect: Gilbert Oliver.
Interior designer: Nancy Brown,
ASID.

**◀ COUNTER IS OUTSIDE
WORK TRIANGLE**

Plenty of cabinets and large
drawers under butcher block
work surface store materials for
flower arranging, gift wrapping,
other projects. Work counter is
at one end of kitchen, out of
sink-range-refrigerator work
triangle.
Architects: Richard Strauss and
Kathleen H. Strauss.

WORK AREAS/OFFICES

Space for a tiny desk or a complete office

Probably the most obvious uses for a kitchen desk are meal planning and shopping-list writing—good reasons to have the desk convenient to the pantry. Space for recipe files and cook books is important; so is room to spread out the newspaper's supermarket specials. You may want to include space for a calculator and typewriter, too—not to mention a home computer.

Many people like to have a telephone in the kitchen so they can answer calls while they cook. Sometimes, this expands into a message center, with an appointment calendar, blackboard or bulletin board, and intercom.

◀ KITCHEN ISLAND DOES DOUBLE DUTY

Stepped down from food preparation height to desk height, island does double service. Desk's design provides space for chair, telephone connection, and file drawer. Desk end of island is away from focus of meal preparation. Architects: Fisher-Friedman Associates.

Sometimes it's occupied with menu planning or schedule organizing; at other times, entire counter is taken over for baking or serving. With wall phone at one end, mixer on hinge-up shelf at other end, book shelves above, and chair space below, this counter is ready for any use.
Architect: William Zimmerman.

UPDATING A ROLL-TOP ▶

Traditional advantages of a roll-top desk—quick concealment of projects-in-process, convenience of having everything still in place when you return—are retained in this built-in kitchen desk. New appeal comes from its unobtrusive location around the corner from kitchen work area, yet close to pantry cabinets. Style and materials of desk match rest of cabinetry.
Architect: Robert C. Peterson.

TELEPHONE'S TUCKED INTO ISLAND

Long, narrow niche in this oak island conceals wall phone. Bank of drawers is handy for telephone books, pencil, and paper; expansive island top provides work surface.
Designer: Alison Ruedy.

▼

KITCHEN HANG-UPS

Find a strategic spot to hang up kitchen gear

Your kitchen may already have lots of places to attach hooks and hangers: under cabinets, over pipes, or directly to ceiling beams or wall studs.

If not, you can find or build any number of devices that create a framework on which to put hooks and hangers: metal or plastic grids, perforated hardboard or plastic, latticework, and custom or commercial pot racks.

Wherever you put your hooks and hangers, you'll want your tools low enough to reach but high enough to avoid bumps on the head. It's best to plan around the height of the cook in your household. Also, make sure hanging storage won't block the swing of cabinet doors or obstruct access to shelves.

LADDERLIKE POT RACK

Tiny 12-volt lights shine on sparkling copperware hung from horizontal "ladder" with copper tubing rungs. Oak frame extends around sides of range hood. Brass S-hooks were purchased at a marine supply store.
Architect: Kathleen H. Strauss of Don Olsen Associates.

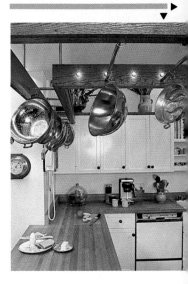

DOWEL RUNS ALONG WALL

Supported every 3 feet by track-and-bracket hardware, 2-inch-thick dowel runs parallel to long wall. S-hooks slip over dowel to hold cooking gear.
Architect: Richard Sygar.

PLASTIC WALL HANGERS

Accessories are stored around cooktop on four different wall-hung units: a spice rack, a potholder hook, a small utensil bar, and a food processor accessory rack. White plastic hangers harmonize with kitchen's soft gray and white color scheme.
Architect: Guy McGinnis.

◄ BASKETS ABOVE PENINSULA COUNTER

Visually dividing kitchen from breakfast area, basket collection accents ceiling beam. On kitchen side, S-hooks slip over flat iron bar attached to side of beam. On wall, antique utensils hanging on nails include an English pan scraper and a fork for catching eels.

KITCHEN HANG-UPS

From modest pegboard panels to sleek high-tech grids

Are countertop appliances, gourmet cookware, dinnerware, and utensils eating up valuable work and storage space in your kitchen? Overcrowded countertops and full-to-overflowing cabinets and drawers are a common problem.

Hanging devices can help you turn almost any vacant surface—ceilings, walls, cabinet doors and sides, the undersides of shelves and wall cabinets—into extra storage space. These hanging devices include simple hooks, baskets, shelves, wall units such as grids and perforated hardboard (pegboard), and racks for ceilings, walls, and cabinet doors.

Hanging devices offer tremendous versatility. Many can be moved as the need arises; many can be modified with components such as shelves, bins, and hooks; and most can accommodate a wide assortment of items, from produce to paella pans.

Fasteners—whatever you use to attach a hanging device to the wall or ceiling—are another consideration. They must be capable of supporting the weight of the items that will be stored—as well as the weight of the device itself. A sizable pot rack, for example, with a cook's collection of pots and pans, weighs a good many pounds. Also, some fasteners work better for certain holding jobs than others. So be sure you read manufacturers' suggestions carefully when choosing from the array of suction, magnetic, stick-on, screw-in, and nail-in hooks and fasteners, as well as such heavy-duty fasteners as togglebolts, expansion bolts, and sleeve-type anchors.

Remember, too, that when you use hanging storage devices in your kitchen, whatever you're storing will be in plain view. For an organized effect, group objects according to their function, shape, or size.

**WALL DISPLAY ▶
OF POTS AND PANS**

As pleasing to look at as they are convenient to use, shiny copper and copper-bottom pots and pans decorate white wall next to cooktop.

PEGBOARD PULL-OUTS FOR POTS AND PANS

Functional—and easy—solution to cabinet full of disorganized pots and pans is one or more ¼-inch pegboard panels that slide loosely between 1 by 2s screwed to top and bottom of cabinet. Cut each panel slightly smaller than height and depth of cabinet. Attach a small knob near front edge of each panel so it can be pulled out easily.

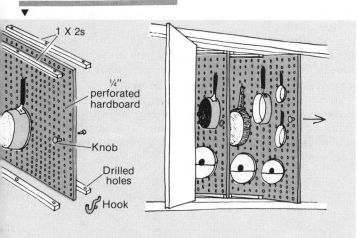

1 X 2s

¼" perforated hardboard

Knob

Drilled holes

Hook

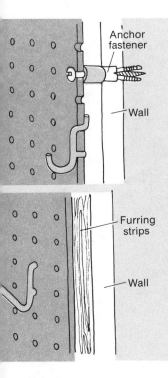

Anchor fastener

Wall

Furring strips

Wall

◄ PERFORATED PANELS FOR A MULTITUDE OF USES

Perforated hardboard, also called pegboard, is perfect for wall storage. Though you may associate it with tool storage in the garage, pegboard works equally well on kitchen walls, especially if it's brightly painted and edged with molding.

Purchase pegboard panels from hardware or lumber stores. Attach them to wall on 2 by 2 wood furring strips screwed into wall studs; or use sleeve-type wall anchor fasteners with spacers that hold panels slightly away from wall to allow clearance in back for hooks.

Another similar and versatile wall storage system is plastic, pegboard-type panels with components that hook on—shelves, bins, knife holders, and hooks. System can be screwed to wall vertically or horizontally.

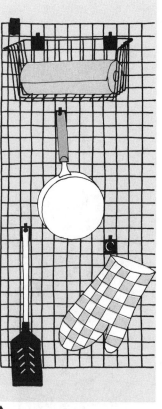

▲ HIGH-TECH GRID

Vinyl-coated or chrome wire grid panel lets you hang utensils, cookware, paper goods, and foodstuffs on racks, shelves, bins, and special hooks. Panel is either screwed directly into wall or clipped onto fasteners screwed into wall. Grid can also be suspended from ceiling on long hooks.

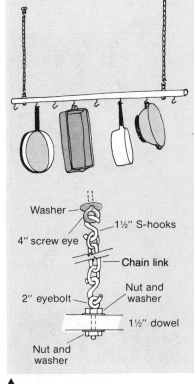

Washer

4" screw eye

2" eyebolt

Nut and washer

1½" S-hooks

Chain link

Nut and washer

1½" dowel

Nut and washer

▲ SUSPEND POT RACK FROM CEILING

Simple pot rack frees cupboard space in kitchen where storage is at a premium. To construct this lightweight rack, attach row of screw hooks to 1½-inch-thick dowel. At each end, drill hole and insert 2-inch eyebolt, nuts, and washers (as shown). Use S-hooks and metal chains to suspend dowel from two 4-inch screw eyes secured to ceiling joists (usually 16 inches apart). Adjust rack to convenient height.

KIDS' CORNERS
Play area storage

Children love to be in the kitchen. After all, most of them have spent a lot of time there sitting in a highchair, crawling on the floor, banging on pots and pans.

Because they're around the cook so much, kids need a section of the kitchen where they won't be underfoot or exposed to the dangers of steaming pots and sharp knives. To separate *your* work from *their* play, locate the children's area where the traffic patterns of play and cooking don't constantly cross.

In a large kitchen, it's fairly easy to child-proof one end and set aside places to draw pictures and scatter toys. Small kitchens with more limited storage require tighter planning.

Design your children's activity center for their convenience. Toddlers need to have their playthings on low open shelves; older children enjoy a small desk for drawing or counter space for their own culinary concoctions.

Consider adjustable racks and shelves of metal, plastic, or wood. Short, movable shelves on wall tracks are handy for an older child; one can serve as a work counter. A stack of drawers can be made available to the growing child successively, starting from the bottom drawer and moving upward. Keep toys organized in pull-out bins or baskets. If you have available wall space, hang a cork board nearby for art work and favorite pictures.

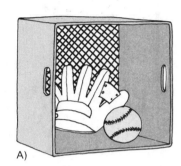

A)

C)

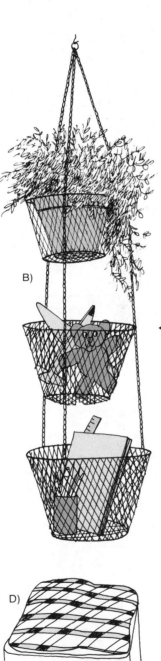

B)

◀ "RIGHT NOW" STORAGE

There comes a time in every parent's day when toys and projects must be cleaned up— the faster, the better. Then kids and parents alike will appreciate simple storage units like the ones shown here. Consider **A)** inexpensive plastic boxes, **B)** hanging three-tier wire mesh baskets, **C)** baskets with handles, or **D)** sturdy plastic cubes.

Cubes and boxes can be stacked conveniently and pushed under a counter out of the way. Some cubes double as low stools with storage compartments underneath.

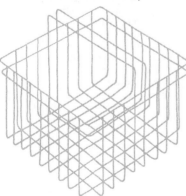

D)

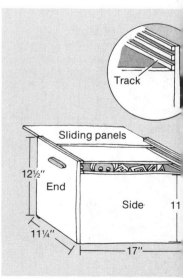

Track

Sliding panels

12½"

End

Side 11

11¼"

17"

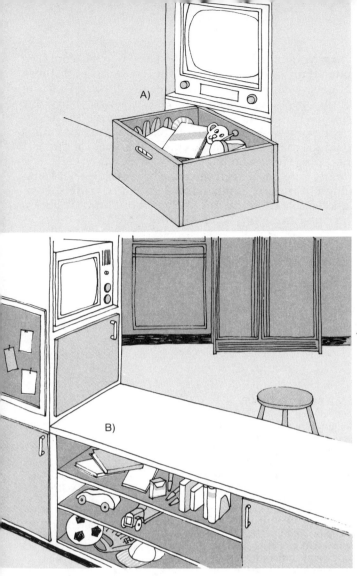

◀ TELEVISION GARAGES

For television watching in the kitchen, place TV where kids can see it and not be underfoot.

A) Kids will appreciate television parked low (about a foot above floor) in a cubbyhole of a base cabinet; arrangement features a pull-out toy box underneath. Leave enough space around TV to pull out or adjust set.

B) If you're remodeling, build TV niche over divider between kitchen and dining area; screen is visible not only from kitchen and counter seats but also from play area.

PLAYTIME MINI-CART ▲

Cart with three or four stacked baskets moves easily from kids' rooms to kitchen and back again, conveying a full playday's supply of trucks, stuffed animals, games, and books. On some carts, baskets pull out for easy access.

◀ DRAWING-SURFACE TOY BOX

Toddlers can stow toys inside portable box and use cover as a drawing table. From ½-inch plywood, cut two side pieces 17 by 11 inches, and two end pieces 11¼ by 12½ inches. Attach handles to end pieces. Make grooves by gluing and nailing three ¼-inch-square by 11¼-inch-long wood strips to top inside of both end pieces. (Allow enough space between strips for panels to slide easily.) Cut bottom to fit. Using nails and glue, assemble box with ends overlapping sides.

From ¼-inch hardboard or plywood, cut two cover panels 11¼ by 16⅞ inches. (They'll slide apart to make a good-size drawing surface.) Sand and finish.

DISCOVER SPACE ▶ UNDER A SHELF, ON A WALL

Even if your kitchen's layout limits active play, a few of your children's quiet-time toys can be kept within reach. **A)** Two-story rack of vinyl-coated wire steals little wall space. **B)** Pocketed wall organizer hangs over desk or work counter. **C)** Hang-up canvas bag holds bulky toys. **D)** Shelf of vinyl-coated wire slips into place beneath existing open shelf. Roomy enough for books and drawing materials, wire shelf is easy to relocate.

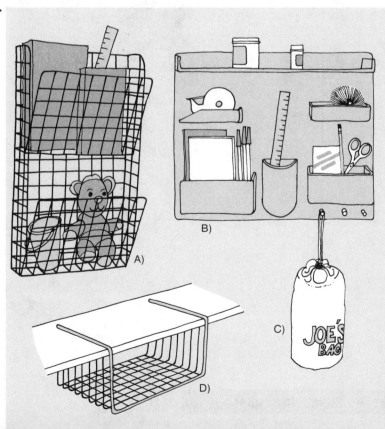

SURPRISE STORAGE
Discovering unused spaces

When your kitchen is storage-starved, what could be better than finding an unexpected place to park those gadgets, dishes, or baskets that are lined up on the counter, waiting for a spot to call their own. Take a few minutes to scrutinize your kitchen. Observe the width of the window ledges—plants or a row of coffee mugs could go there. That blank end of the wall cabinet is a good place for a family bulletin board.

How long has it been since the broom closet held anything but clutter? Remove the door, add a wide shelf at desk height, attach narrow shelves above for cook books, and you have a tiny kitchen office.

Eyebolt

Chain or nylon rope

Hooks

◄ A SUSPENDED DOOR

Hanging from ceiling on nylon rope or chain, door provides lots of extra storage. Suspend door (finished to match kitchen cabinets) from eyebolts or hooks securely anchored in open beams or in ceiling joists (usually spaced 16 or 24 inches apart).

Top of door is a deck for lightweight baskets; hooks on underneath surface hold pots and pans at a convenient—and safe—height. Hooks go through door and are secured with large-diameter washers and nuts on top of door.

KICK-SPACE STORAGE

Don't let odds and ends—screwdrivers, hammer, tape, string—take up precious space in base cabinet drawers; add kick-space drawers below base cabinets for extra storage.

Suppliers of European cabinetry offer kick-space drawers that fit below their specially designed base units (see photo on page 48). In Europe, kick spaces are 8 inches high, twice their height in North America.

But even the traditional 4-inch space can be useful. Cut out a section of the kick-space panel and install a shallow drawer; fill with children's art supplies. Or conceal a tray for silver and other valuables behind kick-space panel.

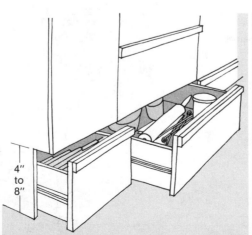

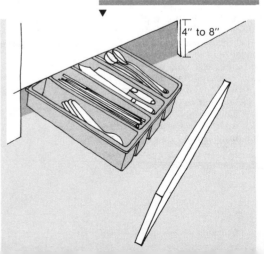

4" to 8"

4" to 8"

◀ MINI-PANTRY AROUND THE CORNER

Bottles, canned goods, and spices can be tucked into unexpectedly convenient spots on shallow shelves that keep labels visible.

Mini-pantry around the corner from stacked ovens (or refrigerator) is created by extending wall 6 inches beyond sides of ovens. Shelves adjust on tracks attached to inside of wall extensions.

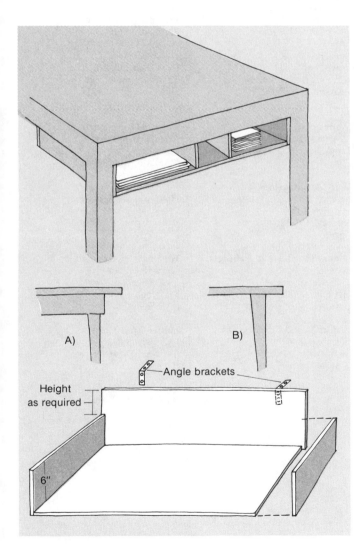

A)

B)

Angle brackets

Height as required

6"

◀ STORAGE SHELF UNDER TABLE

A kitchen table is a blessing both for family meals and as an extra work surface. It's even handier with an added-on storage shelf at one end for placemats, napkins, even a few dishes. Space can double as single-row wine rack.

Build bottom, sides, and back from pine shelving or ½-inch plywood. Make front opening approximately 6 inches high. Unit should be wide enough to fit snugly under top of table and against legs. Sand and finish shelf before attaching it to table.

For skirted table (**A**) or Parsons table, make shelf unit with a high back; use angle brackets to fasten back to underside of table. Screw sides to legs. On country-style table (**B**), make back same height as sides. Fasten shelf to table as described above.

To use shelf as wine rack, glue and nail wood dividers into unit to make compartments about 4 inches wide.

SOURCES

Manufacturers of kitchen cabinets and storage products

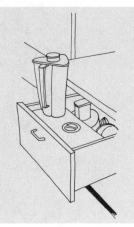
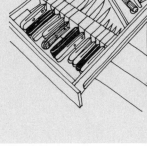

When you're trying to transform an old kitchen into one that's innovative and workable, you'll find a wealth of ideas in the brochures put out by the various manufacturers of kitchen storage units. Here's a selection of major cabinet and storage product manufacturers who will send you information on request; they can also tell you about local outlets or distributors for their products. The entries are coded to identify what each company manufactures; importers of European cabinetry are indicated as well. The product codes and addresses in this list are accurate as of press time.

The Yellow Pages of your telephone directory and the National Kitchen & Bath Association (124 Main Street, Hackettstown, NJ 07840), can help you locate kitchen showrooms, cabinetmakers, designers, architects, and other sources near you.

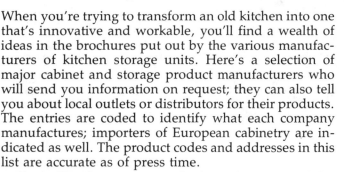

(C) custom cabinets	(m) metal
(S) stock cabinets	(p) plastic
(SO) special order cabinets	(pv) plastic laminate veneer
(SP) storage products	(w) wood
	(i) imported

Akro-Mils
1293 S. Main Street
Akron, OH 44301
(SP/m,p)

Allmilmö Corporation
P.O. Box 629-S2
Fairfield, NJ 07006
(SO/pv,w,i)

ALNO Kitchen Cabinets, Inc.
P.O. Box 10474
Charleston Heights, SC 29411
(C/pv,w,i)

Amerock Corp.
4000 Auburn Street
Rockford, IL 61101
(SP/m,w)

Ampco
P.O. Box 608
Rosedale, MS 38769
(C/m)

AristOKraft Cabinets
P.O. Box 420
Jasper, IN 47546
(S, SO/pv,w)

Artcraft Wire Works
230 Fifth Avenue
New York, NY 10001
(SP/m)

Beck Lumber Co.
5102 S. Washington Street
Tacoma, WA 98409
(S/pv,w)

Beylerian Limited
11 E. 26th Street
New York, NY 10010
(SP/p)

Birchcraft Kitchens, Inc.
1612 Thorn Street
Reading, PA 19601
(C,S/pv,w)

Boro Industries, Inc.
P.O. Box 11558
Fort Worth, TX 76109
(C/pv,w)

Copco, Inc.
50 Enterprise Avenue
Secaucus, NJ 07094
(SP/p)

Coppes, Inc.
401 E. Market Street
Nappanee, IN 46550
(C/w)

Craft-Maid Custom Kitchens, Inc.
P.O. Box 4026
Reading, PA 19606
(C/pv,w)

Custom Furniture & Cabinets, Inc.
N. 55 Cedar Street
Post Falls, ID 83854
(C/pv,w)

Custom Wood Products, Inc.
P.O. Box 4516
Roanoke, VA 24015
(C/pv,w)

Diamond Cabinets
P.O. Box 547
Hillsboro, OR 97123
(S/w)

Elfa/West, Inc.
170 McCormick Avenue
Costa Mesa, CA 92626
(SP/m,i)

Grayline Housewares
1616 Berkeley Street
Elgin, IL 60120
(SP/m)

Haas Cabinet Co., Inc.
625 W. Utica Street
Sellersburg, IN 47172
(S/w)

Hager Manufacturing Co.
1522 N. Front Street
Box 1117
Mankato, MN 56001
(C/w)

Heidapal Designs, Inc.
719 Swift Street, No. 1
Santa Cruz, CA 95060
(C,SO/pv,w,i)

Hoffmeister Cabinets of Nevada
3069 Sheridan Street
Las Vegas, NV 89102
(C,S,SO/pv,w)

Home-Crest Corp.
P.O. Box 595
Goshen, IN 46526
(C,S/w)

Imperial Cabinet Co., Inc.
P.O. Box 427
Gaston, IN 47342
(SO/w)

Ingrid, Ltd.
3061 N. Skokie Highway
North Chicago, IL 60064
(SP/p)

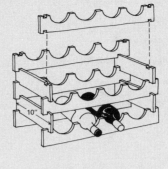

J-Wood
P.O. Box 367
Milroy, PA 17063
(C/pv,w)

Kapri Kitchens
P.O. Box 100
Dallastown, PA 17313
(C/w)

Kemper
701 South N Steet
Richmond, IN 47374
(S/pv,w)

Kent Moore Cabinets, Inc.
P.O. Box 3206
College Station, TX 77840
(C,SO/w)

Kitchen Kompact, Inc.
P.O. Box 868
Jeffersonville, IN 47130
(S/w)

Long Bell Cabinets
P.O. Box 579
Longview, WA 98632
(S/w)

Macor, Inc.
Cabinet Division
912 E. High Street
Mundelein, IL 60060
(C,S,SO/pv,w,i)

MasterCraft Industries Corp.
6175 E. 39th Avenue
Denver, CO 80207
(S/pv,w)

Medallion Kitchens, Inc.
810 First Street South
Hopkins, MN 55343
(S,SO/w)

Merillat Industries, Inc.
2075 W. Beecher Road
Adrian, MI 49221
(S/pv,w)

Merit Industries, Ltd.
12185 86th Avenue
Surrey, B.C.
Canada V3W-3H-8
(S/pv,w)

Micell Cabinet Corp.
501 Washington Avenue
Carlstadt, NJ 07072
(C/pv,w)

Overton Co.
P.O. Box 849
Kenly, NC 27542
(C,S,SO/pv,w)

Pacific Cabinet Corp.
Spokane Industrial Park
Building 26
Spokane, WA 99216
(C,S,SO/pv,w)

Pennville Custom Cabinets
P.O. Box 1266
Portland, IN 47371
(C/w)

Perfection Wood Products
7645 York Street
Denver, CO 80229
(C,SO/pv,w)

Plastics Unlimited, Inc.
Depot and First Streets
Youngwood, PA 15697
(C,S/pv)

Poggenpohl USA Corp.
P.O. Box 10
Teaneck, NJ 07666
(C/pv,w,i)

Prestige Cabinet Corp. of America
29 Rider Place
Freeport, NY 11520
(C/pv)

Prestige Products, Inc.
P.O. Box 314
Neodesha, KS 66757
(S/w)

Quaker Maid
Route 61
Leesport, PA 19533
(C,S/pv,w)

Quality Cabinets of Houston
6048 Westview
Houston, TX 77055
(C/w)

Rainier Woodworking Co.
16318 S. Meridian
Puyallup, WA 98371
(C/pv,w)

Rene Products
8600 Harrison Road
Cleves, OH 45002
(C,S/pv,w)

Rich Maid Kitchens, Inc.
Route 422
Wernersville, PA 19565
(C/w)

Rubbermaid Incorporated
1147 Akron Road
Wooster, OH 44691
(SP/p)

Rutt Custom Kitchens
Route 23
Goodville, PA 17528
(C/w)

Saint Charles Manufacturing Co., Inc.
1611 E. Main Street
Saint Charles, IL 60174
(C/pv,w)

Sawyer Cabinet, Inc.
12744 San Fernando Road
Sylmar, CA 91342
(C,S,SO/m,pv,w)

H. J. Scheirich Co.
P.O. Box 21037
Louisville, KY 40221
(S/w)

Schmidt-Haus
5237 Verona Road
Madison, WI 53711
(C,SO/pv)

Style-Line Manufacturing Co., Inc.
2081 S. 56th Street
West Allis, WI 53219
(C,S/pv,i)

Syroco
P.O. Box 4875
Syracuse, NY 13202
(SP/p)

Transco Plastics Corp.
26100 Richmond Road
Cleveland, OH 44146
(SP/p)

Triangle Pacific Corp.
P.O. Box 220100
Dallas, TX 75222
(C,S,SO/pv,w)

Waldorf Kitchens
Box 578
Waldorf, MD 20601
(C,S,SO/pv,w)

Wood Metal Industries
Wood Mode Cabinetry
Kreamer, PA 17833
(C/w)

XA Cabinet Corp.
16930 Valley View
La Mirada, CA 90638
(C,S/pv,w)

Yorktowne
P.O. Box 231
Red Lion, PA 17356
(S,SO/pv,w)

INDEX

PHOTOGRAPHERS

Glenn Christiansen: 10, 21 bottom. **Robert Cox:** 18, 71 bottom left and bottom right. **Jack McDowell:** 12 left and right, 13 left and right, 14 left and right, 15 top left, 16 right, 17 top and bottom, 20, 21 top, 22 left and right, 24 top, 33, 34, 36 left, 37 bottom, 38 top, 39 top, 40, 41 bottom, 43 top left and bottom right, 44, 45 left and right, 46 left and right, 47 left, 48 right, 57, 58 right, 60 bottom, 61 top left and bottom, 64 top and bottom, 65 top, 66, 68, 69 top left, 70 top, 71 top left. **Steve W. Marley:** 16 left, 19 left, top right, and bottom right, 24 bottom, 35 top right, 39 bottom middle, 41 top, 42, 43 top right, 47 left, 58 left, 59 top and bottom, 60 top, 62, 63 top left and bottom, 65 bottom left and bottom right, 69 right, 71 top right. **Don Normark:** 11 left, 72. **Rob Super:** 9 top and bottom, 11 right, 15 top right and bottom, 23 left and right, 35 bottom left, 36 right, 39 bottom right, 48 left, 63 top right, 67, 69 bottom left. **Darrow M. Watt:** 35 bottom right, 37 top, 61 right. **Tom Yee:** 38 bottom, 70 bottom.

Sunset Ideas for
Bedroom &
Bath Storage

By the Editors of Sunset Books and Sunset Magazine

LANE PUBLISHING CO. • Menlo Park, California

We gratefully acknowledge the many architects, designers, and homeowners whose ideas have come together in this book. We also extend special thanks to Kathryn L. Arthurs, Hilary Hannon, and Marian May for their assistance in assembling the color section.

Editor, Sunset Books:
Elizabeth L. Hogan

Sixth printing March 1989

Cover: A whole wall of closets distinguishes this handsome redwood bedroom. The section on the right includes a rod for hanging full-length garments; cubbyholes for sweaters and extra bedding; and a handy slanting shoe rack. To the left of the bathroom doorway are cubbyholes and a bank of drawers for shirts, lingerie, and other foldables; a tie rack; and a convenient dressing mirror. Further down the wall, double-decker rods (not shown) hold shorter garments.

The closet doors are louvered for ventilation; and to combat that closet pest, the moth, the closets feature cedar interiors. Architect: Donald Olsen. Interior design: Andrew Delfino. Photographed by Steve W. Marley. Cover designed by Zan Fox.

Supervising Editor:
Helen Sweetland

Staff Editor: **Susan Warton**

Contributing Editor: **Scott Atkinson**

Design: **Roger Flanagan**

Photo Editor: **JoAnn Masaoka Lewis**

Illustrations: **Joe Seney**

Mark Pechenik

Contents

Bedroom Storage

If you're concerned about making the most of space in your home, take a moment for this short quiz: Where do you watch Pavarotti at the Met? Where do you balance the family budget? Where do you iron? Where do your children play? Where do you accumulate those books you're planning to read? Where do you listen to your favorite record albums? And where do you enjoy a late-night snack?

Almost for sure, the answer to some or all of these questions is "in the bedroom." Because space is at a premium in most homes, bedrooms must perform a dual role—at least.

Take an inventory. Beyond the obvious bedroom basics, what extraneous items wind up in this room? How are you going to keep them easily usable, cared for, and housed in harmony with the bedroom decor? With a little ingenuity, you can organize supplies for hobbies, work, and precious moments of relaxation to keep your bedroom from becoming a center for uncontrolled clutter. Look at pages 16 and 17 for examples of well-organized double-duty bedrooms.

Children's rooms that double as play areas are shown on pages 24 and 25.

Looking at your bedroom with fresh eyes? Consider the largest space-gobbler of all—the bed. There's no real need for a bed to take up valuable space in today's small-scale bedrooms. If your ceiling is high, how about raising the bed off the floor? Sleeping lofts uncork gallons of space below for whatever activity you choose; we show some on pages 28 and 29. Or you may be interested in more down-to-earth ideas, such as the space-saving hideaway beds shown on pages 14 and 15.

When your bed must occupy a position of importance in the room, make it serve as a major storage spot. If you explore custom designs, you'll discover clever ways to tuck things around and under the bed. The headboard end of the bed offers plenty of storage potential too. Some attractive and practical storage headboards appear on pages 10 and 11, and bedside and underbed storage on pages 6 through 9. Included in this section is the ultimate bedside system, offering headboard, nightstand, bolster bins, and foot-of-the-bed storage.

You certainly won't have to sacrifice storage if you choose to use the head of your bed as a room divider—take a look at the dual-purpose headboards on pages 12 and 13.

When it comes time to rest, you'll want to surround yourself with amenities. Do you need to lodge (and possibly conceal or camouflage) bulky equipment for musical or televised entertainment? You'll find ideas on pages 18 through 23.

What about nighttime reading? Are a couple of shelves adequate—or will you need a wall-length bookcase, as shown on page 18?

On pages 26 and 27 you'll find ideas for accommodating such bedtime comforts as extra pillows and quilts—items too bulky to reside easily in the average linen closet or bureau. Instead, pouf them into a hollow headboard or under a convenient window seat.

What you need to store, of course, depends on how you live. The storage units or systems you choose are a matter of taste and budget. You may be among the people who like the relatively informal, open look of simple bins or baskets—sometimes the things we need to store look pretty enough to display at the same time. Or you may prefer to shut away most of your possessions behind closed drawers, doors, or draperies. In either case, efficiency should be a common denominator.

Happily, reorganizing bedroom space doesn't necessarily require that you hire a contractor, or even a carpenter. This chapter offers many ideas you can use even if your carpentry skills are limited (the *Sunset* book *Basic Carpentry Illustrated* might be just what you need). Or you can take your suggestions to a cabinetmaker or designer for the ultimate in individualized storage.

Whatever your storage requirements, whatever your taste, you'll find a bounty of good ideas to stimulate your thinking as you leaf through the forthcoming chapter.

A Bedside Storage System

Four easy-to-build units that you can use separately
—or in various combinations—to boost bedside storage

Build just one component—or build them all

A small bedroom, especially one that doubles as a home office or den, is a storage challenge. One way to maximize bedroom space is to make the bed itself (a space-waster for two-thirds of the day) as storage-efficient as possible.

The system shown here almost frames your mattress with places to stow things. Since you may not need this much storage at once, the four pieces—a headboard, a nightstand, a bolster with bins, and a foot-of-the-bed chest—are designed to work independently, as well as in various combinations. Just choose what fits your storage needs, your room layout, and your taste; alter the suggested dimensions as you wish. The four components are described in detail below and on the facing page.

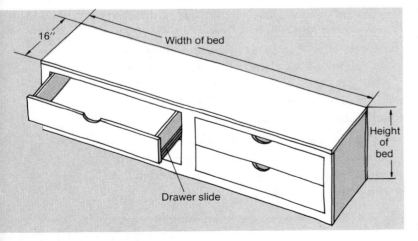

The foot-of-the-bed chest

A low chest of drawers at the foot of a full-size bed has nearly the same storage capacity as a traditional bedroom bureau, yet it's not nearly as bulky. It can also double as a bench or television shelf.

You can buy a unit built especially for the foot of the bed; or try one designed for a different purpose (such as storing engineers' maps and blueprints).

To put together a chest like the one shown, build a frame from ¾-inch plywood, then install four custom-made drawers on standard slides. Make the chests the same height and width as your bed and approximately 16 inches deep.

Another foot-of-the-bed chest appears on page 26.

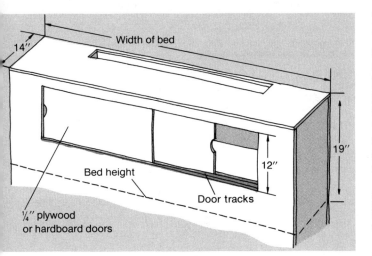

The headboard

This simple yet handsome unit has a storage compartment with handy sliding doors to hide clutter. Its flat top offers a useful surface with an inset at the back that's just deep enough to display magazines and books. The portion of the headboard above the mattress should be approximately 19 inches high and 14 inches deep; the width and overall height of the headboard will be determined by the size of your bed. Sheets, blankets, quilts, and bedspreads alter measurements, so it's wise to measure when these are in place.

Build the headboard from ¾-inch plywood. Use ¼-inch plywood or hardboard for the sliding doors, and install plastic, wood, or metal door tracks. Finish the unit with enamel.

You'll find another easy-to-build headboard on page 27.

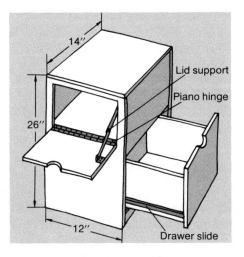

The nightstand

Two storage compartments are stacked inside this compact unit. The top one is a cubbyhole with a hinged, drop-down door in front; below it is a roomy drawer that pulls out from the side.

The nightstand shown here is approximately 12 inches wide, 14 inches deep, and 26 inches high; you can adjust these dimensions to suit your own needs. (To use the nightstand alone, you'll probably want to make it both wider and deeper, with a bottom drawer that pulls out from the front.)

Build the unit from ¾-inch plywood. Buy a ready-made drawer—or build your own—and install it on standard drawer slides. Finish the nightstand with enamel.

The bolster bins

The padded lid of this bedside box hinges open to reveal storage bins for bedding, out-of-season clothing, sewing or sports equipment, or miscellaneous bedroom clutter. The whole assembly—bottom, sides, dividers, and lid—is made from ¾-inch plywood.

Build the box the same height as your bed (or a few inches shorter); box length will be determined by the length of your bed and by the arrangement of the other pieces in your bedside storage system. Twelve inches is a convenient width for the unit, making it unobtrusive, yet wide enough so the bolster can double as a dressing seat or midnight-snack counter. Attach the lid with a piano hinge, and cover all the exposed surfaces of the box (or just the lid) with carpet or foam-backed fabric.

Use bolster bins on one, two, or all four sides of your bed.

Underbed Storage

If the area under your bed collects nothing but dust,
add chests or pull-outs—or a custom-designed storage
platform—to utilize that wealth of wasted space

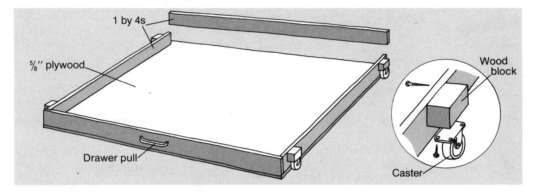

1 by 4s
5/8″ plywood
Wood block
Drawer pull
Caster

Make your own roll-out drawers

Even a standard metal bedframe can accommodate underbed storage. Add casters (remembering to allow an
inch or so for clearance—more for thick carpeting) to
ready-made shallow drawers—or to ones that you build
yourself.

To construct a simple underbed drawer, fasten strips
of 1 by 4s around the edges of a 5/8-inch plywood
bottom (as shown), then add the wood blocks and
casters, and attach a handle. A plywood lid will keep
stored items free of dust—but you'll have to either pull
the drawer out completely for access, or hinge the lid in
the center.

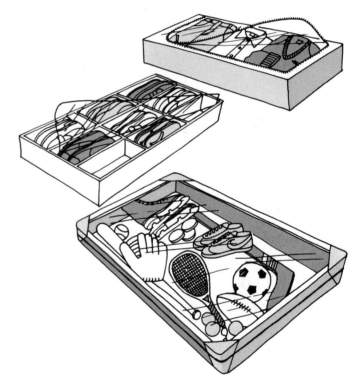

Custom bed holds roll-around cart

Designing a new bed?
Consider leaving space
for a handy roll-around
cart with storage com-
partments, like the one
shown here. Tucked
away, the unit blends in
with the rest of the un-
derbed cabinetry. Pulled
out, the cart doubles as a
nightstand or breakfast-
in-bed table.

Ready-made containers slide under standard bedframes

Trays and chests made expressly for underbed storage
are commercially available in plastic, wood, and cardboard. Many have dividers; most have lids or see-
through vinyl covers. These inexpensive storage aids are
perfect for shoes, out-of-season clothing, bed linens.
Look for them in the notions sections of department
stores, or in mail-order catalogs.

Cabinetry creates base for platform bed

This 120-square-foot guest bedroom/office boasts more storage space than many bedrooms twice its size—thanks to a handsome platform bed with banks of drawers and a cabinet built in. Guests climb up to the sleeping level on three steps which are incorporated into the adjoining desk. Architect: Violeta Autumn.

Bedframe features double-decker drawers

Two levels of drawers are built into this striking bedframe, which is coated with glossy black lacquer. The upper level is perfect for sweaters and lingerie; the lower level is roomy enough for extra bedding. Heavy-duty metal slides let the drawers open and close smoothly. Architect: Wendell Lovett. Interior design: Suzanne Braddock.

Headboard Storage

The head of a bed can do much more than prop up pillows

Bed-hugging headboard

Warm wood cabinetry wraps comfortingly around the head of this bed. Long and sleek, yet somehow snug in appearance, the sweeping headboard furnishes individual niches for a number of bedside conveniences. It even houses a stereo system, a luxury far too cumbersome for most headboards to accommodate. Just behind the slanting backrest, three hatches keep a telephone (its jangle muffled) and extra bedding hidden from view but easy to reach. Design: Richard Pennington.

Headboard appropriates a whole wall

Commodious and versatile, this headboard wall system provides generous storage for everything from books to clothing to Christmas tree lights, while catering to bedside needs. Tucked into its custom-fitted alcove, the head of the bed has behind-the-pillows storage and a ledge for midnight snacks. For reading, there's ample light from the recessed fixtures above. Design: Eurodesign Modular Furniture.

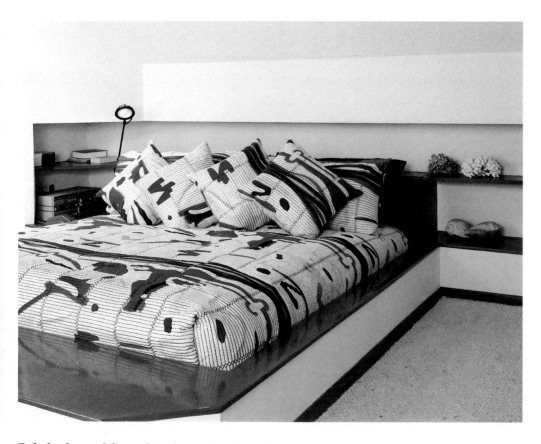

Polished wood for a shipshape sleeping alcove

This handsome platform bed sports a wraparound deck of glossy mahogany. Extending from the deck at the head of the bed are a slanted backrest/headboard with a flip-open top for storage, and open shelves that carry as much or as little bedside paraphernalia as the owners wish, from audio equipment to seashells. Design: MLA/Architects.

Open-and-shut case for bedside storage

Flap-door bins at the head of this bed hide bulky items such as spare linens and pillows. Closed, the doors double as a slanting backrest. (For safety, the doors are never left open when the bed is occupied.)

The compartment on the left houses provisions for nighttime comfort and security: an intercom and light controls for the entire house. Drawers on each side of the bed provide additional storage. Design: Ron Yeo.

Room-dividing Headboards

A two-faced approach to both spatial and storage needs

Floating island in a tranquil setting

In this pretty, pale bedroom, the bed takes center stage—it's a serene island of comfort as well as hard-working storage. Its massive yet sleek headboard is the focal point, partitioning the room into sleeping and dressing areas. On the sleeping side, almost hidden behind the bed pillows, cabinet doors cover storage crannies for bedside necessities; above them, an airy alcove more than accommodates reading lamps, books, a clock-radio, and a pretty plant. On the opposite side, the headboard serves up a dozen drawers, topped with a mirrored niche for toiletries and a jewelry box. Architect: Phoebe T. Wall.

Extra warmth on one side, extra storage on the other

In a bedroom of generous size, this freestanding fireplace wall separates a cozy sitting area from the sleeping quarters. On the headboard side of the wall, bookshelves surround a center panel that offers swing-arm lamps—and plenty of space to prop pillows—for bedtime reading. Architects: The Bumgardner Architects.

Handsome, clever, and capacious

More than compensating for the bedroom's single small closet, this vast bedframe-headboard-wardrobe unit also creates a private dressing corridor behind the bed. In front, tawny oak shelves climb nearly to the ceiling, framing an upholstered backrest. In back, the same rich oak forms a capacious set of cabinets and drawers. Design: The Butt Joint.

13

Hideaway Beds

For small bedrooms, guest bedrooms, double-duty bedrooms—
sleeping facilities that literally come out of the woodwork

Sleepy? Just pull down the wall

Mr. Murphy's popular patented invention of 1905 tilted out of a closet. Today's streamlined versions operate in similar fashion, concealing themselves during the day behind a door or a "secret panel," like the one shown here. The homeowners just pull on the painting's frame, and down comes a full-size platform bed—a ready-made, commercially available unit that was incorporated into a new wall during remodeling. Architects: The Burke Associates.

Daytime seating becomes nighttime bedding

Nestled in a nook of a none-too-spacious cedar cabin, the built-in bench pictured above gets in nobody's way during the day. And when it's bedtime, the base and cushion fold out separately, transforming the seating area into the double bed shown on the left. Separate supports for the sleeping platform are kept in a drawer beneath the bench during the day. Architects: Larsen, Lagerquist & Morris.

Double-duty Bedrooms

Managing the paraphernalia when sleeping quarters share space with hobbies or homework

In the mode of yesteryear

Dressmaking is one of those hobbies that are notorious for clutter. Yet neatness really counts when you're thick in the folds of a complicated project. In this sewing corner, functional antiques and a home-designed wall cabinet handle quantities of dressmaking supplies without disturbing the old-fashioned look of the bedroom.

On the left, thread spools parade their colors in a turn-of-the-century display case. The lace-bedecked figure above it is a child-size Victorian dress form. These days an electric machine stands on the antique treadle cabinet. Above it, the sewing notions sit in small drawers made from aluminum bread pans faced with wood.

Corner cutout for paperwork in privacy

For book-balancing or tax forms, thank-you notes or PTA flyers, epic poems or crossword puzzles, a small home office certainly aids achievement. But where to put it? Most homes nowadays lack spare rooms that aren't already reserved for the television or visiting relatives.

As this situation shows, a bedroom corner may provide the ideal location—out of traffic's way and relatively private. This office is neatly tucked into an alcove originally intended as a closet. The angles of the desk allow for leg room and a bank of drawers, as well as vertical slots large enough for sketch pads and blueprints; the wraparound desktop offers ample work space. Overhead, a small bookcase completes the corner. Architect: David Jeremiah Hurley. Interior design: Jois.

Camera cache in a closet

Most of us connect closets with clothing. Naturalists may think first of moths, psychiatrists and genealogists of skeletons. But to an enthusiastic photographer, the closet in a spare bedroom can serve quite a different purpose: safely storing all the delicate and valuable apparatus of his craft. Here, floor-to-ceiling adjustable shelves behind bifold closet doors keep cameras and gear in tidy, easily accessible order. There's even room on the closet floor for a small refrigerator for film. Closet interior: Just Closets.

Bedroom Wall Systems

Cabinets, drawers, open shelves keep your private world in order

Bedroom bibliotheque

At the end of a weary day, some of us hit the hay, some of us hit the sack, and some of us also hit the books, at least for a little while before we doze off. For inveterate bedtime readers, bookshelves figure significantly in bedroom storage arrangements. Here, an orderly and cheery wallful of literature offers abundant possibilities for collecting, rearranging, perusing, lending, borrowing, displaying and, of course, reading. Architects: Rachlin Architects.

Wall-length whatnot

What, exactly, a whatnot holds is entirely up to its owner's fancy. While this one is less ornate and more purely functional than what Grandma might have called a whatnot, it certainly has all the versatility of those nostalgic storage pieces. Like the cabinetry shown on pages 20 and 21, it houses a television, as well as books and clothing, and then extends itself into a dainty glass-topped writing desk. Architects: Woody Dike and Tom Moore. Cabinet design: L. W. Grady.

That's entertainment!

On display here are some of the essentials of a bedroom entertainment center: stereo components, a library of record albums, and several shelves of books. For stow-away storage, this attractive wooden wall system also offers drawers and more drawers, cabinets and more cabinets. Three cubbyholes along the countertop have the same kind of covering found on roll-top desks. For ideas on storing the bedroom TV—another entertainment essential—turn to pages 20 and 21. Architect: Robert C. Peterson.

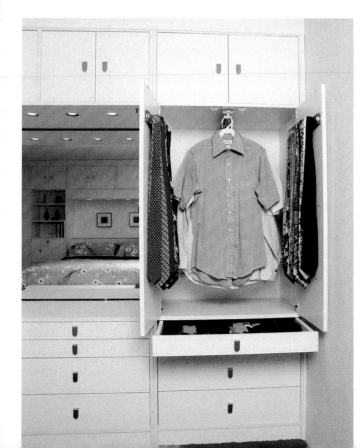

In a nutshell—it's natty

Open the big doors in this wall unit, and what do you find but a handy small-scale closet. Crisp shirts on a pullout rod line up along its center, while neckties hang neatly from racks placed high on either cabinet door. With nary an inch of wall space wasted, cabinets and drawers abound, surrounding the counter and recessed mirror. Design: Eurodesign Modular Furniture.

Television Storage

Keeping the set out of sight when it's out of mind

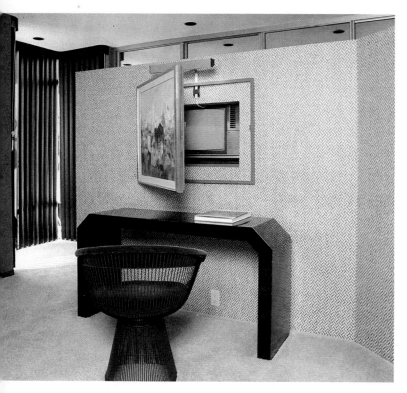

Artful camouflage

A framed painting swings back against the wall, allowing this television set to retire modestly from view when nobody's watching it. Without intruding on the sleek bedroom decor, the set is still ready for action when Bogart wakes up the wee hours of the TV schedule. Architect: William W. Hedley, Jr. Interior design: Charles Falls.

Sharing space with the shirts

The owner of this handsome, custom-built armoire can watch the morning news as he selects a shirt for the day. The television is bolted securely to a swivel-topped pull-out shelf, so it can be turned or brought forward for easier viewing. But when TV time is over, and the armoire doors are closed, there's no hint of the screen—or the shirts.

Even in antique storage pieces, there are often nooks and crannies that can be used for television storage; two antique hideaways are shown on pages 22 and 23. Interior design: Anona Colvin.

Cornering a super screen

For people who like wide video horizons, projection television has become a popular new luxury in home entertainment. But what about those times when you'd like it to be out of sight and out of mind? One simple solution, decoratively effected here, is to place the whole works in a vacant corner, then hide it all behind tall bifold doors. Interior design: Curt Graham.

Now you see it, now you don't

In a little hole-in-the-wall of its own, this television nestles discreetly under the sill of a greenhouse window. Cabinet doors shut it away from view when it's not being used. The drawer below and the narrow cabinets on either side provide additional bedroom storage. Architects: Ted Tanaka and Frank Purtill.

Antique Storage Furniture

Yesterday's chests and dressers still hold their own as storage units

From the Far East—a *chan jang*

Originally a Korean kitchen cupboard, this good-looking antique now accommodates the needs of a Western bedroom. A unique catch-all, it neatly tucks away shoes, handbags, sweaters, sewing paraphernalia, books, and even a tiny television set.

Crafted in the 19th century of elm wood, the wonderfully mellowed piece has been lined with pages of calligraphy from an old Korean book. Small drawers at the top serve handily for such items as jewelry, scarves, or billets-doux. *Chan jang* courtesy of Sloan Miyasato.

A bit of old Peking, by way of Europe

During the late 19th century period that we usually associate with Art Nouveau, French aristocrats took a liking to the exotic yet rustic look of Chinese furnishings designed at the time expressly for export to Europe. This dresser, of burnt bamboo and woven cane, may once have graced a fashionable country boudoir in the south of France. Today its deep drawers hold a multitude of 20th century foldables. Interior design: Ruth Soforenko Interiors.

Victorian hideaway for books, TV

Last century's clothes-keepers can be refurbished to suit contemporary tastes and to hold one of this century's most popular inventions. This richly carved Victorian armoire, American-made of oak, was stripped, bleached, and finally waxed to show off its natural golden color. The interior has been lined, and the doors upholstered, in a fabric that matches the bedroom wallpaper. Finally, a swivel-topped, pull-out plywood tray was added to hold a television set. Interior design: Ruth Soforenko Interiors.

Eastlake's "plain" is modern-day fancy

True to the dictates of Charles Eastlake's *Hints on Household Taste,* published in 1872, this charming dresser of the "golden oak" era looks almost austere for a Victorian piece. But its simple ornamentation (carved rather than superficially stamped into the solid wood) and pretty round mirror lend eye-catching style to this present-day bedroom.

Children's Rooms

Storing toys so they're easy to reach,
easy to put away, and easy on the eyes

Tomato-tone lockers for play area

Playtime paraphernalia can be stashed in metal lockers just like the ones used in schools and gymnasiums. (To find dealers in your area, look under "Lockers" in the Yellow Pages of your telephone directory.) Sandwiched between the lockers are baskets of vinyl-coated wire for visible storage; they slide in and out on their own heavy-duty plastic framework. A butcher block countertop ties the system together and provides additional storage space. The cork bulletin board above displays posters and drawings—and keeps the walls free of tacks and tape. Interior design: Joan Simon.

Bunkbeds with built-in storage bunkers

An expansive drawer slides out from beneath these clean white plastic laminate bunkbeds to deliver toys to the adjacent play area. At the end of the beds is a mini-armoire with adjustable shelves for clothing, as shown here, or for additional toys. The cabinet top doubles as a nightstand for the upper bunk. Furniture courtesy of Julianus Associates.

The building blocks of a toy storage system

Versatile storage modules do more than organize mountains of playthings. They can be combined to form desks, platform beds, room dividers, and wall systems—then rearranged to suit the changing needs of growing children. You can buy ready-made modules in wood, particle board, or plastic—or you can build your own.

Construct your modules from ¾-inch plywood suitable for painting. A convenient size for each module is 16 inches square; for compatibility, make rectangular ones 16 by 16 by 32 inches. Add shelves (they double as vertical dividers when you rearrange the modules), hinged doors, even simple drawers; use wood molding or veneer tape to hide the plywood edges. Finish the modules with enamel—a single bright shade or a rainbow of colors.

If you stack several modules, be sure to bolt them to the wall or floor—or to each other—for stability.

Drawing desk holds a row of rolling toy bins

With the lid down, a toy bin or two pulled out, and a small chair pulled up, this handy unit serves as a drawing desk. But when playtime is over, the toy bins slide under the desktop to form a single, compact storage unit. Desk sides and lid are built from ¾-inch plywood; the bottom of the divided tray is made of ⅜-inch plywood or ¼-inch hardboard; and the tray frame is built from fir 1 by 4s. The unit illustrated is 19 inches high, 20 inches deep, and 48 inches wide, but you can adjust these dimensions to suit your child's needs.

Assemble the desk with glue and woodscrews or finishing nails. Attach the swing-up lid with a piano hinge, and add a lid support (or chain) at each end. Depending on the dimensions of your unit, the drawers of an old file cabinet might furnish ready-to-use bins (just add casters); or make your own bins from plywood. Finish the desk and bins with bright-colored enamel.

Stuffed animals on display

A doll tree can store a whole crowd of cuddly companions. Made from a closet rod 1⅜ inches in diameter, the tree stands in a Christmas-tree holder which has been bolted to the floor for extra stability. To attach the dolls, sew small plastic rings to their backs, and hang them from cuphooks screwed into the "trunk" of the tree.

Oversize Storage

If bulky items are a king-size storage problem,
try one of these large-capacity solutions

Capacious compartments under seat cushions

Window seats aren't merely delightful places to curl up with a novel and a mug of coffee. Below those comfortable cushions are jumbo-capacity drawers, pull-out bins, or simply a large enclosed space that's reached through a hinged top or cabinet doors.

Window seats are basically either "built-in" or "built-out." The first type is usually built into a window alcove during construction or a major remodeling. The second type, which can be added on later, is essentially a long, narrow cabinet that's built out from the wall below an existing window. You can extend a built-out window seat along an entire wall—or around a whole room. Or, to achieve a built-in effect, you can install a wall system on both sides of a window, and build a seat in the "recess" created below the window.

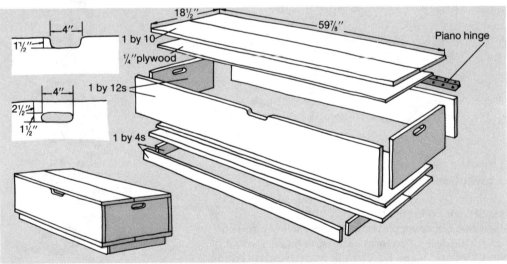

Get a firm foothold on oversize storage

There are scores of chests commercially available that can handle foot-of-the-bed storage—from steamer trunks and footlockers to rattan hampers and handsome cedar chests. But it's easy—and inexpensive—to build one of your own.

With a cushion on top, this clear pine storage chest doubles as a dressing seat. The four sides are cut from 1 by 12s; the lid and bottom are each made from two side-by-side 1 by 10s backed with one piece of ¼-inch plywood (the plywood pieces are cut slightly smaller—17 by 58⅜ inches for the chest illustrated here—to slip between the 1 by 12 frame); and the entire unit rests on a base made from 1 by 4 strips. The dimensions shown are for a queen-size chest, but you can adjust them to fit your own bed.

For another foot-of-the-bed idea, see page 6.

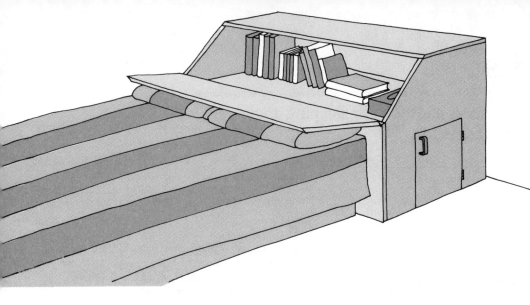

Easy-to-build hollow headboard

With two storage levels, this good-looking headboard has plenty of room for bulky items such as pillows and comforters. What's more, the door of the upper compartment doubles as a slanting backrest.

The depth of the unit is 24 inches. Make the headboard 12 inches taller than your bed and 2 inches wider. The backrest/door slants back at a 45-degree angle just above mattress level.

Build the headboard from ¾-inch plywood. Before assembly, cut a door out of each side piece (for access to the lower compartment). Assemble the pieces, nail 1 by 3 cleats to the inside of the headboard to hold the interior shelf, and attach the backrest/door with a piano hinge. Reattach the side-piece doors with hinges, and add door pulls and magnetic catches. Finish the headboard with enamel.

For another easy-to-build headboard and more bedside storage ideas, **see page 7**.

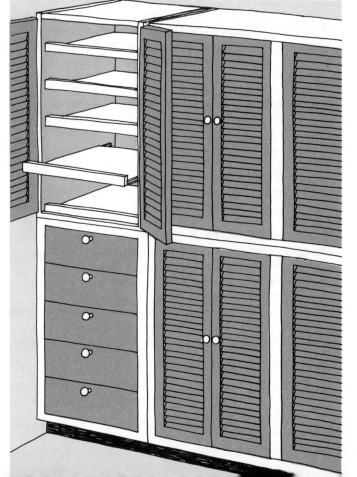

Towering pillar for paraphernalia

A floor-to-ceiling storage column offers space enough for everything from sweaters and lingerie to extra blankets. It might be part of a larger wall system, or it can stand alone in an otherwise unused corner.

Ready-made storage columns are available in furniture showrooms and home centers. You can also have a cabinet-maker design a unit to fit your special needs.

Sleeping Lofts

If your bedroom has a high ceiling, elevate your sleeping area
to open up storage or living space below

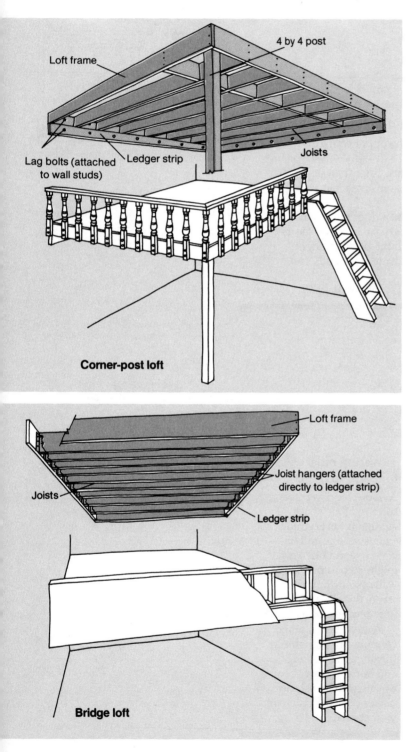

Corner-post loft

Loft frame

4 by 4 post

Lag bolts (attached to wall studs)

Ledger strip

Joists

Loft frame

Joist hangers (attached directly to ledger strip)

Joists

Ledger strip

Bridge loft

Lofty ideas

Lofts are simply elevated platforms that add floor space
—and visual interest—to a room. They're especially useful in studio apartments (renters should check with the
landlord before building, of course) and in bedrooms
that double as work or entertainment centers.

Ceiling height, obviously, is a critical factor. As a
practical guide, consider 6½ feet the minimum headroom needed for standing below a loft, and 4½ feet the
minimum headroom needed for sitting up in the bed
above. (But always check your local building codes; the
requirements for your area may be different.) Add
another foot for the structure of the loft itself, and you'll
find that you need a ceiling that's about 12 feet high. If
you have the 8-foot ceilings that are standard in so
many newer homes, you'll have to remove all or part of
the existing ceiling, or be content with the more "down-
to-earth" forms of underbed storage (see pages 8–9).

Two basic loft designs are illustrated here. The corner-
post loft is supported by a ledger strip on one wall and
two corner posts, or by ledger strips on two adjoining
walls and one corner post. The bridge loft touches three
adjoining walls and is supported by ledger strips on the
two opposing ones. A third type (not shown) is a freestanding loft, which requires support posts on all four
corners with braces to prevent sway. But the freestanding
loft is not as sturdy as the other two, and it's more complicated to build.

Once you've determined your design and dimensions, check them with your local building department.

Use structural fir for the loft frame and wall ledgers.
(Essentially, you're building a new floor and supporting
it above the existing one, so the size of your structural
lumber will depend on the number of feet the loft will
span. Check local codes.) You'll also need ¾-inch plywood for the loft floor, 4 by 4s of structural fir for any
corner support posts, and materials for a ladder and
safety rails.

You'll probably want to furnish your loft simply, in
keeping with its small scale. And remember that it's a
sleeping loft—not designed for heavy storage.

Some ideas for using the new space *under* your loft
are illustrated on the facing page.

Mini-library

Need a peaceful retreat for reading or listening to music? Create a cozy den below your sleeping loft by adding shelves for books, records, and stereo components. If you have a bridge loft (see facing page), just fasten shelves to the walls underneath it using L-braces or adjustable tracks and brackets. With a corner-post loft, let the backs of freestanding bookcases define the walls of your new mini-library. For comfort, add your favorite chair, an area rug, and a good reading lamp.

Office or sewing room

Turn your underloft space into a compact office by setting up a desk or drawing table, bookshelves for reference books and supplies, a telephone, and a file cabinet. Or create a sewing room by installing a sewing machine, a counter for cutting out material, drawers for fabric and patterns, a wall organizer for thread and notions, and perhaps a pull-out ironing board. If you have a bridge loft—or if you've added walls beneath your corner-post loft—you can hang cabinets or shelves from the wall studs and not encroach on precious floor space.

Walk-in closet & dressing room

Install a closet rod or two beneath your loft, then add a bank of drawers and a dressing table with a lighted make-up mirror, and you've created a walk-in closet that doubles as a dressing room. Sliding or folding louvered doors will keep the area private yet well ventilated. For more closet and dressing-room ideas, see the next chapter, pages 30–53.

Closets & Dressing Areas

Many of us, preoccupied with our busy lives, turn a negligent eye to the state of our closets until the calendar announces the season for old-fashioned spring cleaning. And sometimes even that isn't enough to nudge us.

At the same time, just about everyone would really like to have a nice, orderly closet—a closet so well planned and tidy that a beloved garment could be easily found, and in sparkling condition, rather than crumpled from crowding. Though they may seem insignificant in the larger context of life, the small details of what we wear actually have quite a resounding effect on how we feel about ourselves throughout each day. In the upcoming chapter, you'll find many good ideas to make your closets more accommodating and to make you feel better about your wardrobe—and yourself.

The closet that comes with the home you move into—unless specifically designed otherwise—is likely to be either a roomy walk-in closet (especially in an older home) or a shallow, but lengthy, wall closet. Both have particular advantages. In general, clotheshorses prefer the walk-in style, simply because it usually holds more (see pages 36 and 37). Of course, with good space planning and double-decker closet rods, a wall closet can accommodate the most extensive collection of clothing. Some fine examples appear on pages 34 and 35.

And then there's the matter of doors. Here walk-ins have another advantage: a standard door that can usually carry accessories on specialized racks and hooks. Wall closets are most often equipped with sliding doors. These can be vexing, either because they occasionally jam or slip off their tracks or just because they never disclose a full view of a wardrobe. Accordion-fold doors, made of two or more hinged panels, are preferable. These fold back to each side, so you can review your closet's contents with one sweeping glance. But any closet door— standard, sliding, or accordion-fold—will be more effective if it's also louvered for ventilation.

Have you ever considered using a closet *without* doors? We show this new approach to clothing storage—the unabashed open look—on pages 38 and 39.

If you have space for a dressing area (or a separate dressing room), you'll find plenty of ideas for organizing and decorating it on pages 42 through 45. Some dressing areas can even perform a dual role. The one on page 44, for example, doubles as a laundry/ sewing room; the dressing room shown on page 45 also serves as an exercise studio.

Maybe you spend vacations at a small mountain cabin, or have college-age children who drop in, temporarily, at home. In either case, you'll find some useful ideas on pages 52 and 53, which are devoted to temporary and portable closets.

Is your youngster's closet a jumble of toys and crumpled clothing? Some delightful ideas for organizing kids' clothes quarters can be found on pages 40 and 41.

Carefully planning your closet storage means avoiding wasted space. Throughout this section you'll notice that closet rods are doubled; most of our apparel nowadays simply doesn't need the full 64-inch height generally provided by the single pole that is standard in traditional closets.

Having saved space with double-decker rods, you may be able to fit in several levels of shelves, drawers, or pull-out bins (see pages 32 and 33). In

this chapter, you'll see how bins of vinyl-coated wire have the triple advantages of cheerful good looks, maximum ventilation, and quick visibility of contents.

Shoes need shelving, too, so allow them an appropriate amount of closet space. Stored up off the floor, your footwear stays bright and dust-free. And you'll find it's much less frustrating to slide a vacuum cleaner quickly across an uncluttered closet floor.

Accessories also need places to call their own. Look at pages 48 and 49 for clever ideas on organizing them with special hangers, custom racks, baskets and barrels, and hooks and pegs.

To combat that closet pest, the moth, who has been dining on silks and woolens since they were first woven, you can line the closet with cedar, an effective but expensive solution. Or you can use repellent, taking care to keep it out of the reach of children.

After you've organized your closet and before you fill it once again, review your wardrobe, sorting it by categories of "Absolutely love this," "Not sure," and "Why did I buy this?" By keeping only the first two categories, you'll look—and feel—much better in your clothing.

A Closet System

Open shelves, drawers, and multilevel rods
work together to organize your clothes quarters

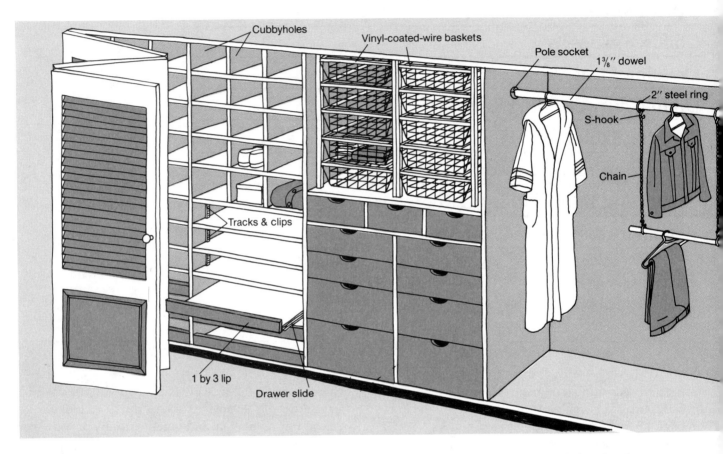

Cubbyholes · Vinyl-coated-wire baskets · Pole socket · 1⅜" dowel · 2" steel ring · S-hook · Chain · Tracks & clips · 1 by 3 lip · Drawer slide

Open shelves

Shelves are probably the most versatile components in a closet system. They accommodate items in a wide variety of shapes and sizes (from ten-gallon hats to handkerchiefs); they keep stored items visible; and they're easy to install. And if you use an adjustable system of tracks and clips or tracks and brackets, shelves are also easy to rearrange.

Fir and pine are good choices for closet shelving; so are ¾-inch plywood and particle board, especially if your shelves will be deeper than 12 inches. If you're planning a shelf longer than 4 feet (3 feet if it's particle board), be sure to add a mid-span support.

For added interest—and convenience—use vertical dividers to form clusters of cubbyholes, or convert some of your shelves to pull-outs by adding standard drawer slides and lipped edges made from 1 by 3s.

Drawers & pull-outs

Simplify your dressing routine—and gain valuable floor space in the bedroom—by eliminating your bulky bureau and adding a new drawer system in the closet. If you want a built-in unit, construct a frame to accommodate drawers custom-made to desired dimensions. Or buy a modular set of drawers. For visible storage, try a system of vinyl-coated-wire bins that glide in and out on their own framework.

Multilevel rods

In updated closets, the primary space waster—the traditional single closet rod—has given way to multiple rods whose heights are determined by the owner's clothing. But you needn't make any major structural changes to convert your closet to multilevel rods. Just buy an adjustable suspension bar, or make one of your own from a metal bar or wood dowel, steel rings, S-hooks, and some lightweight chain (as shown).

Closet metamorphosis

Before the new storage system was installed (see inset), this all-too-typical closet broke virtually every rule for good closet design and organization. Its one long shelf was crammed with hats and handbags, books and bedding, while the extra foot of space between the shelf items and the ceiling above was totally unused. Clothes were jammed together on the one long closet rod, which was low enough to make long dresses and robes dust the floor, yet high enough to leave several feet of wasted space below jackets, skirts, and blouses. Impossible to vacuum, the closet floor was a dusty jumble of shoes, boots, handbags, and luggage.

With the new organizers in place, the closet holds everything it did before—and more—with room to spare. Five different levels of closet rods make sure that each item gets the space it needs. The closet floor is clear (and dust-free) now that shoes and handbags are lined up on shelves of their own. And, best of all, the owners were able to eliminate their bulky bedroom bureau—thanks to a stack of large-capacity closet drawers and some roomy open shelves for sweaters and other foldables. Closet interior: Just Closets.

Wall Closets

A custom design can double—even triple—
your closet's storage potential

Wardrobe at a glance

Many of us have closets we're only too glad to shut the door on. But this one offers a compartmentalized network so neat that it's actually pleasing to contemplate from the vantage point of one's bed at 6 A.M. (The slide-out tie rack just to the right of the mirrored center panel is shown more closely on page 48.)

When the bifold doors are closed, an expanse of mirrors not only aids grooming but creates the illusion of doubled room depth. Interior design: Alan Lucas & Associates. Closet interior: Minimal Space.

Planning ingenuity creates a closet for two

A little engineering carved ample storage for both his wardrobe and hers in a relatively compact space—leaving the rest of this bedroom serenely uncluttered. Baskets of vinyl-coated wire offer several advantages over traditional, and bulky, chests of drawers: they allow ventilation, they make it easier to find your favorite pullover, and they hide neatly behind the closet doors. Architect: N. Kent Linn. Interior design: Joan Simon. Closet interior: Minimal Space.

Predawn efficiency

For many a commuter, every morning minute counts in the race to catch the train, bus, or carpool, and an efficiently arranged closet like this one can pare down dressing time and ease those important first decisions of the day. Thanks to the bifold doors, even sleep-filled eyes can take in most of the wardrobe at a glance. In the center of the closet, accessible from both sets of doors, are two rods offering double-decker storage for shirts, jackets, and slacks; at the far left, longer coats and robes hang at standard height. Shoe shelves eliminate floor clutter, and a stack of drawers and open shelves keeps folded shirts and other clothing in good order. Closet interior: Just Closets.

Cozy cache in a corner

Like the intricate honeycomb of a hard-working beehive, this remodeled high-and-narrow Victorian closet leaves scarcely a centimeter to chance disorder. New double-decker closet rods carry twice the freight of the original single one, and the newly installed bank of open shelves accommodates volumes of sweaters and other foldables without crush or confusion. Closet interior: Just Closets.

Walk-in Closets

Luxurious spots to shelter a wardrobe—some so spacious
they double as dressing rooms

**Within easy reach
of the bath**

Housing your garments
adjacent to the bathroom can
save flurry and flutter as you
race the clock on weekday
mornings.

Such convenience was
feasible here without threat
of moisture damage to the
wardrobe. The spacious bathroom is well ventilated (a must
for this kind of arrangement),
and a sliding door seals off
the adjoining closet.

Lighting for the closet is
supplied by fluorescent
tubes above the cornices.
Architects: Designbank.

High-rise housing for clothing foldables

Good-looking enough to display books or collectibles, the wall unit at one end of this spacious walk-in is a private cache for quantities of foldable clothing. Cubbyholes at mid-level hold clear acrylic bins full of small items such as socks and lingerie. Double rods along one side of the closet, double shelves and a rod along the other, accommodate two extensive wardrobes neatly and without crowding. Design: Philip Emminger.

For clotheshorses, a spacious livery stable

Most walk-in closets are big enough to comfortably accommodate wardrobes for two people—even when each person makes frequent sartorial acquisitions. In this closet, there's space for floor-to-ceiling shoe shelves, a built-in chest of drawers, and a necktie rack. Double closet rods on either side offer an uncrowded abundance of raiment. And everything is easy to see—thanks to good indirect fluorescent lighting. Architect: Ron Yeo.

Open Closets

Honest, upfront clothes quarters to flaunt your finery

Letting it all hang out

Tucked under an eave, a man's collection of striped, plaid, and tattersall clothing makes an unobtrusive, tidy display that pleases the eye and detracts not a whit from the bedroom's striking design. During the day, skylights illuminate clothing colors; when the sun goes down, that function is performed by wall-mounted fixtures that look like jumbo dressing-table lights.

Above the closet is a compartment with sliding doors; to the left is a tall built-in unit with a white-enameled cabinet topping a dozen black-lacquered drawers. Architect: Wendell Lovett. Interior design: Suzanne Braddock.

Haberdashery, unabashedly on display

Looking something like an opened-up steamer trunk, this movable wall unit holds a man's wardrobe in natty good order. A covering curtain or screen for the closet would only make this small bedroom seem smaller. But as an honest display—sporting neckties like pennants and crowned with crisscrossed tennis rackets—this arrangement serves as a personal haberdashery, letting the owner make mental selections before he even gets out of bed. Closet design: Just Closets.

Two wardrobes separate bed and bath

Curved and compact, this room divider doubles as an open armoire for two people. Reminiscent of the voluptuous furniture styles of the 1930s, the closet curiosity has room for everything from brogues to silk dresses. The curved section offers open shelving, necktie pegs, a pull-out bin for laundry, and deep drawers of clear acrylic for small foldable items. Around the bend, facing the bathroom, there are additional nooks and crannies for towels and toiletries. Architect: Gary Allen.

Children's Closets

Organizing kids' clothes quarters for easy upkeep

Closet revamp encourages tidiness

With all his personal effects piled in a jumble, either on the floor or high up out of reach, it was hard for the eight-year-old owner of this closet to find things or put them away (see inset, right). But built-in shelves and drawers, plus an extra closet rod placed at just the right height for him, brought order out of frustrating chaos. At the same time, as with any well-planned closet remodel, space was cleared for storing at least twice as much. Closet interior: Just Closets.

Small girl's wardrobe makes a fetching display

Her mother's serendipitous shopping trips turned up unusual and elegant organizers for a five-year-old's wardrobe. Pretty hats and colorful dresses hang from an antique coat rack. Below that, a handsome wooden towel rack from a bath accessory boutique holds everyday play clothes. And, most imaginatively, her small-scale footwear lodges in a divided wicker desk tray originally designed to hold stationery. The entire arrangement makes a charming display in a small bedroom that has no built-in closet.

Nooks for Baby's needs

Naked we come into this world—but we don't stay that way for long. Before you can say "Dr. Spock," most babies have acquired a veritable mountain of clothes, linens, and other possessions. To stow it all in orderly fashion may be a major challenge.

In this nursery closet, there's a nook for every need. A short, low closet rod encourages Baby, as she grows, to hang up her own clothes. Baskets of vinyl-coated wire allow both ventilation and easy viewing of contents. Architect: N. Kent Linn. Interior design: Joan Simon. Closet interior: Minimal Space.

Dressing Areas

Create a corner—or a luxurious separate room—
where you can retire to attire

Plenty of doors and drawers

Behind the large double doors in this dressing room,
you'll find a tidy double-rod clothes closet; behind the
smaller doors are individual cubbyholes for as many as
thirty pairs of shoes. Below the counter, built-in drawers
of varying depths provide streamlined accommodation for
folded items. Architect: Charles L. Howell.

Athletic esthetics

Dubbed "The Locker Room," this spacious dressing hall
features an amenity not often included in dressing-area design. Down its considerable length runs a sturdy locker-room
bench, crafted of wood. Beyond its good looks, it provides
a place to sit for lacing up running shoes or toweling off after
a shower.

Other noteworthy features are a full-length mirror (with
plenty of room to back away for a long look), adjustable
track lights, a Chinese basket that functions as a clothes
hamper, and—of course—an efficiently arranged closet with
double-decker rods and adjustable open shelves. Architects:
Rachlin Architects.

Reflections on the art of dressing

Look beyond the stunning hammered brass sink and brass-trimmed tile counter, and you're aware of something equally impressive reflected in the mirror: a spacious closet on the opposite wall of the dressing room proudly displays its beautifully stacked, stored, and suspended wares. Louvered for both good looks and good ventilation, its trifold doors hinge back to reveal an entire wardrobe. Architect: David Jeremiah Hurley. Interior design: Jois.

Horseshoe headboard creates a dressing corridor

Unless you're back there deciding on something to wear, you don't notice the expansive wardrobe accommodations formed by this tall, horseshoe-shaped headboard. Placed toward one end of the bedroom, the arrangement creates a private dressing corridor—narrow, but with comfortable elbow room for pulling on a turtleneck, zipping into a dress, or lacing up shoes. Other behind-the-headboard dressing areas are shown on pages 12 and 13. Architects: Jacobson and Silverstein.

Double-duty Dressing Rooms

Stretching beyond their usefulness as places to don your duds

Bedroom annex is a clothing-care center

Dressing with both care and efficiency is easier when you keep your clothes and all
the appliances needed for their upkeep in one handy location. This combination dressing-
laundry-sewing room includes open shelves, drawers, closets (not shown), a washer and
dryer, sewing machine, and fold-away ironing board. All are ready for instant service,
whether you need to store, wash, dry, or repair your clothing—or just press something at
the last minute. Architects: Olsen/Walker. Cabinetry: The Butt Joint.

Next to the bath, a home figure salon

Everything a body might need to keep in shape is right here—doctor's scale; expansive mirrors for checking apparel—or one's ballet posture; an exercise bar for morning workouts (it's mounted with strong handrail brackets); and a tall chest full of clothing to put on a newly trimmed-down, toned-up figure. On the right (behind the scale) is a closet for hanging garments. Architect: Jennifer Clements.

Dressing Tables

Sitting down to all the accouterments of good grooming

Chic import swings open for your toilette

Displaying its wares from cleverly swiveling trays, this portable make-up center conceals all the trappings of good grooming within a trim plastic façade. And there's even more storage potential inside the padded vinyl stool. A costly import from Italy, this handsome vanity pivots and folds together when not in use, its compartmentalized trays, mirror, and storage seat transformed into a sleek stack.

Cosmetics corner

Find an empty corner and fill it—this is one of the fundamentals of clever storage. Here, a custom-designed dressing table turns an otherwise wasted bedroom corner into an essential part of its owner's grooming regimen. Decoratively paneled bins swivel out from the wall to proffer their cargo of cosmetics, then swivel back under the vanity shelf. The triple mirror is framed with the same oak detailing that decorates the drawers.

The romantic allure of wicker

An appealing beginning— and end—to each day are practically guaranteed at this charming little wicker vanity. Its simple, arched design catches the eye and may even divert attention from the clutter that all dressing tables inevitably collect. The unobtrusive glass shelves are easy to wipe clean. Furniture courtesy of de Benedictis Showrooms.

For today's fair lady, antique beauty

"The Fair each moment rises in her Charms/Repairs her Smiles, awakens ev'ry Grace/And calls forth all the Wonders of her Face." So wrote Alexander Pope early in the 18th century, addressing himself to the mysteries of a lady's toilette. For many of us, such marvelous transformations would be aided by an inspirational setting. Here's the very thing—an elegant Louis Philippe vanity with upholstered bench, both crafted of walnut. Lighting— essential to any dressing table—is stylishly supplied by smartly draped windows and a pair of lamps.

Organizing Your Accessories

Use baskets and barrels, hangers and holders
to arrange those all-important extras

Fold-up, slide-away tie ladder

The sides of this ladder rack swing up for easy access
to more than four dozen ties on six dowels. Once the tie
selection is made, the sides swing back down for compact storage. The entire unit slips in and out of the
closet on standard drawer slides. Design: Minimal
Space.

Hidden jewelry storage

Tucked away in the back of a closet and concealed behind hanging garments is this clever hideaway for
jewelry. Built between the wall studs, the cabinet houses
eight fabric-lined, shallow drawers. For camouflage, the
outside of the cabinet door is painted the same color
as the rest of the closet wall, and the door opens by
means of a touch-latch. Design: Philip Emminger.

Put baskets & barrels to work as handy holders

Use baskets—wire or woven—to organize socks, lingerie, gloves, and scarves. Place them on closet shelves, tuck them into drawers, or suspend them from the closet ceiling.

Try a fiber drum, a small wine barrel, or an enameled metal drum to hold those tall, skinny items that are propped up precariously in the back corners of your closet: umbrellas, walking sticks, and sports equipment such as fishing rods, skis, baseball bats, and hockey sticks.

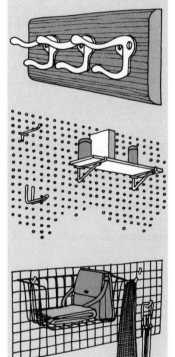

Closet hang-ups

Stylish or mundane, a system of hang-ups in your closet can organize and display belts, ties, scarves, hats, handbags, and even necklaces. You might use simple plastic holders with adhesive backing, an antique oak taproom rack with fancy brass hooks, or a high-tech grid system of vinyl-coated wire.

Improvised hooks and pegs are equally effective; try china knobs, cabinet pulls, old railroad spikes, or even common carpenter's nails.

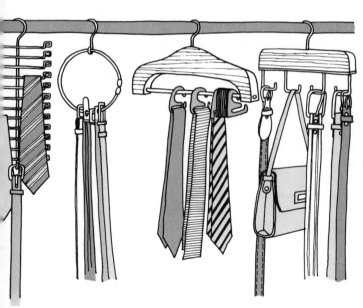

Hangers that major in accessories

Some smart-looking accessory holders, like the ones shown here, are designed to slip right over the closet rod. Available in the notions sections of most department stores or through mail-order catalogs, these specialty hangers hold belts, ties, scarves, handbags, or various combinations of accessories.

Organizing Your Clothing & Footwear

Keep your wardrobe under control with these inexpensive closet products and easy-to-build storage aids

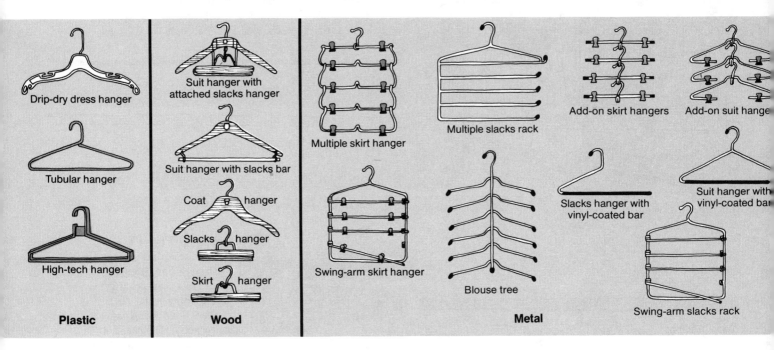

Drip-dry dress hanger

Tubular hanger

High-tech hanger

Plastic

Suit hanger with attached slacks hanger

Suit hanger with slacks bar

Coat hanger

Slacks hanger

Skirt hanger

Wood

Multiple skirt hanger

Swing-arm skirt hanger

Multiple slacks rack

Blouse tree

Add-on skirt hangers

Add-on suit hanger

Slacks hanger with vinyl-coated bar

Suit hanger with vinyl-coated bar

Swing-arm slacks rack

Metal

Trade in those wire hangers

Do your clothes a favor and discard the wire hangers you've collected over the years from dry cleaners and laundries. Never meant for long-term use, they crease folded slacks, misshape garment shoulders, and sag under the weight of winter coats and heavy jackets. Worst of all, they seem to multiply in your closet and always end up in a tangle. Why not replace them with colorful plastic hangers—or wood or metal hangers designed for particular garments?

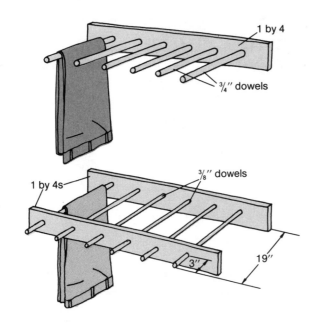

1 by 4

¾″ dowels

⅜″ dowels

1 by 4s

3″

19″

Easy-to-build slacks rack

Your closet gains a custom touch with the addition of a simple slacks rack. To build the horizontal ladder shown, run 19-inch lengths of ⅜-inch doweling through corresponding holes in parallel 1 by 4s; allow the dowels to protrude 3 inches beyond the front 1 by 4 to form accessory pegs. Secure the dowels with white glue spread inside each drilled hole. Choose a ladder length that fits between opposing closet walls or vertical dividers. The rear 1 by 4 is fastened to wall studs with 3-inch-long lag screws; then the front is attached to both walls with angle brackets.

If you'd rather slide your slacks onto a rack from the front (instead of looping them over from above), attach ¾-inch dowels to a back 1 by 4 only.

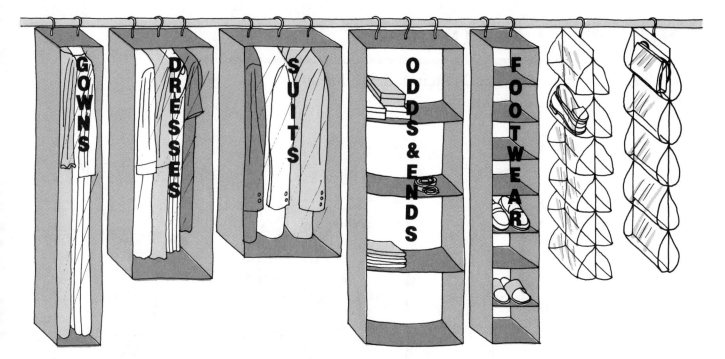

Hanging garment bags are practical protectors

For storage of shoes, hats, handbags, and out-of-season or seldom used clothing, consider purchasing a handy hanging garment bag—or a whole matching set of them. Bags made for clothing on hangers are sized for long evening wear, dresses, or suits; accessory bags with shelves come in two sizes—one for shoes, and one for hats, handbags, sweaters, and other bulky items. Made from clear, colored, or patterned vinyl, the bags have front or side zippers for easy access.

Also available on hangers are vinyl organizers with pockets for shoes or handbags.

You'll find garment and accessory bags in the notions sections of large department stores or in mail-order catalogs.

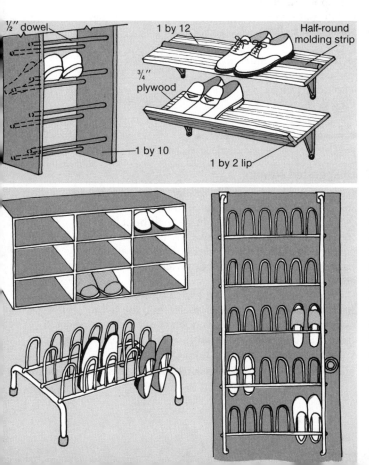

Footnote on shoe storage

Among the chief contributors to closet clutter are shoes. If you store them on the closet floor, sometimes it's a chore just to dig out two that match, and when you do, they may be covered with dust. Ready-made shoe racks (over-the-door models, floor racks, vinyl wall pouches) can solve these "pedi" problems. Or, with some inexpensive materials, a few simple tools, and a little know-how, you can put together a custom rack of your own.

Shoe shelves are easy to build from 1 by 12 lumber or 3/4-inch plywood. Use regular L-brackets to hang them right on the wall, or use straight or angled brackets in an adjustable track-and-bracket system; with the latter you can make slanting shelves. Add a half-round molding strip as a heel stop (see illustration), or, if your shelves are made of plywood, put a 1 by 2 lip along the front to keep shoes from sliding and to hide the plywood edge. (Since there's no overhang, be sure your lipped shelves are at least as deep as your shoes are long.)

Another good choice is a dowel rack—reaching to the ceiling, if you like. First, cut two side pieces from a pine or fir 1 by 10, then drill holes for pairs of 1/2-inch dowels, offsetting them (as shown) for a forward tilt.

Temporary & Portable Closets

Versatile storage pieces on hand when you need them—
and out of the way when you don't

Movable closets serve as a room divider

These practical units allow you to convert a spacious room, such as a family room or large bedroom, into two private sleeping areas—without making any structural changes. What's more, they provide each sleeping area with a roomy closet of its own.

Built from ¾-inch plywood, each of the units shown here is 40 inches wide, 24 inches deep, and 3¾ inches shorter than ceiling height. (Of course, you can adjust these dimensions—or add additional units—as necessary.) Each closet has a tall space with a rod for hanging clothing, and a two-shelf cabinet above for shoes, hats, and bulky sweaters.

The closets are brought into the room on a dolly and slid into position on a continuous sill built from 2 by 4s, with one unit facing into each sleeping area. Since the 2 by 4 sill is actually 3½ inches high, you'll have just enough overhead clearance (¼ inch) for a tight fit. For extra stability, the units can be secured to the ceiling with molding strips or angle brackets.

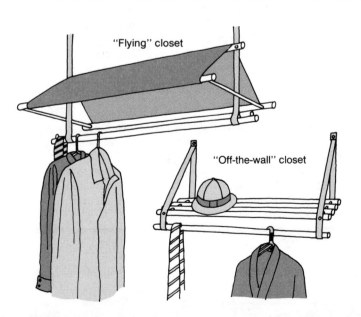

Suspended storage

Here are two commercially available hanging closets that are easy to carry and quick to install.

The "off-the-wall" closet has a shelf built from natural-finish hardwood dowels with another dowel suspended below as a closet rod. The whole assembly hangs from natural-color cotton webbing straps that are attached to the wall studs.

The "flying" closet is suspended on cotton webbing from two mounting hooks screwed into the ceiling joists. Garments hanging on the wooden closet rod are protected from dust by an attractive natural-color canvas awning. Closet designs: Richard Pathman.

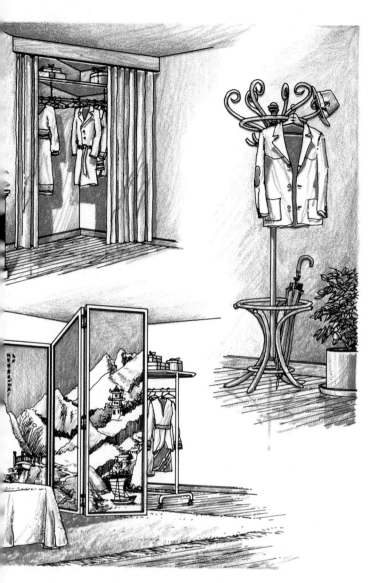

Almost-instant closets

Empty corners in a bedroom are prime quick-closet candidates. Simply install a shelf on the diagonal, suspend a closet rod from it, and close off the triangular area with blinds, curtains, or a Roman shade. If you prefer traditional doors, build a frame from 2 by 4s covered with plywood strips or wallboard.

Other quick-closet ideas: hide a commercial garment rack behind a beautiful folding screen, or try the original open closet—the coat tree.

Antique wooden wardrobe

Contemporary wardrobe of plastic laminate

Metal-framed cardboard wardrobe

Freestanding wardrobes go where they're needed

Whether they're carved and mirrored antiques, sleek contemporary pieces of glossy plastic laminate, or inexpensive metal-framed cardboard units, freestanding wardrobes are as practical as ever. The original portable closets, they're a solution for bedrooms with little or no built-in closet space.

Bathroom Storage

Of all the rooms in the house, the bathroom tends to be the smallest—and the least seriously considered in terms of effective space planning. Yet, in recent decades, many of us have begun to collect more and more paraphernalia (including bulky electrical grooming appliances) that we use most often in the bathroom.

Your answers to the following questions will help you plan your bathroom storage requirements: What supplies do you need and use regularly in the bathroom besides a toothbrush, soap, and towels? Many people store cosmetics, medicines, small appliances, extra toilet and facial tissue, magazines and books, and cleaning supplies. Can the items you use regularly be housed conveniently in your present bathroom storage space? If not, you'll welcome this chapter's wealth of practical and attractive solutions to bath storage problems.

When it comes to basic bathroom storage units—cabinets and drawers—you have a wide range of materials, styles, and colors to choose from. Some new designs in traditional wood cabinetry are shown on pages 58 and 59, and on pages 60 and 61 you'll find some of the sleek European imports of plastic laminate. If you're thinking of building your own cabinetry, you can get ideas and instructions from these *Sunset* books: *Basic Carpentry Illustrated, Bookshelves & Cabinets,* and *Wall Systems & Shelving.*

Is the inside of your cabinetry as hardworking as it could be? On pages 56 and 57 we show ideas for storing supplies in racks, pull-outs, and lazy Susans that hide behind cabinet doors.

You'd rather *display* colorful towels and stacks of soap than tuck them behind closed doors? Take a look at the attractive open shelving on pages 62 and 63.

Medicine cabinets are a standard feature in bathrooms, but your medicine cabinet needn't be humdrum if you choose one of the novel designs or arrangements presented on pages 66 and 67. Laundry hamper ideas appear on pages 70 and 71. And for housing the burgeoning number of appliances that shave, curl, tweeze, or dry your hair, improve complexions, and clean teeth, see the ideas on pages 76 and 77.

On pages 74 and 75 you'll see a selection of towel racks to buy or make. And on pages 72 and 73 we offer an equally fine selection of racks for paperbacks and periodicals.

Provided the room has adequate space and ventilation, you may choose to store your linens in or near the bathroom. You'll find some examples of effective and modern linen closets on pages 64 and 65.

Take a good look around your bathroom. Search for potential storage space in now-wasted areas. Likely locations include the space between the medicine chest and the sink, the space above the toilet (leave 12 inches above the tank for servicing the mechanism), corners that you could fill with triangular units, and the bathroom door on which you can install hooks, pegs, racks, or baskets.

What about that empty space above the tub? Either narrow cabinets or open shelves placed above the bathtub will dramatically expand your bathroom storage capacity. One caveat: Make sure the storage units and the items to be stored are impervious to moisture. Nothing dampens the spirits more than clinging bath powder or flaking paint from improperly finished cabinetry.

If moisture isn't a problem in your bathroom, and if you have space to spare, you might consider moving in furniture—an attractive old chest or bookcase can add good looks as well as storage.

As in planning your bedroom or reorganizing your closets, what will work best for you really depends on what you need and use frequently, how much space you have to work with, and what resources are available. Whether you build or buy your storage units or hire a design consultant, your best resource is your own imagination, combined with practical ingenuity.

Cabinetry: The "Inside" Story

Clutter-swallowing helpers that hide behind closed cabinet doors

Problem-solving pull-outs

There's no need to grope around in your bathroom cabinets in search of that extra tube of toothpaste or the bubble bath you got last Christmas. With pull-outs like the ones shown here, bath supplies glide right out for easy access. Available in wood, regular and vinyl-coated wire, and plastic, pull-outs can be installed on standard drawer slides or on their own special framework.

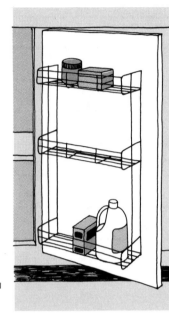

Back-of-the-door bonanza

A wood or vinyl-coated-wire storage rack mounted to the inside of a cabinet door can help you organize soaps, shampoos, and other cosmetics, as well as bathroom cleaning supplies.

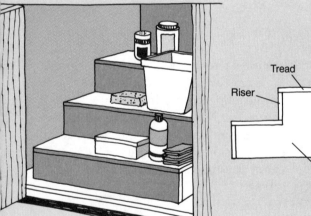

Bath-supply bleachers

This generous grandstand for bath supplies assures that nothing will be overlooked in the back of the cabinet. Graduated storage steps put an emphasis on visibility: you see your entire inventory of paper products and cosmetics at a glance.

Once you've designed a bleacher unit to fit your needs—and your cabinet—cut treads and risers from 1-inch lumber and stringers from ½-inch plywood. With finishing nails, assemble the pieces as shown; coat the unit with varnish or enamel, then slide it into place inside your cabinet.

Not-so-lazy Susans

These hard-working storage-go-rounds help keep bathroom paraphernalia from finding its way into the far reaches of your cabinetry. Single-level or tiered, a lazy Susan rotates so that everything you store is visible and accessible. Be sure to measure your cabinet carefully—allowing for drainpipe clearance, if necessary—before you buy or build one of these organizers.

These cabinets put away plenty

Imported from Germany, this plastic laminate bath cabinetry carries all the soaps, cleansers, lotions, creams, and scents you'll need for some time to come. The gleaming chrome towel rack swings out of the way to allow easy access to the spacious undersink compartment; the cabinet on the left features swivel-out trays in various sizes. Cabinetry courtesy of European Kitchens & Baths.

A parade of pull-outs

Hidden most of the time behind closed doors, these under-the-sink pull-outs glide into clear view when you need to get at their contents. Ranging from deep bins to shallow sliding shelves, they serve up everything from daintily folded guest towels to scented dusting powder. Topping the wooden cabinetry is a counter of blue plastic laminate; the glamorous basin is made of brushed aluminum.

Cabinetry of Wood

The traditional raw material of the cabinetmaker's art, shown here in designs that are far from ordinary.

A touch of the peaceful East

Oriental influence is serenely apparent in the soft-toned simplicity of the wood detailing, the spacious proportions, and the quietly beautiful tile design that draw the mind away from the cares of a busy day. In addition to the traditional undersink cabinet and bank of drawers, there is a generous tiled dressing bench with a single substantial drawer below for linens. Cabinet design: The Butt Joint

Hollywood glamour, right at home

Curving cabinetry and theatrical make-up lights add star quality to this sleek sink and storage area. The mirrored panels at either end of the unit are actually mirror-faced doors for twin medicine cabinets. And below the sink, a cupboard and bank of drawers offer roomy recesses for tucking away towels, lotions, and other accouterments of glamorous grooming. Architects: Olsen/Walker. Cabinet design: The Butt Joint.

Orderly without, organized within

There's nothing trendy about this bathroom storage wall and sink counter. The attractive traditional-style wood cabinetry and a mirrored medicine cabinet just look great and do their job—keeping bath necessities and even clothing in their proper place—while giving the whole room a pleasing sense of order. Who could ask for more? When open to view, the drawers and doors disclose a wealth of storage organization, including a roomy set of wooden pull-outs. Design: Dennis O'Connor.

Cabinetry of Plastic Laminate

The sleek, chic European imports
are a bold new bath-storage option

Plastic pizzazz, Italian-style

From the ultra-modern approach of northern Italian design comes this factory-molded sculptural elegance for the bathroom. The clever countertop towel rack whimsically plays with terrycloth tones, creating vertical stripes that balance the horizontal strokes of navy blue on the wall above. Drawers and cabinets are anything but boring—they're concave or convex; they can be pulled or swiveled. And even the vanity stool stands for more than just plain seating—it stores things, too. Cabinetry courtesy of Dahl Designs.

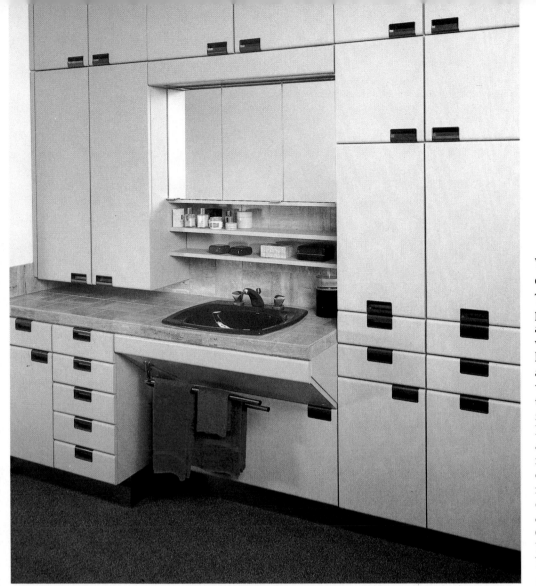

Wall-covering cabinetry

This German cabinetry puts every square inch of a bathroom wall to work—with precision. The fine-lined pattern on drawers and cabinet doors provides an interesting texture that's resistant to fingerprints, as well. Behind the beautiful façade are cleverly designed interiors to accommodate everything from cosmetics to laundry. (You can peek behind the doors on pages 57 and 71.) Cabinetry courtesy of European Kitchens & Baths.

Not corners, but curves

This sand and charcoal-colored cabinetry presents a rounded look that's a refreshing contrast to the harsher, predominantly angular environment of many bathrooms. So there are no handles to interrupt the smooth façade, all cabinets open with touch-latches. The bottom cabinet on the far side (shown open) features a swing-out towel rack. Cabinetry courtesy of Dahl Designs.

Open Shelves

Out-in-the-open storage puts towels
and other bright bath supplies on display

Tubside art enhances the bath

Surely one of the most sumptuous of life's simple pleasures is a good, hot soak in a bubbly bath. To enrich the experience, this bathroom provides a colorful gallery of miniature folk art for bathtime viewing. Besides display space, the handsome cedar shelves offer storage for bright towels, and even for a few books. Architect: William Abbott.

Towels sit high up in brassy splendor

In days gone by, this vintage piece held luggage overhead in a cramped train compartment. Today, in a crowded bathroom, it keeps extra towels out of the way, yet within reach. Its brass mesh shelf and filigree framing are a treat to view from underneath. Design: Rand Hughes.

Greenhouse windows offer shelf space

Greenhouse popouts, available from building-supply and home-improvement centers, can provide extra space and daylight, as well as wide views of the leafy world outside. At the same time, they offer attractive shelf space for both practical and decorative items. Since the room faces a shady corner of the garden, there's no worry that sunlight might fade the towels. Design: Woody Dike.

Mini-library for private browsing

Many people appreciate the privacy bathrooms afford for reading in undistracted solitude. Here, a colorful collection of paperbacks offers not only food for thought, but hospitality and decorative cheer as well. You'll find more ideas for bathroom libraries on pages 72–73. Design: Jeanne Kleyn.

Graceful niche for bath necessities

An arched alcove, traversed by a single glass shelf, creates open wall storage with a clean and airy feeling. The rectangular opening just below houses a fluorescent light behind a frosted glass panel; more glass functions as sliding doors for the base cabinet.

Under the window, a laundry hamper disguises itself as a simple ledge when its lid is closed. Architects: Ted Tanaka and Frank Purtill.

Linen Closets

Orderly accommodation for the bulk of your bed and bath needs

Closet chic

Clean-as-a-whistle white shelving etches a crisp border around stacked sheets and towels in this walk-in linen closet.

Derived from an industrial design, these vinyl-coated-wire shelves are available for the home through specialty shops, interior designers, and home centers. Besides their look of high-tech sophistication, they offer other advantages: good air circulation, light weight, quick installation, and easy access to their contents. Architect: John Galbraith.

Sleek exterior, hard-working interior

One basic aim of good storage design is an everything-in-place look that's gentle on the eyes. When all its doors and drawers are closed, this floor-to-ceiling storage wall blends unobtrusively into its all-white bathroom surroundings—only the glistening brass hardware calls attention to its function. Behind the cabinet doors, colorful linens are neatly arranged on lipped, pull-out shelves. Architects: Fisher/Friedman Associates.

Stowaway space, unlimited

This meticulously planned storage wall swallows more than enough linens to meet the bed and bath requirements of even a large family.

Cabinets midway up the wall feature doors that swing down on piano hinges to become counters just right for folding and sorting laundry. Adjustable shelves inside the upper cabinets provide flexible storage spaces. Architect: John Galbraith.

Medicine Cabinets

Handy, high-style housing for home remedies
and prescriptions, first-aid supplies and cosmetics

Pops open at a touch

Just give this medicine cabinet door a little push and it'll pop right open— thanks to the convenient touch-latch. Since the door opens upward, you'll want to position the cabinet low enough for adults' convenience, but high enough to prevent bumped foreheads. Cabinet courtesy of Plus Kitchens.

Low-lying cabinets leave room for a view

For many of us, the first sight of the day, as we splash cold water on our faces, is somewhat less inspiring than a gentle garden view. But as this thoughtful arrangement makes clear, the traditional over-the-sink mirror is not compulsory. Here, you can have it both ways: twin medicine cabinets with mirrored sliding doors are recessed into the back-splash area, leaving space for a window above one sink and for a mirror above the other. Architects: Ted Tanaka and Frank Purtill.

Prescription for storage

Built in between the wall studs, this wooden medicine chest is compact yet roomy, with storage space on the inside of the cabinet door as well as on the interior shelves. Small-diameter wooden dowels keep door-stored items in place. Design: Jeanne Kleyn.

Cabinet puts corner to work

Tucked into a corner between the sink and bathtub, this jumbo medicine cabinet holds cosmetics, remedies, and bath supplies for the whole family. Below it is a tip-out laundry hamper (you see it open on page 70). Architect: William B. Remick.

Showerside Storage

A berth for every bathing need

Tile frames supplies—and scenery

Bright blue tiles wrap the storage niches and window that make this tub/shower combination special—as well as convenient for family use. Plastic tub toys, soap, and hair care needs are right at hand, and the glimpse of the outdoors is a bonus. Architects: Fisher/Friedman Associates.

Towels greet you as you round the bend

Just around the corner is a roomy shower, tiled in bright white from floor to ceiling. But here, tucked in a tall, tiled recess, are thick and thirsty towels that stay well out of moisture's way—yet handy for drying you off as you emerge dripping from a steaming shower. Design: Philip Emminger.

Shower heads have hang-ups, too

Short of perching your shower supplies precariously on a windowsill or tub ledge, no storage system could be simpler than this clear acrylic device that slips over and hangs from the shower head. Available in department stores and bath boutiques, shower caddies usually have a small rack for a washcloth, a ribbed tray for soap, and a shelf that's slanted to keep water from pooling under the shampoo bottles.

Sheer beauty from Italy

Imported from Italy and sold for a pretty American penny, this prefabricated cylindrical shower stall comes with storage compartments as sleek-looking as those racy Italian sports cars. While you're getting wet, the towels and toiletries stay dry behind a curved, clear acrylic sliding panel. Architect: William B. Remick.

69

Hampers & Scales

A fresh, new look at those bathroom basics

Hatch lifts up to catch clothing

The sturdy fir deck around this bathtub provides more than just good-looking surroundings for a sudsy soak. It also makes efficient use of the space between the tub and a wall by offering a roomy built-in laundry hamper. When the lid is closed, the spot doubles as a dressing bench. Design: James Fey.

Tip-out bin for a tight spot

In this bathroom, a tip-out laundry bin takes clever advantage of the corner between the sink and bathtub. It serves its purpose smoothly in a tight-cornered room where a conventional freestanding hamper would only be in the way. Architect: William B. Remick.

For towel-tossing

Flip open this sleek tilt-down cabinet door and you find a laundry hamper just waiting for you to play doff-and-toss. The vinyl-coated-wire basket lifts out so that after you've flung your clothing and towels into it, you can carry the whole works over to the washer. Cabinetry courtesy of European Kitchens & Baths.

Between truth sessions, scale disappears

Mommy and Daddy might cringe to read what they weigh, but to a youngster it's a real thrill to gain a pound or two. This young lady stands on a niftier-than-average bathroom scale. When not dispensing good or bad news, it folds up and into the wall (like a miniature version of the Murphy idea shown on page 14). Not only does the bathroom floor remain free of underfoot obstacles, but the scale stays protected, too. Design: Judy Aptekar.

A Very Private Library

Racks to display your current collection
of periodicals and paperbacks

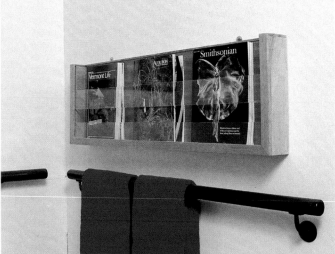

Three-in-one wall unit

With a small bathroom, you can't afford to waste even the awkward space between the toilet and the adjacent wall. The handy redwood unit shown here offers a lot in a limited area: a shallow yet roomy cabinet for extra soap and paper products, a tissue holder, and a very simple magazine rack. (Magazines stand on top of the supply cabinet and are held in place by two redwood trim strips.) Design: Marshall Design-Built.

See-through strips let magazine covers brighten bath

In this wall rack, magazines are held in place by two strips, as in the rack shown on the left. But instead of redwood, the strips here are made of clear acrylic to give a sleek, contemporary look—and to let colorful magazine covers show through. The rest of the unit is simply a shallow, three-sided wooden box. Design: John Matthias.

Cabinet creates a paperback perch

Spanning a toilet alcove, the top of this wooden medicine cabinet is home to a collection of paperback books. Open shelves are an appealing—though often overlooked—option for bathroom storage; pages 62–63 show several other ways in which creative homeowners and designers have put them to work. Design: The Butt Joint.

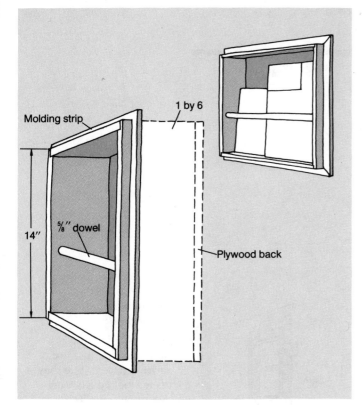

Molding strip

1 by 6

14″

⅝″ dowel

Plywood back

Between-the-studs box library

This recessed rack for reading matter is a simple box that fits snugly between two wall studs. Since wall studs are usually 16 or 24 inches apart (center to center), your box library will probably need to be 14½ or 22½ inches wide; 14 inches is a convenient height for it. Locate the studs, measure and mark your wall carefully, then remove only enough wallboard to accommodate the box. (Pick a location for your box library where you won't run into electrical wiring and plumbing lines inside the wall.)

Use fir 1 by 4s or 1 by 6s for the box frame (1 by 6s will add extra depth, but they'll stick out slightly from the wall). Before assembling the frame drill shallow holes in the side pieces to hold a ⅝-inch dowel (see illustration). Assemble the frame and add a ¼-inch plywood back. Slide the unit into the wall cutout, and side-nail the box to one or both wall studs. Add molding strips or wood trim around the box to hide the rough edges and give a built-in look. Finally, finish the unit with enamel, varnish, or polyurethane. Design: John Schmid.

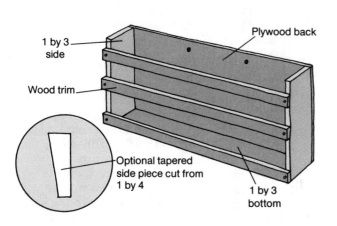

1 by 3 side

Plywood back

Wood trim

Optional tapered side piece cut from 1 by 4

1 by 3 bottom

No-frills wall rack

This simple wall rack is remarkably easy to build. Cut two side pieces and a bottom piece from pine or fir 1 by 3s, and cut a back from ¼-inch or ⅜-inch plywood. Assemble the rack, then nail ¼-inch-thick strips of wood trim across the front to keep magazines and books in place. Finally, drive two woodscrews through the back of the rack and into the wall studs and apply a paint, varnish, or polyurethane finish. The unit illustrated is approximately 12 inches high and 20 inches wide, but these dimensions can be adjusted to suit your needs and wall space.

If you must get fancy, build the rack with tapered side pieces (cut from 1 by 4s) so your reading matter tilts forward for easier access.

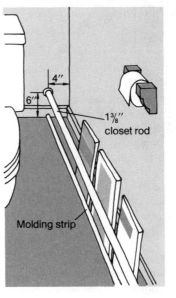

4″

6″

1⅜″ closet rod

Molding strip

Closet rod corrals magazines

A 1⅜-inch wooden closet rod, mounted 4 inches out from the wall and 6 inches above the floor, can keep magazines rounded up in what would otherwise be wasted space. A molding strip attached to the floor (as shown) will keep magazines from sliding forward. If your bathroom floor tends to collect water, add a narrow wooden platform (with the molding strip on top) to keep your reading matter high and dry.

73

Towel Hang-ups

A whole raft of racks, rails, rods, and rings
that you can buy or build

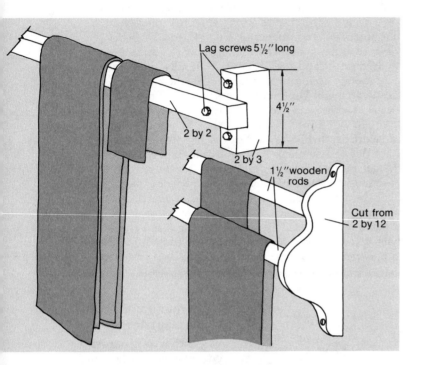

Lag screws 5½" long

4½"

2 by 2

2 by 3

1½" wooden
rods

Cut from
2 by 12

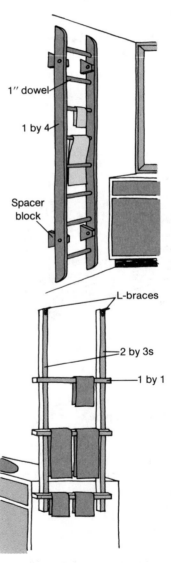

1" dowel

1 by 4

Spacer
block

L-braces

2 by 3s

1 by 1

Redwood & towels—two ways to go

Here's a pair of easy-to-make variations on the basic
towel bar theme. One is a no-nonsense rail; the other is
a fancier, and slightly more challenging, two-rung rack.

The rustic rail is made from a long redwood 2 by 2
held out from the wall by 4½-inch-long end blocks
made of 2 by 3s. Lag screws 5½ inches long attach the
rail to the end blocks—and the end blocks to the wall
studs. (Be sure to find the wall studs before you decide
on a length for your rail.) If lag screw heads seem too
rustic, you can countersink them and cover them with
dowel plugs.

For the two-rung rack, use 1½-inch wooden rods and
redwood, fir, or pine 2 by 12s. From the 2 by 12s, cut two
curved wall mounts like the one shown; smooth them
with a rasp and sandpaper. Drill shallow holes in the
mounts to support the rods, positioning the lower rod in
front of the upper one, as shown. Two screws fasten each
mount to the wall studs. (Again, determine the length
of your rack after you've located the wall studs.)

A bathroom's humid climate can be tough on unfinished wood, so be sure to protect your new towel bars
with several coats of polyurethane finish or penetrating
resin.

The lowdown on ladders

Floor-to-ceiling towel
ladders make the most of
narrow spaces while they
make a bold decorating
statement. They're also
very easy to build.

Recess 1-inch dowels
into matching holes in
two parallel 1 by 4
uprights; glue the dowels
in place and clamp
them securely until dry.
Or simply nail 1 by 1
strips to the front edges of
two parallel 2 by 3 up-
rights. Fasten your ladder
to the floor and ceiling
with L-braces (be sure to
allow at least ¼ inch
between the top of the
ladder and the ceiling for
clearance), or attach it to
spacer blocks that you've
screwed into the wall
studs.

Redwood is an excel-
lent material for towel
ladders because of its
handsome appearance
and moisture resistance.
Hardwoods are also
good, but somewhat
more expensive. Which-
ever material you
choose, be sure to pro-
tect it with a polyure-
thane finish or penetrat-
ing resin.

Trellis treatment

What makes this attractive towel rack a gift from the garden? It's actually a redwood trellis that has been carefully sanded to remove any splinters, then varnished for moisture resistance and screwed to the wall studs. Hooks were added for towels, accessories, and small electrical appliances.

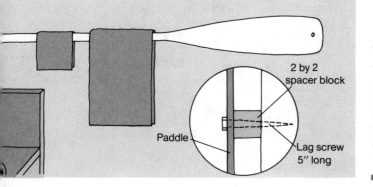

2 by 2
spacer block

Paddle

Lag screw
5" long

This paddle stays high & dry

This sleek 5-foot towel bar is actually a canoe paddle that was purchased for under $10 at a marine supply store. It's attached to the wall studs with two 5-inch-long lag screws that run through holes drilled in the paddle and in two spacer blocks cut from a 2 by 2. Several coats of clear marine varnish make this unusual towel bar "weatherproof."

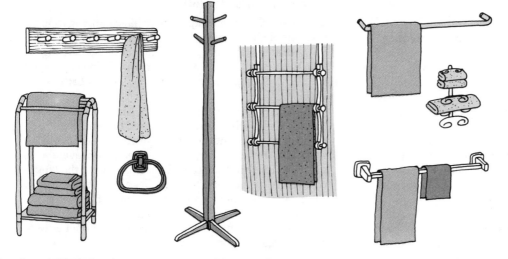

Ready-made racks

If you'd rather buy a towel rack than build one, you'll find a large selection of ready-mades. Standard bars and rings, sold individually or as components in matching accessory sets, are available in a wide variety of materials—from brass to chrome, from oak to plastic. If you have floor space to spare, consider a freestanding rack, such as a towel tree or a floor stand with room for both hanging and folded towels. Other options include wall racks with brass hooks or wooden pegs, and handy over-the-door organizers.

Small Appliance Storage

Here are several solutions to the problem of where to stash your burgeoning collection of grooming gadgets

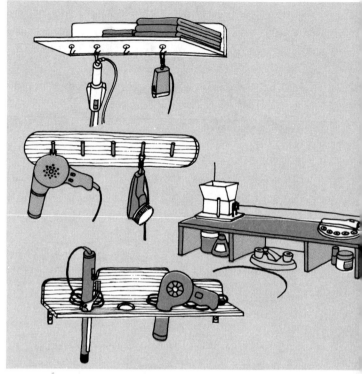

Ready-made solutions to appliance storage problems

The popularity and proliferation of personal-grooming gadgets have put bathroom storage at an even greater premium. We have electric toothbrushes and water jets; blow dryers, curling irons, and electric rollers; shavers, tweezers, complexion brushes, and manicure machines—but how can we keep them all organized and within reach?

A clear acrylic appliance caddy is an attractive, though fairly limited, solution. Designed to sit on a countertop or hang on a wall, it has a large holster for a blow dryer and side compartments for other small appliances and grooming aids.

Storage aids not designed specifically for small appliances can be easily pressed into service: consider shower caddies (remember that they can be hung on an open wall as well as over a shower head), wall-mounted vinyl pouches (often sold as closet organizers), and undershelf baskets of vinyl-coated wire.

Perhaps the most flexible approach to small appliance storage is a vinyl-coated-wire grid system. Appliances with hanging loops can be suspended on hooks; those without loops can be stored in the bins and baskets that are available as components of such systems.

Some improvised solutions

If your small grooming appliances have hanging loops, then simple hooks or pegs are all you'll need for storage. Put together a taproom rack from a redwood backing strip and some brass hooks or hardwood-dowel pegs; or simply screw cuphooks to the underside of a bathroom shelf.

If you'd rather not hang your appliances, consider a narrow shelf with carefully measured holes drilled through it to form holsters for your curling iron, your shaver, or the nozzle of your blow dryer. For several large or heavy appliances, try a wider shelf running the length of the sink counter and 6 to 8 inches above it; support the shelf with wood blocks spaced to form counter-level cubbyholes for cosmetics and grooming aids. For moisture protection, finish wood shelves with enamel or two coats of clear polyurethane.

A pair of in-the-wall cabinets

These two recessed cabinets feature built-in electrical outlets and space for several personal-grooming appliances. The cabinet on the left is recessed into an open wall and can be camouflaged with wallpaper or paint. A mirror mounted on the inside of the cabinet door allows one-stop grooming.

The cabinet on the right makes use of the space between the medicine chest and the countertop below. Its mirrored door extends the look of the medicine chest mirror; a piano hinge and two lid supports allow it to swing down 90 degrees to form a handy counter.

Hidden door catches—magnetic for the mirrored cabinet, a touch-latch for the camouflaged one—add sleekness to both storage units. Plastic laminate keeps the inside of the cabinets bright-looking and easy to clean.

Countertop hideaway

A cabinet right on the counter can be a convenient place for the grooming gadgets you use daily. Here, an electric shaver and a dental water jet fit inside a plywood-frame cabinet that was tiled to match the bathroom counter. The appliances swing out on a hinged plywood shelf, ready for use. Cords run through a hole in the counter and down to an outlet in the cabinet below. Design: Larry Meyer.

Bath Accessories

These handy holders can give your bath a brand-new look

For a custom look— a coordinated collection

Changing accessories is an easy and inexpensive way to update your bath. Coordinated lines usually include towel racks, bathroom tissue holders, facial tissue dispensers, soap dishes, toothbrush holders, and sometimes even medicine cabinets and magazine racks. Matching non-storage items, such as electrical outlet covers and drawer pulls, are sometimes offered, too. Available in a variety of styles and price ranges, coordinated accessories are appearing now in materials such as pine, oak, plastic, brass, and chrome—as well as the popular ceramics.

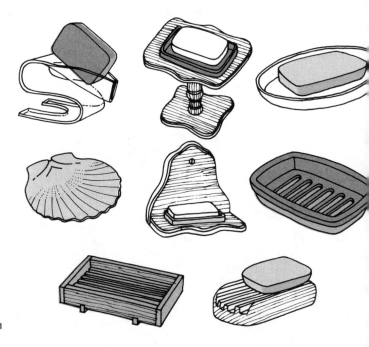

Distinctive dish designs

Soap dishes come in styles, materials, and colors to suit every bathroom decor. There are standard countertop dishes, pedestal models, and wall-mounted units; materials include ceramics, clear acrylics, glass, plastic, and the popular clear-finished woods. Most dish designs include holes or slats to facilitate drainage and save soap; or you can add one of the ribbed or spiked plastic inserts that are designed especially for this purpose.

If made-for-the-bathroom soap dishes don't appeal to you, consider using a pretty porcelain dish—or a beautiful seashell—instead.

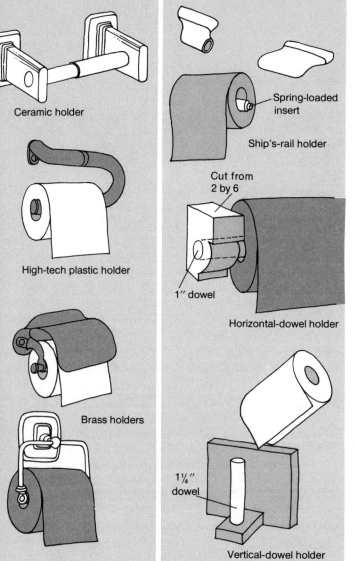

Ceramic holder

High-tech plastic holder

Brass holders

Spring-loaded insert

Ship's-rail holder

Cut from 2 by 6

1" dowel

Horizontal-dowel holder

1¼" dowel

Vertical-dowel holder

Tissue holders to buy or build

Tissue holders are available in a wide variety of styles and materials—from traditional steel or ceramic holders with spring-loaded inserts, to high-tech plastic models in bright colors, to costly antique reproductions in solid brass. But tissue holders are also very easy to make, and the handsome wooden ones shown here are fine examples.

The two ends of a teak ship's rail (from a marine supply store) make a very stylish holder. Just drill a small hole in the inside edge of each piece to accommodate a spring-loaded insert (available at most hardware stores), and add shims, if necessary, to increase wall clearance. (Remember that a new roll of tissue is about 5 inches in diameter, so the insert's center must be at least 2¾ inches from the wall.)

The horizontal-dowel holder substitutes a 1-inch dowel for the spring-loaded insert. Cut two end pieces (in any shape you like) from a fir 2 by 6. Then drill a 1-inch-diameter hole halfway through one end piece and a corresponding hole completely through the other end piece (so the dowel can be removed). Allow at least 4½ inches clearance between end pieces (that's the width of a standard roll).

With the vertical-dowel holder, the tissue roll stands on end. Use scrap blocks of fir, oak, or redwood and a 5-inch-long 1¼-inch dowel. Assemble the pieces (as shown) with woodscrews and glue.

Mounting tissue holders may require some patience. Some end pieces are easier to mount if they are first bridged by a backing piece which is then attached directly to the wall. Try to anchor a holder to a wall stud; if that's not feasible, use expanding anchors or toggle bolts.

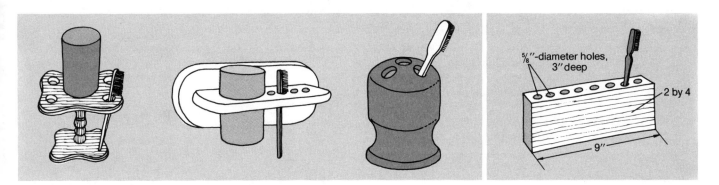

⅝"-diameter holes, 3" deep

2 by 4

9"

Dental details: a brush-up course

Choose one of the many commercially available toothbrush holders—freestanding or wall-mounted, with tumbler or without—or make one of your own from a scrap block of oak.

Begin with a 9-inch-long 2 by 4. Into one edge, drill eight ⅝-inch-diameter holes, each 3 inches deep (see illustration). Smooth the entire holder with fine sandpaper. Finish the wood with two coats of clear polyurethane to protect it from the humid bathroom climate—and from dripping toothbrushes.

Index

Photographers

Richard Fish: 21 top. **Jack McDowell:** 10, 11 bottom, 12, 15, 18, 19 bottom, 20, 21 bottom, 22 bottom, 23 bottom, 35 bottom, 37 bottom, 39, 42, 44, 45, 46, 47 bottom, 57 bottom, 59 bottom, 62, 63 top left and bottom, 64, 65 bottom, 66 right, 69 top, 71 bottom, 72 top right. **Steve W. Marley:** 9 bottom, 11 top, 13, 14, 19 top, 36, 38, 43 bottom, 47 top, 58, 59 top, 60, 61 bottom, 63 top right, 65 top, 67, 68, 69 bottom, 70, 72 top left and bottom. **Rob Super:** 22 top, 24, 34 bottom, 41 bottom. **Tom Wyatt:** 9 top, 16, 17, 23 top, 33, 34 top, 35 top, 37 top, 40, 41 top, 43 top, 48, 57 top, 61 top, 66 left, 71 top.

Sunset
Garage, Attic
& Basement
Storage

By the Editors of Sunset Books and Sunset Magazine

LANE PUBLISHING CO.•Menlo Park, California

We wish to thank the architects, designers, and homeowners whose innovative ideas for storage are included in this book. A special thank-you goes to Kirsten Fedderke for her assistance in assembling the color section.

Cover: Boxes, baskets, bins, shelves…these are tools of the storage trade. Labels and see-through panels make them especially convenient; pegboard, hooks, and brackets make them adaptable. Photographed by Jack McDowell. Cover design by Zan Fox.

Photographers

Gerald Fredrick: 28. **Gene Hamilton:** 36, 60 left, 62. **Jack McDowell:** 3, 4, 5 top and bottom left, 11, 12, 13 bottom, 14, 19, 20, 21 left, 22, 29 left, 35, 37, 38, 43, 44, 45 top, 46, 51, 53, 59, 60 right, 61. **Steve W. Marley:** 5 bottom right, 27 left, 30. **Ells Marugg:** 29 right. **Rob Super:** 45 bottom left. **Tom Wyatt:** 6, 13 top, 21 right, 27 right, 54.

Editor, Sunset Books:
Elizabeth L. Hogan

Sixth printing March 1989

Supervising Editor:
Maureen Williams Zimmerman

Staff Editors: **Susan E. Schlangen**

Susan Warton

Contributing Editor: **Scott Atkinson**

Design: **Roger Flanagan**
Photo Editor: **JoAnn Masaoka**
Illustrations: **Rik Olson**

Contents

Behind sturdy blonde doors, *this custom storage wall works hard at organizing a garage-load of goods. Architect: Glenn D. Brewer.*

About This Book...

Some of life's greatest pleasures are associated with the possessions we own and must store—garden tools that help ensure fragrant blossoms in spring, sleek new skis that sink into fresh powdery snow, sturdy old suitcases that wear the scars of travel as surely as we carry the memories. It seems that the more we enjoy life, the more we have to store.

What's *your* storage situation? Do you know where you'll stack the firewood to stoke the new wood stove you've been thinking about? How will you put to use the knowledge gained at that great wine class, if you don't have a proper place to store wine? What do you do with your multiplying financial records, mystery novels, family photos?

We think it's best to start simply. That's why our first section (pages 6–11) is devoted to storage units and accessories. You'll be pleased at how much even a few hooks, racks, and bins can do. For specific belongings, we've included an item-by-item storage section (pages 12–59). Filled with ideas, it's an alphabetical showcase that tells you what to do with items—outdoor furniture, sports equipment, and workshop supplies—that may be stumbling blocks in your storage path. The section also contains special features about auxiliary storage areas—the patio, deck, and garden shed—and a feature on storage safety.

Crowded garages, stuffy attics, and wet basements receive in-depth treatment in the back of the book (pages 60–79). Here, we explain ways to remedy some of the more complicated but common problems of garage, attic, and basement storage.

A place for everything *and everything in its place. Pine boards and vertical plywood spacers form cubbyholes—large ones for basketballs and ice skates, small ones for wine and miscellany. See pages 8–9 for more shelving ideas. Design: Richard and Sandra Pollock.*

Open doors reveal *garbage cans, counter, shelves for supplies, and combination woodbin and pass-through. Architects: The Hastings Group.*

Loft frees floor space *below for table saw, freezer, extra refrigerator. Commercial fold-down stairs offer easy access to lightweight storables. For more on lofts, see page 65.*

"Tools" of the Storage Trade

Pegs, hooks & racks • shelving • boxes & bins • cabinets & closets

Simple storage aids *can handle complex storage needs. Here, a modest shelving unit corrals camping gear and gardening equipment, nails grip tennis rackets, and a bin brims with sports gear. The bike dangles from ceiling hooks.*

It's the hottest day of the year, and you still haven't stored your winter woollies, holiday decorations, and snow tires. Don't worry; you're suffering from a common ailment. And here you'll find some tested remedies—the most basic storage units and accessories.

This section is like a catalogue, with some tips to help you select the kinds of storage units and accessories best suited to your needs. The emphasis is on simple, utilitarian storage aids that are easy to build or install: pegs, hooks, racks, shelves, boxes, bins, cabinets, and closets. Many of these items can be purchased in a variety of colors, materials, and designs.

You'll probably want to choose a combination of open and closed storage. Open storage—for example, heavy-duty hooks securely fastened to garage wall studs—may be ideal for hanging up your snow tires. Fragile holiday decorations, on the other hand, require closed storage— say, cardboard boxes on track and bracket shelves —for protection from dust, moisture, and accidents.

By adding a few storage aids, you'll open up more floor space and gain better clearance—important benefits in full garages, attics with steep walls, and basements. You may even discover new space for work or play.

Consult *Sunset's* companion volumes, *Wall Systems & Shelving* and *How to Make Bookshelves & Cabinets*, for more details on tools, techniques, and materials.

Pegs, hooks and racks

Pegs and hooks are the simplest storage aids, great for items that you want immediately accessible. Use them to hang objects from walls, ceiling joists, rafters, shelf undersides, and cabinet interiors. Rack systems, which make use of pegs and hooks, provide great storage diversity and capacity.

Pegs and hooks are particularly easy to install. For pegs, you can use large carpenters' nails hammered into wall studs or rafters, dowels recessed into drilled holes, spring clips, and even cabinet pull knobs hung on the wall. The range of hooks available includes coat hooks in many sizes, shapes, and materials; cup hooks screwed into shelf undersides; and large hooks for hanging such heavy items as bicycles (see page 15).

Wall racks are great for organizing garden tools, outdoor clothing, folding lawn chairs, hand tools, sports equipment, and many other items. The classic rack system for garages is a pegboard equipped with various hooks and hangers. Pegboard, or perforated hardboard, is made in ⅛ and ¼-inch thicknesses; install ¼-inch board for heavy-duty use. When you install pegboard, use spacers to hold it slightly away from the wall, allowing clearance for hooks.

Racks made of steel and vinyl-coated steel have either horizontal or vertical metal tracks or grids that attach to the wall. Both kinds can be equipped with a range of accessories—from hooks to shelf brackets to hanging bins—to handle specific storables.

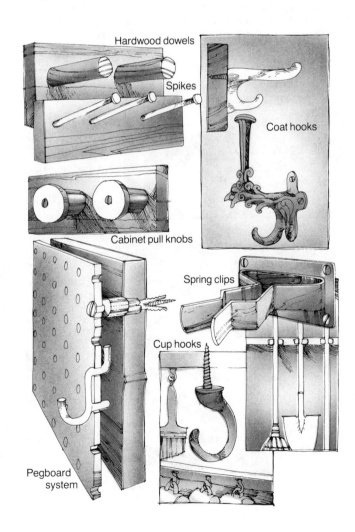

Hardwood dowels

Spikes

Coat hooks

Cabinet pull knobs

Spring clips

Cup hooks

Pegboard system

Shelves

Shelves and storage go hand in hand... the two words are almost synonymous. Shelves can be hung from the wall, suspended from the ceiling or rafters, or used to span an enclosed frame or opposing walls. Adjustable shelves and freestanding shelf units give you more flexibility, but are less stable for heavy loads.

Formal shelving units are unnecessary in storage areas. Instead, consider the following simple, less expensive ways to assemble basic units or fasten individual shelves to walls or ceilings.

Materials. What materials make good shelves for storage? Sturdy utilitarian shelves can be made from solid fir or pine, plywood, or particle board. Fir is stronger than pine, but pine is less expensive. Plywood is best for shelves more than 12 inches deep. Larger platforms can be fashioned from hollow-core doors or plywood and supported by a solid lumber frame (see page 65). You can cut your own shelves, ask lumberyard personnel to cut them for you, or purchase precut or preassembled units. Easy-to-clean plastic laminate shelves are handy for laundry or crafts areas.

Shelf spans. When planning your shelving, follow this rule: no shelf should have a span of more than 48 inches. For light loads, 1-inch thick lumber spanning 32 inches is ideal; for medium to heavy loads, shorten the span to 24 or even 16 inches, or use 2-inch-thick lumber. For very strong shelves, sandwich together two layers of ¾-inch plywood with glue, and reinforce with 1 by 2-inch strips around the edges (see drawing below). Heavy particle board shelves tend to sag, regardless of the load; if you use particle board, keep the spans very short.

Blocks and boards. Stack bricks or cinder blocks to support solid lumber or plywood shelves, preferably against a wall. If your stack is higher than 5 feet, anchor the top shelf to the wall.

Brackets. Common shelf brackets (with or without gusset supporters), continuous Z-brackets, or L-braces are easiest for fastening individual shelves or a small series of shelves to the wall.

Cleats and ledgers. Made from 1 by 2 trim or L-shaped aluminum molding, cleats and ledgers can be used to support shelves that span opposing walls and rafters or the insides of closets and cabinets. Cleats hold up the shelf ends, and a ledger runs along the back edge (see drawing below). For extra support, use 2 by 4s.

Ropes and chains. Suspended from eyescrews attached to ceiling joists or rafters, ropes and chains provide sturdy shelf support. Rope is knotted—or clamped with electrical cable clamps (see drawing below)—to secure shelves. Chain-supported shelves

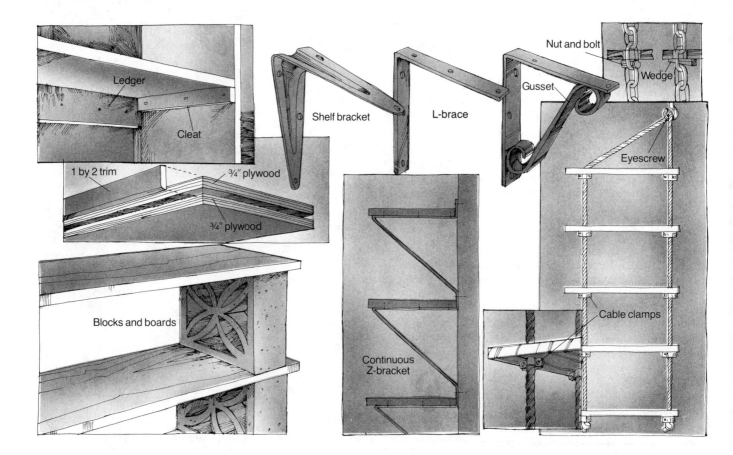

Ledger

Cleat

1 by 2 trim

¾" plywood

¾" plywood

Blocks and boards

Shelf bracket

L-brace

Continuous Z-bracket

Nut and bolt

Wedge

Gusset

Eyescrew

Cable clamps

must be wedged in place with wood scraps or secured with nuts, bolts, and washers below each shelf. Attach chains to the eyescrews with S-hooks. For added stability, also attach the ends of the ropes or chains to the wall behind.

Ladder supports. Use old ladders or build them from 2 by 2 or larger lumber. Suspend them from ceiling joists or rafters, or tie them together with cross braces for a freestanding unit. Nailing shelves in place will help stabilize the unit.

Adjustable shelving hardware. Track systems—tracks and brackets, or tracks and clips—have become the most popular way to hang a series of adjustable shelves. Generally, bracket systems are hung on a wall, and clips are used within a cabinet frame or other enclosed area. Brackets are available in several styles and finishes; the most common sizes accommodate 8, 10, or 12-inch-deep shelves, but some systems will support shelves up to 24 inches deep. For heavy loads, use industrial systems. Adjustable clips are made in two designs: gusseted and flush (see drawing below). The gusseted type holds more weight.

Tracks should be fastened to wall studs if possible, especially if your shelves will bear a lot of weight. If you must fasten tracks to wall coverings alone, you'll need spreading anchors or toggle bolts for the job. If your walls are block, brick, or solid concrete, you'll have to use masonry fasteners (see pages 78–79).

Boxes and bins

Midway between shelving and more formal cabinetry are boxes and bins—containers more casual than cabinets, more protective than shelves.

Bins: tilt-outs and roll-outs. The most useful storage bins tilt or roll out from beneath a counter, from inside a cabinet or closet, or from along a room's perimeter. They're excellent space savers. Roll-out bins are good for moving items to and from a congested work area; tilt-outs angle down for quick top access.

Boxes: build, buy, or recycle. When stacked with some kind of support, cardboard boxes and wood crates don't clutter up the floor or fall apart. Try organizing them on wide shelves, or on a frame made as shown below.

Wood boxes can be hung from wall studs with nails or screws, or attached to a piece of plywood.

Box modules. A set of box modules consists of plywood boxes that you construct. They fit together well because they're all alike or have complementary dimensions. Rectangular units (see drawing below) should be exactly twice as long as square modules.

Build modules from ¾-inch exterior plywood, then finish them with enamel or polyurethane. Bolt high stacks together or bolt them to the wall. Add simple doors or pull-out drawers for a fancy system.

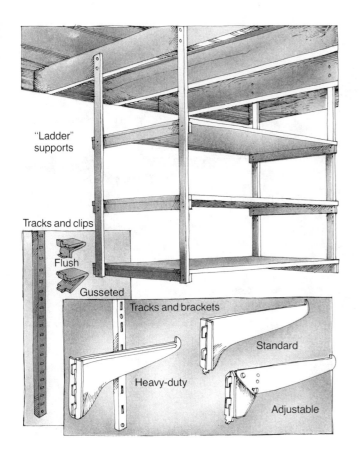

"Ladder" supports

Tracks and clips

Flush

Gusseted

Tracks and brackets

Standard

Heavy-duty

Adjustable

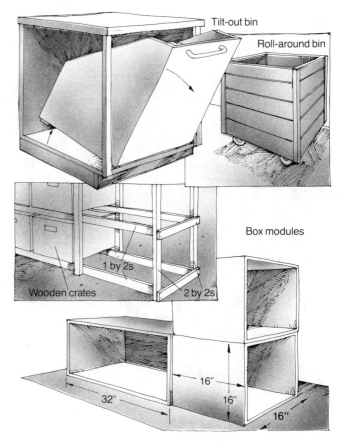

Tilt-out bin

Roll-around bin

1 by 2s

2 by 2s

Wooden crates

Box modules

32"

16"

16"

16"

Cabinets, closets, or both?

Cabinets and closets rank above other kinds of storage units in usefulness, complexity, organization, and cost. Efficient cabinets and closets—whether freestanding, framed in, or hung from a wall or ceiling—often include other storage components such as shelves, drawers, rods, and hooks. For ultimate flexibility, an integrated storage wall of both cabinets and closets is ideal. Consider the following features when shopping for premade units or when building or refurbishing closets and cabinets for the garage or basement.

Doors. You have several choices: hinged, sliding, folding, and roll-up. A hinged door—whether of the flush, lip, or overhanging type—gives you quick access to what's inside; it's also the most secure and weathertight kind of door. However, hinged doors on large units may be heavy and unwieldy, and hinged doors require more clearance than other kinds of doors. Sliding doors—with wood, metal, or plastic tracks—demand no clearance, but allow access to only half of a closet or cabinet at any one time. Bifold doors are a good compromise for large units; they're usually louvered, which allows for ventilation. Roll-ups of plastic or canvas are economical choices, but not as durable or protective.

Drawers. Odds and ends that have a way of getting lost need drawers. Ideally, drawers should be no deeper than 30 inches and no taller than 12 inches.

You can build your own drawers—a sticky task for the uninitiated—or choose from a large selection of manufactured drawers or "drawer frames" (drawers, hardware, and the support frame). Before building or buying, select your drawer guides. Commercially made guides are usually the smoothest. However, simpler systems of wooden strips or plastic channels work adequately for most loads. Lightweight drawers that won't carry much weight can slide in and out without guides.

The case for closets. Large, open closets are effective for storing seasonal clothing, garden and house maintenance goods, cleaning supplies, firewood—even roll-out bins and power tools on casters. Design your closet for many uses: add clothes rods, hooks, or pegboard walls inside; shelves or cabinets above; and a bank of drawers. This kind of unit is especially useful if security is a problem; the outer doors can be locked.

Security and safety. Depending on the contents and location of your cabinet or closet, you may want to make it secure. To foil burglars, use a heavy-duty padlock with a steel or solid brass case and a hardened steel shackle attached to an integral bolt and security hasp. When closed, the hasp should cover the screws that attach it to the unit. If you're worried about keeping your children out, a simpler, less expensive lock and hasp should do. Purchase rust-resistant locks, bolts, and hasps. Standard hinged doors, especially with hinges mounted to the inside of the unit, offer the most protection.

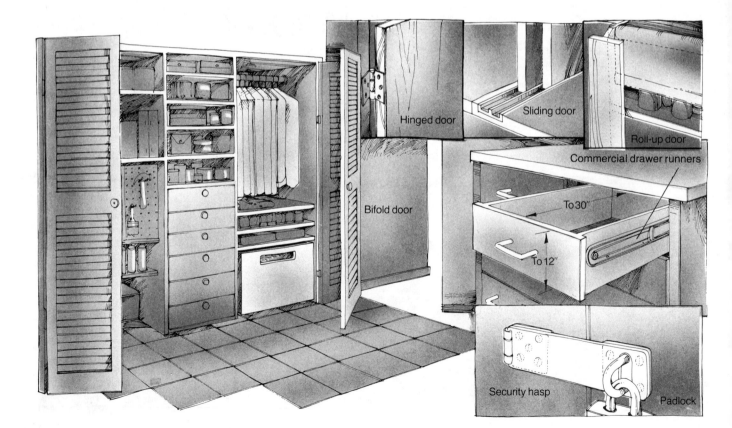

Hinged door

Sliding door

Roll-up door

Bifold door

Commercial drawer runners

To 30"

To 12"

Security hasp

Padlock

Storage bays. *To gain storage space without crowding cars, bays were built in three walls of this new garage. Each projection hangs from the rafters and features narrow side windows. Two include plywood shelves on a frame built of 1 by 4s; the third has a workbench instead of shelves. The projection in the side wall shown at right takes advantage of an underused side yard. A similar bay can be added to an existing garage as part of a remodeling project. Architect: William Patrick.*

Item-by-Item Storage Ideas

From bicycles and books to workshop tools and wines

Reels on redwood door. *Fishing reels and fishing line hang on the inside of a redwood door. Items are placed so the door closes without disturbing tackle boxes and other gear on shelves. Design: Jean Chappell.*

All in a line. *Everything has its place on this brightly painted garage wall. Tools, some of which dangle from cords looped through holes drilled in the handles, hang on nails. Fuel is stored in safety cans.*

Sideways rungs: a storage switch. *Simple wooden racks, securely attached to the garage beams and positioned for convenience and clearance, support an extra-long ladder. Cars are removed when ladder is being loaded and unloaded. Design: Emil Marent.*

Bicycle Bulk

Space-saving ways to keep bikes off the floor, out of harm's way

If your family has caught the cycling bug, you've no doubt discovered that those bikes take up a lot of space. To accommodate bicycles, you can add an extension to your garage (see below), make do with available parking space, or look for another likely storage spot around the house or yard.

In the garage, get lightweight 10-speed bikes off the ground if possible. You'll save floor space and probably boost the life of your tires, which tend to crack and go flat when left sitting on the floor over long periods of time. A solid bike rack or hook can be especially handy at repair time: while the rack holds the bike in place, your hands are free to do the work. Heavier bikes should be stored on floor stands such as the ones shown in the drawing on the facing page.

No garage? If you have to store bikes in a carport, security can be a problem. Lockable, walk-in closet units are one way to guard against both theft and weather. A patio or garden shed can also provide shelter for your bikes.

Angle parking without a scratch

A bicycle shed in a garage? Sure! This 3 by 16-foot extension provides enough space to angle-park a family of bikes—and even wheel them in or out alongside a parked car. Pushed-out garage side wall and extended foundation made it all possible; a shingled roof and matching redwood siding nailed to studs completed the project. New side wall is ideal for hanging storage, and alcove at end keeps wood scraps in order.

Clever hang-ups

Brightly colored screw hooks from the cycling shop, driven into wall studs or ceiling joists, support bicycles with ease. More elegant braced wall brackets—originally intended for a closet rod—give better clearance from the wall (secure them solidly with ¼ by 3-inch screws). Stagger single hooks to hang several bikes close together; two brackets secure both wheels of a bike high above the floor.

Hoist them high

This handsome, easy-to-build rack made from fir 2 by 4s and 1 by 3s keeps bicycles off the floor and out of the way. Notches in each upright board slip over a ceiling joist and are secured with 4-inch carriage bolts; lap joint notches at the opposite ends cradle the 1 by 3 racks. Adjust the diagram dimensions to fit your bikes, the garage height, and the height of cars beneath.

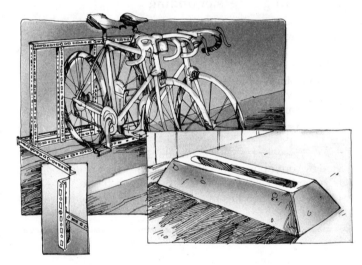

Stand them, school-style

Bicycle floor stands—like those from the school playground—are very convenient at home. Buy commercial racks or build your own from L-shaped slotted metal channel and nuts and bolts from hardware stores. Or check with local building suppliers for cement bike blocks that have slots for front bicycle wheels. Though heavy enough to stay put when you want, bike blocks can still be moved as needs and seasons change.

Books, Documents & Photographs

Pamper paper—it damages easily

Books, magazines, personal documents, financial records, photographs, and correspondence: no collection grows faster, is more difficult to keep organized, and requires such stable storage conditions. Light, moisture, heat, insects, and poor ventilation are all enemies of stored paper products.

What conditions are ideal? Librarians recommend temperatures between 60 and 75° and humidity between 50 and 60 percent for storing most papers. If you use good quality storage units that permit air circulation, a dry and insulated attic or basement should be fine. For photographs and papers that need to be perfectly preserved, hot attics and damp basements are out (see pages 68–73 and 74–79 for more details and solutions).

If you store paper items in cardboard boxes, the lids or flaps should be loose enough to allow a free flow of air. Pack books and magazines loosely, and check occasionally for signs of dampness or mold. Metal units or units lined with metal (see drawing on page 75) will protect paper from insects and rodents. Boxes—whether of cardboard or metal—block out light, as well.

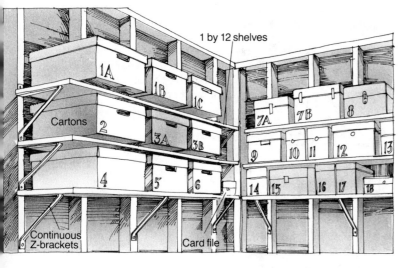

1 by 12 shelves

Cartons

Continuous Z-brackets

Card file

Orderly filing for easier finding

An organized collection of cardboard or metal containers for household records, receipts, documents, and correspondence will meet the storage needs of most homeowners.

Individual filing boxes or cartons handle large items. Also available are canceled check organizers with filing inserts, slipcover letter files, and binding cases for documents. Metal and cardboard card files—manufactured in many sizes—make compact containers for lots of bits and pieces of paper.

Arrange your box system on 1 by 12-inch shelves supported by continuous Z-brackets or individual shelf brackets. To keep track of what's where, number each box to match a corresponding index card listing the contents of the box.

Space-saving file cabinets: Safe as houses, almost as strong

A metal office file cabinet, with one to five stacked drawers, is a very efficient and safe way to store important documents and photo negatives. If appearance and neatness count, recess the file cabinet into a knee wall or under stairs, for example, so that only the drawer fronts are exposed. For maps, oversize documents, and art paper, use wood or steel flat files. File cabinets are expensive, but you can reduce the cost by purchasing used equipment; look up "Office Furniture and Equipment—Used" in the Yellow Pages.

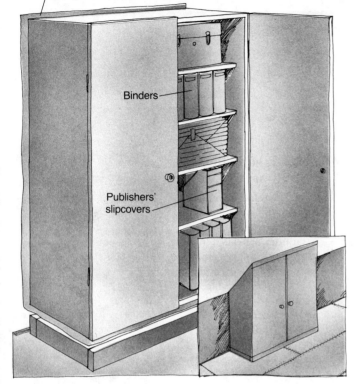

Polyethylene sheet

Binders

Publishers' slipcovers

Catching library overflow

Lovers of the printed word are always running out of shelf space for their collections of mysteries, reference texts, or favorite magazines. Inevitably, part of the library is "off to storage."

Even in the attic or basement, books and magazines should be stored on standard shelves. Set up shelves in a dry area that has a stable temperature. It's all right to store books in a cold area as long as it's dry. Don't place shelves against a wall that hasn't been insulated; fur out the wall (see page 78) or at least place polyethylene sheeting between the wall and shelves. If your books will be exposed to a lot of light, especially direct daylight or fluorescent light, the shelves should be equipped with doors or curtains. Magazines can be stored in slipcover cases or binders sold by publishers or office suppliers.

Protecting photos & film

Fortunately, photographic films and papers are more stable and long-lasting today than they were in the past, but your photo memories can still fade or discolor if exposed to excessive light, heat, or moisture. Keep them in covered boxes, cupboards, or flat file drawers. Place a small amount of silica gel in each container to help absorb moisture. Storage conditions for photo materials must be temperate and dry.

Store color transparencies in boxed projector trays or special clear plastic 8½ by 11-inch sheets. Black and white and color negatives are best kept in negative file sheets inside a binder and drawer. Separate prints with pieces of paper or enclose them in individual rag paper envelopes, and lay them in flat file drawers or boxes.

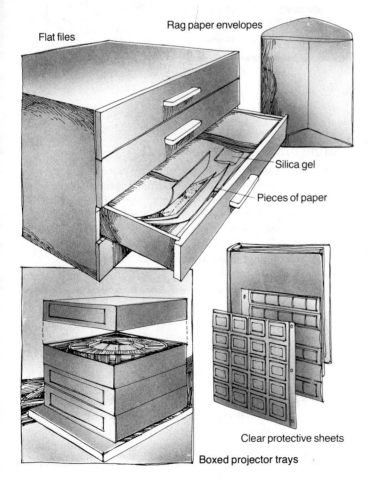

Flat files

Rag paper envelopes

Silica gel

Pieces of paper

Clear protective sheets

Boxed projector trays

Cans, Glass, Newspapers & Discards

Simple sorting systems for home recycling and disposal

Taking out the garbage is a familiar chore, but recycling is a newer responsibility for most of us—and easy enough when you're organized. You'll need up to four adjacent bins for presorting and storing tin, aluminum, glass, and newspaper. An easy-to-carry container located in or near the kitchen will save you extra steps until you have a full load. Bins should be lightweight and made of plastic, metal, or plywood treated for moisture.

Place both garbage cans and recycling bins in any well-ventilated area protected from the elements: a corner just inside the garage door, a carport enclosure, or a small outdoor shelter in the side or back yard (check local building codes before constructing). For convenience, cans and bins shouldn't be too far from either the kitchen or the driveway or street. Prefabricated metal garbage can shelters, whether separate or part of a large garden shed (see pages 42–43), are handy.

Stackable slide-outs save space

Neatly separated recyclables await pickup within a stack of lipped plastic laundry baskets. On recycling days, the baskets easily slide forward and out. A welder assembled the iron brackets shown, but you can attach wooden drawer guides or cleats inside an open cabinet frame to hold each basket. Or for a more finished look, try one of the commercial bin systems that roll on their own frames.

Plastic laundry basket

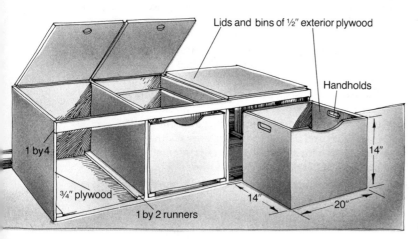

Lids and bins of ½" exterior plywood

Handholds

1 by 4

¾" plywood

1 by 2 runners

14"

14"

20"

Sorting bins swallow plenty

Here's a basic enclosed three-bin recycling system; you can modify it for special needs. Side-by-side bins house recyclable aluminum, tin, and glass. (You might install an extra large newspaper bin, too—papers pile up quickly.) You can leave the hinged tops up for easy access, or flip them down to double as counter space. On recycling days, slide each bin out by gripping the cutout on the front, then carry by using the two side handholds.

Don't lug it. Roll it.

Do you dread the weekly chore of lugging heavy overflowing garbage cans out to the curb and back? A simple remedy is to mobilize those cans. A crisscross dolly on wheels, sized to fit, is the answer for one can; two cans can ride in style on the rolling wagon shown. Pull the wagon up and down the driveway with a thick rope or chain handle.

A messy subject comes clean

Neat alcove solves several dilemmas: the cans are out of view, yet accessible from inside or outside the garage. On pickup day, the cans can be moved while the main garage doors remain locked. Design: Victoria G. Gilmour.

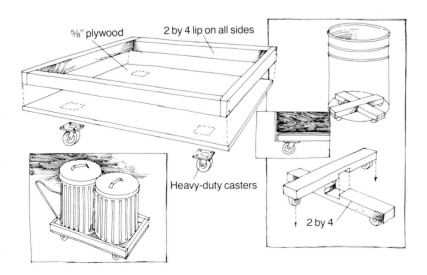

⅝″ plywood   2 by 4 lip on all sides

Heavy-duty casters

2 by 4

Coping with All-weather Wear

How to contain the mess and let outdoor clothing dry

Whether you must deal with snow-caked boots, sandy sneakers, or rain-soaked jackets, a "mudroom" can save both your temper and the garments themselves. In this spot close to an exterior door, clothing can be shed and left to dry.

A mudroom ideally is furnished with a long bench for removing wet boots and rain pants, and pegs or hooks and a long shelf for parkas, gloves, and hats. Equip the area beneath the bench with drawers or a storage chest for dry socks and shoes. Deep, open cubbyhole shelves or a clothes closet and bureau turn

an enclosed mudroom into a changing area.

A complete mudroom might include some source of heat—an adjacent water heater or heating duct—to help clothes dry quickly (for a heated shelf idea, see page 47). A louver or pegboard closet door and a ventilating fan inside the closet help check moisture and odor buildup. A floor cover of removable wooden slats or a galvanized metal grate allows water to drip down to a waterproof floor; the grates and slats also allow air circulation. In truly muddy climates, install a faucet and drain for rinsing boots and rain gear.

Concealed pull-down
The space between the joists in this basement makes room for an overhead pull-down compartment, an easily accessible hiding place for ski boots or other gear. Outdoor clothing for rain and cold weather hangs on a metal closet rod just below the pull-down. Architect: Karlis Rekevics.

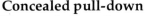

Heel toe, heel toe

Shoes and boots hang on dowels recessed at an upward slant into a thick board. The board is bolted to a wall stud. Easy-care flooring makes cleanup simple. A tension closet rod fits neatly below the sloped ceiling. Architect: James Elliott Bryant.

Corner cache catches all

Before entering the house, family members shed their outdoor wear in a storage corner in the garage. The clothes rack, built of 1 by 2s that rest on triangular supports, holds slickers and jackets. Boots, shoes, and roller skates tuck into bottom compartments. Shelves above organize less frequently used items, including camping supplies and sports equipment.

Clothing in Hibernation

Simple shelters sequester out-of-season wardrobes

The key to storing clothes is protection—from moisture, dust, and insects. Moisture, in the form of condensation or actual seepage, is best controlled within the entire storage area; see pages 75 and 76–77 for details and remedies. Closed units are best where dust or insects are major concerns. Built-ins are the most functional, but steel wardrobes—even the cardboard wardrobes used by movers—provide serviceable closets. To prevent mildew, closed units should be vented with finely screened openings or, for problem cases, an exhaust fan.

A traditional cedar closet or chest will help deter moths. Remember, though, that while cedar repels moths it does not kill them. Cedar-scented moth-controlling substances—spray and solid—can be used inside garment bags, chests, or closets.

Make sure that clothes are thoroughly cleaned before storing them.

A closet for off-season clothes
Make room in bedroom closets by storing out-of-season and seldom-worn clothing in their own portable closet in the garage. When closed, the door protects clothes from dust and light. There's even room for stowing bulky bags and luggage inside and on top.

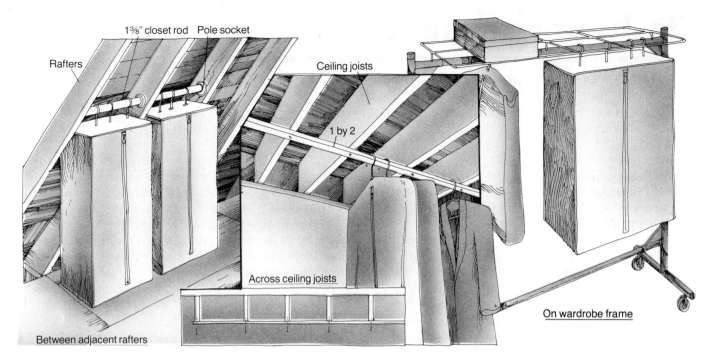

1⅜" closet rod Pole socket

Rafters

Ceiling joists

1 by 2

Across ceiling joists

On wardrobe frame

Between adjacent rafters

Makeshift closets: quick, easy, safe

Open units are the simplest, though least protected, means to out-of-season clothes storage. Lengths of 1⅜-inch closet rod, adjustable metal rods, or 1 by 2s can be strung between opposing or adjacent attic rafters, fastened to the bottom of ceiling joists, or suspended from chains or ropes. A mobile wardrobe frame is both adjustable and collapsible.

Protect clothes and shoes stored in the open with vinyl or fabric garment bags—available in several types and sizes.

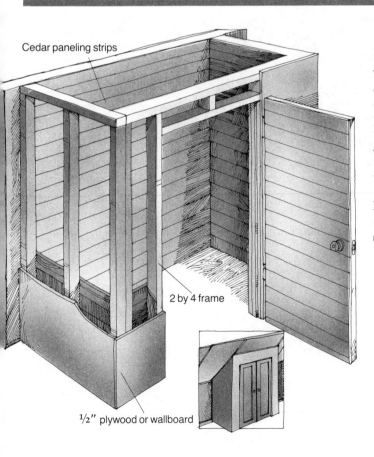

Cedar paneling strips

2 by 4 frame

½" plywood or wallboard

Cedar—for extra care

To fashion your own cedar closet—or to convert an existing closet—line the closet frame inside with tongue-and-groove cedar paneling strips, available in kits from home improvement centers. Just cut the strips to length and lay them in horizontally, one wall at a time, with paneling adhesive and finishing nails. For maximum protection, line the ceiling, floor, and door too. Weatherstrip the door edges tightly.

Don't finish or seal your cedar with varnish—you'll lock the fragrance inside the wood. To revive the fragrance, sand lightly with fine sandpaper.

Stashing Firewood

Protecting wood, seasoning it, getting at it with ease

To an increasing number of people, firewood has become an important supplement or primary alternative to other energy sources which are expensive and sometimes in short supply.

These are basic rules for storing firewood: 1) split the wood before stacking; 2) raise the wood off the ground; and 3) don't pile wood against a house wall—leave some space between the wall and firewood stack.

Wood can be stacked in parallel or perpendicular (crisscross) rows. For safety and neatness, brace tall woodpiles. If you're seasoning wood outside, don't seal it off completely because you'll trap moisture and condensation inside. Instead, store wood under a shed roof in an area sheltered from the elements.

Should you store firewood inside? If you have the space, by all means yes. Wood stored inside dries faster and contains less residual moisture. But before you bring your split wood inside, check it for insects. Don't store infested wood inside. Metal or masonry surfaces below and behind your indoor woodpile will help prevent insects from homesteading in your walls and baseboards.

Snoop around for nooks & crannies

Survey the garage, basement, or carport for likely places to store your firewood. Here are two good places to look: under the basement stairs and below hanging garage or carport cabinets.

Farmhouse idea: the lean-to

This kind of woodshed can be a simple lean-to bin or a full-scale add-on with pass-through access or a door to the house. Keep a simple lean-to open on the sides, and make sure that firewood is raised off the ground. A good roof overhang ensures adequate air circulation and protection from the weather.

Raised off ground

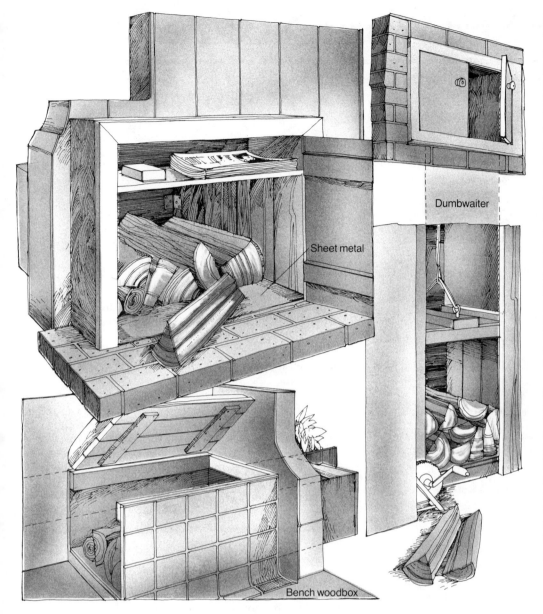

Sheet metal

Dumbwaiter

Bench woodbox

Save toil with pass-through

With a woodpile and a fireplace, the shortest distance between two points is a straight line—that's the idea behind pass-through access doors. If your storage area or add-on woodshed is adjacent to a wall near the fireplace or woodstove, a simple wood box with an interior access door can save you from stepping into the teeth of a gale to stoke the fire on a stormy night. Building codes require that a wood box opening into a garage or carport have a solid-core, self-closing door. To keep insects out of living quarters, line the wood box with sheet metal.

For a stylish variation, store your wood under a fireside bench seat that can be loaded from the outside; when you need a log, just lift the hinged seat. Have a mechanical bent? A basement-to-fireplace dumbwaiter, operated by cables and a hand winch, is a helpful friend to the fire tender.

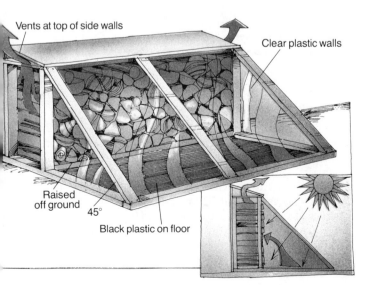

Vents at top of side walls

Clear plastic walls

Raised off ground

45°

Black plastic on floor

Solar seasoning

With this unit, green wood is seasoned in far less time than in the open air. The design can be modified to suit your budget, available space, and architecture. However, you'll want to make sure that the woodshed's positioning, materials, and ventilation are appropriate. The unit's front wall should face south and slope at close to a 45-degree angle. Use clear walls to let the sun in and black plastic or painted plywood inside to absorb heat. Side vents at the top pull warm air up past the wood, carrying moisture out the top.

Food...for Next Winter, Next Week

"Putting by" plenty in pantries, larders, root cellars

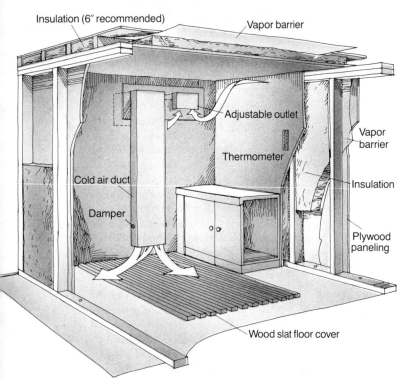

Insulation (6" recommended)

Vapor barrier

Adjustable outlet

Thermometer

Vapor barrier

Cold air duct

Insulation

Damper

Plywood paneling

Wood slat floor cover

Home cornucopia: a food cellar

To build a food cellar in your basement, partition off an area adjacent to a shaded north or east wall and away from heating ducts and pipes. Then insulate the ceiling, new interior walls, door, and (unless the climate is cool year-round) the exterior wall above ground level. Cool ground temperatures and, when the weather is cool, the outside air will keep cellar temperatures low; the insulation will keep out heated air from the living quarters. If possible, choose a site for your cellar with an outside opening—a window is convenient—to provide air flow. Install a cold air duct with a damper, and sliding outlet vent in the opening. A power fan and an automatic thermostat may be useful additions. A floor of sawdust sprinkled with water, with a platform of wood slats laid over it, will maintain humidity at the high level necessary for some food crops.

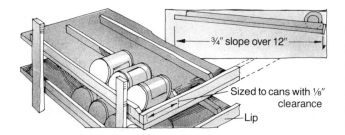

¾" slope over 12"

Sized to cans with ⅛" clearance

Lip

Cans roll right into reach

Food shelves that hold only bulk canned goods can be sloped forward so that cans will roll to the front. No more digging for buried cans—and the shelves can be as deep as you like. Molding strips laid across the front and along each shelf keep cans aligned.

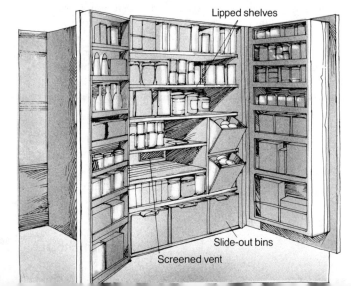

Lipped shelves

Slide-out bins

Screened vent

Granny's larder, revisited

If you'd like a multipurpose food storage area for canned goods, grains, cheeses, and bulk produce, revive an old tradition: the built-in larder. Lipped shelves hold canned goods, jars, and packaged foods securely; the double doors are lined with narrow shelves that provide additional—and highly accessible—storage. Down below, slide-out bins—a commercial system or homemade—hold fruits and vegetables. Screened vents to the outside or to a cool crawl space act as an old-time cooling device, keeping larder temperatures low.

Household food storage can be divided into two categories: pantry or room-temperature storage for canned goods and nonperishables; and root cellar cold storage for fruits, vegetables, staples, and preserves.

You can place cans and jars just about anywhere that's convenient (except near a furnace or water heater) in the garage or basement: on orderly shelves, inside an unused utility closet, or behind cabinet doors. However, most basements are too warm for root cellar storage. One way to bypass the temperature problem in a basement is to insulate a small area for food storage along a cool basement wall (see details shown at left and on page 78).

To cool the food storage area, you can use natural or mechanical methods (see page 77).

An old-fashioned root cellar with a cool dirt floor is another food storage option. Traditionally, root cellars. were dug below the house, into the ground outside, or into a hillside. A modern-day crawl space may be just the place to locate your root cellar (see page 79 for ideas).

Most root crops require moist, cool storage conditions. Other crops, including winter squash and pumpkins, like warmer, drier surroundings. Consult an agricultural extension service for more detailed information about proper food storage. In addition, see the *Sunset* book *How to Grow Vegetables & Berries*.

Harvest headquarters
Metal utility shelves, durable and warp-resistant, are a practical choice for food storage. Lipped edges on the shelves hold jars safely. Adjustable—and available in many sizes—the shelves can be bolted to studs for added stability.

Contoured shelves offer simple-to-see storage
For maximum visibility, cans, jars, and bottles fit one or two-deep on narrow ends of contoured track-and-clip shelves above the counter. Bulkier items are stowed below. The counter is handy for unloading groceries—food goes right onto the shelves or into the freezer or extra refrigerator. The pantry floor is kept clear for the drop-down ladder. Architect: Bo-Ivar Nyquist.

Patio Paraphernalia

Bags of charcoal, comfortable cushions, sun umbrellas, hammocks, badminton and croquet sets, inner tubes and inflatable rafts — sometimes it seems we have as much furniture and equipment for the patio, deck, and pool as for the house. It's most convenient to store such things close to where you need them — wheeling the portable grill just a few feet makes spur-of-the-moment barbecues easier.

Most outdoor equipment does require shelter from an occasional summer shower. Closed storage units and roof or deck overhangs provide needed protection. Units should be built according to durable, waterproof designs, and from good materials: redwood, exterior plywood, and masonry are standards.

Patio, deck, and poolside storage should blend with or complement a house's architecture and landscaping.

Barbecues in dividers or against the house. The most durable barbecue is set into a freestanding unit built from brick, stone, or concrete blocks. Below the barbecue or to the side, you can build in cabinets for starter fluid, charcoal briquettes (in metal or plastic cans with tight-fitting lids to keep out moisture), utensils, and accessories. A barbecue-plus-storage unit often doubles as a divider wall, separating the patio area from the garden or yard.

Portable barbecues rust quickly when exposed to dampness and precipitation. A deep cabinet to house a portable barbecue can be built against the house wall, protected beneath the eaves. Barbecue storage cabinetry could include shelves, hanging pegs, and possibly drawers for tongs, mitts, and rotisseries; a fold-down door could double as a serving counter.

Using space beneath a deck. Even the space beneath a deck is often useful for storage. If yours is a low deck, consider a trap door with a built-in box below for hoses and gardening supplies. The trap door should match the decking materials; it can be set in place or attached with leaf-type hinges set flush with the deck. You might provide access to a larger below-deck space from the side; store lawn furniture or other large items there, protected from the weather.

Corner cabinets for outdoor activities

Barbecuing is a joy when the necessary cooking utensils are close at hand. The three double-door cabinets in this outdoor brick and tile barbecue center offer plenty of convenient storage space. The counter, a perfect buffet table for parties, doubles as a display surface for container plants. Design: Armstrong & Sharfman.

For storage, sunning, sitting

Hinged deck bench holds a cargo of gardening supplies. Solid to keep out the rain, the bench invites snoozing and sunbathing. Design: Ed Hoiland.

Disappearing act

Collapsible director's chairs tuck neatly and conveniently into an outside deck locker. The storage spot is actually space stolen from a corner cabinet in the kitchen. The well-camouflaged door was cut from the deck's wall paneling. Architects: Larsen, Lagerquist & Morris.

Furnishings, Offstage

Out of fashion or out of season, here's how to handle it

How can you make bulky belongings like dining room tables, overstuffed chairs, or china cabinets disappear? Unfortunately, there's no magical solution.

Most furniture is much too heavy or awkward to fit into standard storage units. You may be able to get lighter furnishings up onto overhead platforms (see page 65) or tuck them into "backwater" spots; but the best basic procedure for storing furniture is to keep it out of the traffic flow—in attic or basement corners and against walls—and arrange the pieces as compactly as possible.

Protect furniture by covering it with old mattress pads or blankets. Polyethylene sheeting, canvas, or even newspaper can also help keep the dust off. Lamps, decorations, and breakables should be stored on heavy-duty shelves.

See "Outdoor Furniture" (pages 32–33) and "Luggage & Game Tables" (pages 40–41) for more ideas.

Airy alley for all-purpose storage
Vinyl-coated-wire shelves are ideal for rugs and other storables that require good air circulation to prevent damage. Cartons fit on and under the shelves without blocking access to the back of the space. Architect: David Jeremiah Hurley.

Rugs require rolling

To store a rug or carpet for any length of time, roll it—never fold it—around a pole or cardboard tube. Wrap the carpet in paper or plastic, but leave some room for air to circulate. For rugs and carpets, the storage environment shouldn't be damp or overly warm: excessive drying is as bad as mildew. Moth balls or crystals will help keep insects away, but some fibers react adversely to these repellents. Consult a carpet expert before storing a prized carpet.

Quality quilt care

Ideally, heirloom quilts or fine blankets should be rolled or loosely folded, then inserted into a clean, all-cotton pillowcase or a larger covering made from a sheet. Never store a quilt in a plastic bag (the fibers need to breathe), and keep quilts from direct contact with wood. Take your quilts out of their cases occasionally and refold a different way.

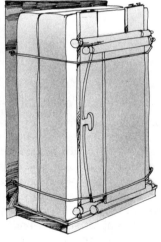

Managing bed bulk

Keep your mattresses and box springs off the floor, and don't let them sag. Stand them upright against a wall. Prop them up with a large sheet of plywood or hardboard, or the bed's own headboard and slats; and secure the whole assembly against the wall, if necessary, with loops of wire, light chain, or rope attached to the wall behind.

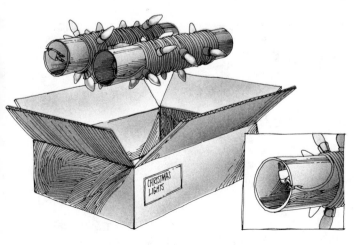

Tangle-free Christmas tip

Here's a way to save aggravation next year when you unpack the Christmas tree lights. This year, save the cardboard tubes from rolls of gift wrapping paper and a few small-to-medium cardboard boxes. Cut the tubes to box length; then push each light strand's plug inside a tube end and secure with masking tape. Coil the lights firmly around the tube, as shown, by rotating the tube; tape the end in place. Tubes then slip snugly inside the box.

A 12-inch-long box and tube will handle a strand of 35 to 50 small twinkle lights. Use a larger box for a big-bulb strand.

Outdoor Furniture

Fair-weather forecast for longer-lasting beauty, service

When the weather prediction is "weekend showers," do you hope for sunny skies because you don't want to move your patio furniture? Whether the weather takes you by surprise or it's time to prepare for a change in season, you need convenient ways and protective places to store your outdoor furniture.

Hang lightweight objects on garage or basement walls, or place them on a loft platform or overhead rack, or inside carport storage units. If necessary, store bulky items in a garden shed (see pages 42–43), patio storage unit (see pages 28–29) or garage extension (see page 67).

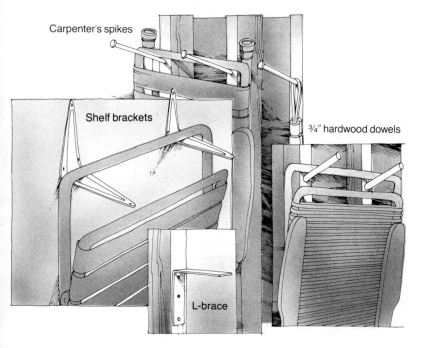

Carpenter's spikes

Shelf brackets

¾" hardwood dowels

L-brace

For fold-ups, easy hang-ups

Save precious floor space by hanging lightweight folding lawn chairs and recliners from wall studs, on ceiling joists, or even high on the rafters. For simple supports, use carpenter's spikes (oversized nails) driven into framing members, or ¾-inch dowels glued and inserted into predrilled holes; common shelf brackets or L-braces are other possibilities. Arrange supports in pairs that fit each piece.

A simple track-and-bracket system, intended for shelving, can also be used for storing furniture on the walls.

High-rise storage for window sections

Storm sashes, screens, and window shades are safely out of the way when placed on parallel wood racks suspended from ceiling joists or rafters. Racks for heavy storm windows should be assembled with bolts; racks for lightweight screens can be built with nails or screws. The hardware on sashes prohibits flat stacking; offset every other sash an inch or two. A similar rack is shown in the photo at the bottom of page 13.

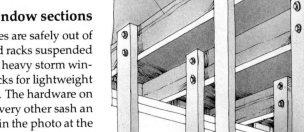

Lag screws

Overhead joist

2 by 4s

4" bolt

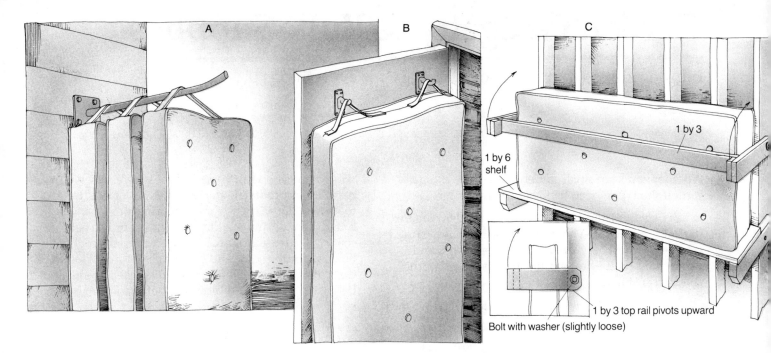

Labels in illustration:
A
B
C
1 by 6 shelf
1 by 3
1 by 3 top rail pivots upward
Bolt with washer (slightly loose)

Airy care for outdoor cushions

Those colorful and comfy cushions deserve some attention when it comes to storage. With a heavy summer storm or the first fall freeze, it's time to bring outdoor furniture cushions inside.

Cushions should be stored off the ground to provide good air circulation, promote quick drying, and prevent mildew problems. A wrought iron rod (A) attached to a wall stud is a handy device for hanging several cushions from their hand loops or from loops you've sewn in place. Metal coat hooks (B) hold individual cushions. Build horizontal racks from fir or pine (C) for long chaise lounge pads; attach the racks to open studs. The upper rail pivots.

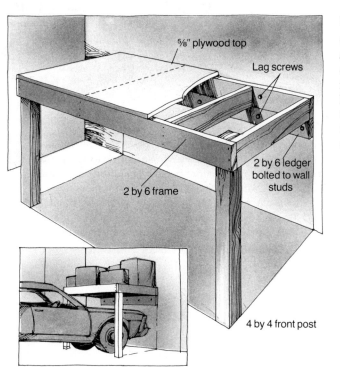

Labels in illustration:
⅝″ plywood top
Lag screws
2 by 6 ledger bolted to wall studs
2 by 6 frame
4 by 4 front post

Up and away in a loft

Get on top of the storage situation by placing patio tables and pool furniture under the garage roof—or better yet, over the car. If you and a helper can lift the furniture, store it on this loft platform. The back of the platform sits on a ledger strip, which is attached to wall studs or to a masonry wall. The front of the platform is supported by sturdy posts that straddle the car hood. For more information and ideas about loft storage, see page 65.

Garden Gadgetry & Bulk Supplies

Pruning shears to potting soil ... a place for everything

Whether you keep small garden tools in the garage or garden shed, you need handy and safe storage.

A pegboard and hanger system is ideal for organizing light to medium-weight tools and supplies. Closed cabinets are best for garden poisons, sprayers, and extra-sharp tools—keep your cabinets locked if small children are afoot.

If you're putting your garden center to bed for the winter, tools need an environment where they won't rust. If rust-producing dampness is a problem, treat tools with liquid rust cleaner, emery paper, or a wire brush; then oil any working parts and apply a light coating of grease to surfaces likely to rust again. Fertilizers, potting soils, and chemicals should be sealed from moisture inside bins or cabinets; metal containers help keep rodents and insects out of grass seed and bird feed.

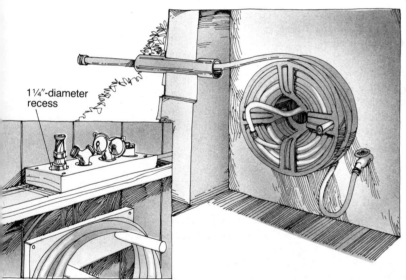

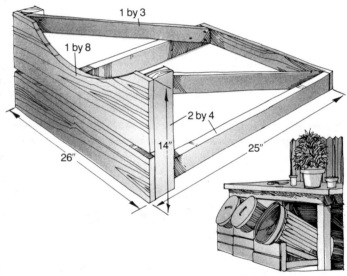

Keeping hoses unsnarled

Wrestling with the garden hose can often be a muddy, tangled proposition. One solution is a reel, mounted next to a water outlet inside a garden shed, garage, or basement. A 20-inch length of 2-inch PVC pipe runs through the wall leading to the garden; you just reel in the hose when it's not in use.

To organize hose nozzles and accessories, drill recesses with a 1¼-inch Foerstner bit into a length of 2 by 4; you could fit the board between wall studs near the hose, or mount it to a wall or fence with L-braces.

Storing soil additives

Tucked beneath a potting table or workbench, these containers make a handy, space-saving addition to any gardening center. Use them to store peat moss, potting soil, sand, and fertilizers. Lay garbage cans atop a slanting wooden rack, as shown; from there, your materials can be transferred directly to pot or wheelbarrow. This rack could be built with a third board across the front to increase the angle.

Sunlit shelving for potted plants

Plywood shelving under the large greenhouse window
provides storage space for empty pots and saucers below,
and a convenient counter on top. Attached to wall studs, the
sturdy potting shelf at left is at comfortable working height;
there's room below for large bags of lawn fertilizer. The high
shelves hold miscellaneous supplies. The window in this
garden storage area bathes plants with light; the plastic roof
and swinging plastic panel overhead keep the corner warm.
Architects: Sortun • Vos Partnership.

Heavy Garden Gear

Big and ungainly machines and tools need space, easy access

Large and bulky garden equipment—power mowers, mini-tractors, rototillers, sprayers, and snowblowers —usually requires a spacious, sheltered floor area (dry to prevent rust) and a clear path to the access door. On the subject of doors: they must be wide enough for your biggest piece of machinery, and the sills must be low, or you'll have to build a ramp or two.

If your equipment inventory is growing steadily, consider building a garden shed (see pages 42–43) or a garage extension (see page 67).

Easy wheeling into the back yard

Gardening equipment rolls conveniently onto a brick walkway through a large sliding door at the back of the garage. Architect: Thomas Jon Rosengren, Inc.

Dowels prop long-handled tools

Brooms, shovels, cultivators, and other garden tools stay vertical, thanks to dowel dividers in this roomy carport closet, just a short walk away from flower and vegetable gardens. The remaining floor space accommodates a garden sprayer and sacks of charcoal. When closed, the sliding doors blend with the wall of the carport. Architect: Buzz Bryan.

Wall space, floor space, even shelf space

Nails in wooden walls do the work of brackets, holding garden equipment. A single shelf stores garden supplies that otherwise might clutter up valuable floor space, reserved here for a mower and bags of potting soil and manure. Architects: Moyer Associates Architects.

Laundry Needs

Tips to save you time, fuss, and mismatched socks

Storage units and accessories above and around your washer and dryer make an efficient work area. Place a long, deep shelf—or shelves—directly above the machines for frequently used supplies. Above the shelf is a perfect spot to install ceiling-high cabinets for cleaning supplies, linens, and overflow storage.

Every laundry area needs counter space for folding, sorting, sprinkling, and mending clothes. Plastic laminate counters are easy to clean. In cramped quarters, a fold-down counter is convenient. You may also want a sink for washing delicate garments or soaking out stains. Hang clothes for drip-drying on a simple metal or wooden closet rod over the sink. A ceiling fan directly above promotes quick drying.

Install more cabinets or a set of large-capacity storage bins below the counter. On the wall attach a narrow cabinet for your ironing board. Close off the area with louvered double doors: they hide clutter and muffle the noise of machines while providing adequate ventilation.

Laundry layover

Custom-fitted to an odd-shaped area in the basement laundry room, these wide-open shelves are a vital link in the laundry assembly line. The cubicles, made of particle board and faced with fir, hold washing supplies and folded laundry; blouses go right on hangers. Architects: Sortun • Vos Partnership.

Out-of-sight ironing board

A full-size ironing board can be stored inside a storage closet near the laundry or in a shallow cabinet of its own. In a storage closet, secure the board with a chain or strap. For greater convenience, build a special slot for the board. A cabinet built to house an ironing board alone should allow several inches around the board for access. The average board would fit in a space 65 inches tall, 21 inches wide, and 5 inches deep; but dimensions vary, so be sure to measure your board.

Built-in ironing boards commonly fold down from behind a door, or pivot or slide out from a slot below the counter top.

Add an electrical outlet inside your board compartment or nearby for your iron.

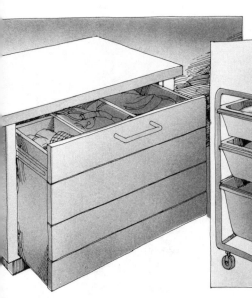

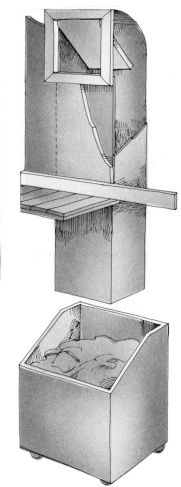

More fun than bother ...a laundry chute

A laundry chute effortlessly directs dirty clothes from your home's main or second floor to a laundry center in the basement or garage below. You can locate the chute opening in an inconspicuous but handy spot—inside a clothes closet in the master bedroom; in a wall, with a hinged or flap door; or inside a bathroom cabinet. If you have curious youngsters on the loose, be sure that the opening is raised high above the floor or measures no more than 12 inches across.

The best time to think "laundry chute," of course, is when you're designing or remodeling your house. Materials? Plywood, sheet aluminum, or 18-inch-diameter furnace heating duct (look in the Yellow pages under "Furnaces," "Sheet Metal Work," or "Plumbing Contractors").

Order out of clothing chaos

Whether below a counter, inside a freestanding island, or stacked floor to ceiling, sorting bins keep clothes ready to go when laundry day arrives. Have at least three large bins for sorting whites, colors, and permanent press items; a fourth bin might hold towels or work clothes.

Below the counter, try wooden tilt-out bins or one large pull-out drawer with internal compartments. Against the wall, you could use a commercial system with bins that slide out of their own frames, or improvise with plastic dish bins on wooden drawer guides (see page 55). A roll-around hamper, or removable bins, can go right with you wherever they're needed.

Luggage & Game Tables

Often awkward to fit anywhere—but here are solutions

Whether you spend your free time traveling to faraway places or enjoying ping-pong or poker at home, you'll face pretty much the same storage problem: because of their special sizes and shapes, neither luggage nor game tables fit neatly into regular cabinets and closets. All too often, these items are stacked clumsily against a wall or take up space in the wrong place.

To store card or ping-pong tables, train or game boards, and suitcases during the off season, you might look for out-of-the-way ledges; or build enclosures specially tailored to their dimensions; or construct a high-up platform. With a pulley system, you can even pull an unwieldy table or trunk up out of the way without having to build a platform.

Tailor-built hideaways

Card tables and folding chairs—for morning bridge parties, late-night poker games, and Sunday afternoon barbecues —always pose a storage problem. It's wise to find them a spot of their own. Some convenient places are (A) inside a cubbyhole cabinet below a staircase; (B) in a narrow, deep slot at the back of a garage storage wall; and (C) in a tilt-out bin built into a cabinet. These places work well for luggage, too.

Before building a cabinet or otherwise modifying a storage area, measure your tables, chairs and luggage. Collapsible tables and chairs require very little depth; luggage needs a little more. Most square tables come in sizes up to 36 inches square, and round tables are usually 30 to 36 inches in diameter. A folded chair is usually 20 to 22 inches wide and up to 38 inches high. Make your hideaway snug enough for tables to stand upright, but allow several spare inches of clearance in width and height for access.

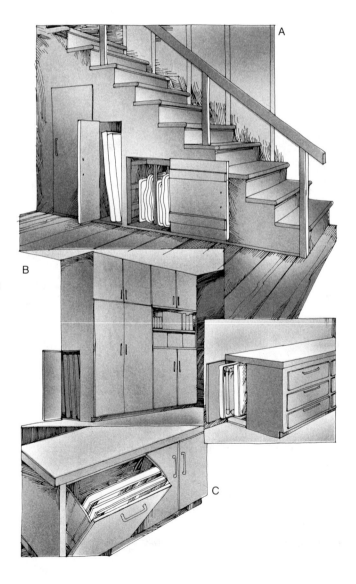

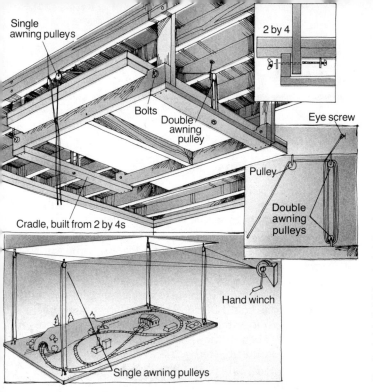

Single awning pulleys

2 by 4

Bolts

Double awning pulley

Eye screw

Pulley

Double awning pulleys

Cradle, built from 2 by 4s

Hand winch

Single awning pulleys

Winch-and-pulley hoist-ups

Nothing eats up basement or garage space like a ping-pong table or model train board. A hand pulley system, or a hand winch and pulleys, can give such storables a big lift. At top, a folded ping-pong table is set onto a wood cradle, then hoisted to the ceiling and secured there with bolts. The train board shown below has matching single awning pulleys above and below, and is raised with a small hand winch. It's always best to have two people around when it's time to hoist your table or board.

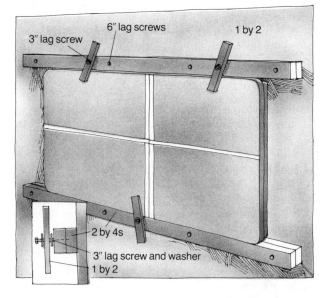

3" lag screw

6" lag screws

1 by 2

2 by 4s

3" lag screw and washer

1 by 2

Put a wall to work

If you have spare wall space inside or a roof-protected space outdoors on the leeward side of the house, here's a basic rack that will hold your ping-pong or card table securely. Nail parallel rails of doubled 2 by 4s across wall studs. Make the space between the rails equal to your table's width plus ¼ inch for clearance. Eight-inch lengths of fir 1 by 2 pivot on lag screws and washers to hold the table in place. To store tables more than 3 inches thick, consider adapting the rack shown in drawing C on page 33.

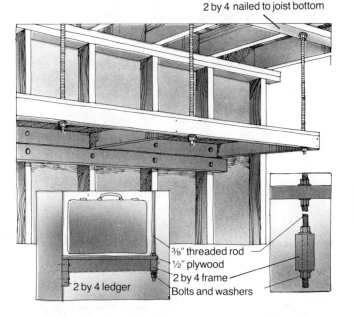

2 by 4 nailed to joist bottom

⅜" threaded rod
½" plywood
2 by 4 frame
Bolts and washers

2 by 4 ledger

Luggage line-up

Luggage and other bulky storage odds and ends line up along this secure ledge, which takes advantage of high wall space in garages or basements. The 38-inch-wide shelf sits atop a 2 by 4 ledger strip fastened to wall studs. It's supported in front by threaded rods tied into a 2 by 4 nailed across ceiling joists or rafters. Line the ledge with carpet scraps to avoid scraping luggage.

Sheds for Storage Overflow

A separate shed serves two storage purposes: garden and yard gear can be near to where you use them, and more space is available in the garage, attic, and basement.

Simple or elaborate, a shed can be a model of efficiency and convenience, actually making it easy to transplant petunias or put away the tricycle.

Check local building codes

Before setting your sights on a certain kind of shed, visit the building inspector in your area. You'll need to find out whether to apply for a building permit and what codes affect your project. Detached buildings are often subject to requirements regarding minimum setbacks from property lines. You may also face limits on installing water and electrical lines or be required to build your shed with fire-retardant materials. Codes vary: sheds aren't allowed in some communities; in others, you can locate a shed almost anywhere on your property, as long as it isn't anchored to the ground or set on a concrete slab.

Should you buy or build?

Depending on how industrious you are, you can erect a metal shed frame from a kit, assemble the parts of a prefab unit, or build your shed from scratch.

If you choose the metal frame, you'll play the roles of a mechanic and carpenter. You can also select what kind of siding and roofing to use: wood, aluminum, fiberglass, or heavy translucent plastic. The heavy plastic can be used to create a greenhouse effect.

Convenient to install, prefab metal sheds come in standard designs; some can be assembled in an afternoon. However, they tend to rust, and it's difficult to attach storage units and accessories to their thin walls. So before buying a prefab kit, find out whether the manufacturer provides a line of shelves, racks, and other accessories especially designed for the metal shed. If accessories aren't available for the design you want, you can always build a wood frame inside the shed.

Wood frame sheds allow you to create an attractive custom design that meets your exact needs and suits your available space. You can easily attach storage units to wall studs or overhead rafters. Unlike a metal shed, a wood shed is flammable; and you'll have to devote considerable time to planning and building.

Shed specifications

A shed should be at least 6 feet wide and a minimum of 4 to 6 feet deep, depending on your needs. If you're building it, plan your access wisely. Install a wide door —4 to 5 feet.

If allowed by code, a shed should be on some kind of foundation to secure it from wind and frost heave. The foundation also prevents wood floors from rotting. Metal sheds often come without floors; a concrete slab is an ideal foundation for these. Some prefab sheds come with special ground anchors or floor supports. Concrete piers and wood beams make a simple, efficient foundation for a wood frame shed.

If your shed floor is above ground level or if the door has a high sill, you'll probably want to use some kind of ramp. A ramp makes access more convenient for wheeling in a wheelbarrow or driving in a mini-tractor. If the floor of the shed is on the ground, elevate equipment on concrete blocks in the winter.

Planning your shed's interior

The rule for storage in tight spaces like sheds is to keep small objects off the floor. Floor space is valuable, and you'll want to use it for access and heavy equipment. You can fasten cabinets, shelves, tool racks, and workbenches to the framing members in a wood shed. If you don't use the manufacturer's storage accessories for a metal shed, consider building a wood frame inside it.

To help you plan your shed's innards, review the following storage ideas:
- Old kitchen cabinets or a counter with built-in drawers are great for a mid-size shed.
- Garden poisons should be locked in a cabinet out of children's reach.
- If you have a hinged door that swings out, install narrow shelves on the back of the door.
- Industrial metal shelves can be used in a shed; they won't warp from dampness, but they may rust.

If your lawn chairs and other outdoor items won't take up all of your shed space, incorporate a garden work center into the shed. Set up a potting counter, and provide garbage cans or tilt-out bins for fertilizer and potting materials; a sink; racks for tools and pots; and small shelves for seeds and bottles. Hang a chalkboard on the wall to record planting timetables and schedule weekly garden duties. See pages 34–37 for specific ideas on storing garden tools and supplies.

Tree-side potting nest

Set against a backdrop of towering redwoods, this potting shed repeats the design and materials of the adjacent structures. The doorway, partial walls, and slatted roof contribute to the open feeling and let light into the shed, making it ideal for growing plants from seeds. Potting supplies fit on shelves that run the length of one shed wall. Along the other walls are a work counter, a utility sink, and below-counter bins. Landscape Architect: G. E. Talbot.

Summer Sports Gear

Ready when you are: boats, bats, balls, rackets, fins, tackle

Summer sports equipment ranges in size from the compact softball to the 16-foot canoe. You'll have to vary your storage methods accordingly. You may want to rotate summer sports equipment by season: keep baseballs and swim fins in less accessible spots during winter months and within easy reach during the height of summer activities.

Some sporting goods, such as baseball bats, tennis rackets, and water-skis, can be stored on organized racks or pegboards. Equestrians might hang bridles and bits on hooks and pegs, and saddles on horizontal "saddleback" rails made with 2 by 4s. For organizing a variety of items of various sizes and shapes—such as

camping and fishing gear—shelves, closets, and storage chests are the most convenient. A stack of deep cubbyhole shelves by the garage door keeps gear immediately accessible. For the dedicated athlete, metal school lockers—either new or recycled—make familiar storage units. A simple nylon hammock strung overhead can keep basketballs, footballs, and sleeping bags from disappearing.

Very light boats can be hung on ropes or racks attached to inside or outside walls; canoes and rowboats are often suspended from overhead joists or collar beams—providing they can handle the weight. For storing heavy or large boats, see pages 50–51.

Angled walls for rifles and poles

Racks mounted on angular corner walls offer out-of-the-way places to store rifles and fishing poles, keeping these items accessible, yet removed from the rest of the garage. Because only fishing nets and boots are on the floor, the storeroom door can swing open without banging into any equipment. Architect: Glenn D. Brewer.

Chains and frame cradle canoe

Attached to the rafters with chains, a strong wood frame supports this heavy canoe and keeps it out of the way of cars. Neatly stacked firewood functions as a windbreak at the back of the carport. Architect: James Van Drimmelen.

An ace of a storage place

Custom cabinetry keeps tennis equipment and running gear neatly packed away. Sets of double doors open into mini-clothes lockers with room for bags at the bottom. The lower unit is fitted with cubbies for shoes, dividers for rackets, and racks for cans of tennis balls. Design: Betsie Corwin and William G. Florence.

Winter Sports Equipment

Safe stashing of skis, skates, saucers, sleds

During the winter, you might want to keep your seasonal sports gear where it's ready for a quick weekend trip to the mountains or a morning visit to the slopes. In the spring, winter equipment can trade places with golf clubs, baseball bats, or camping equipment, and go into less accessible areas—up into attic corners, against the ridge line or rafters, or into a crawl space.

The rule for most winter storables, in and out of season, is to hang them up. Skis are easily hung by the pair or grouped in a rack. Snowshoes, saucers, skates, and small sleds are best hung on nails, spikes, pegs, or hooks (see page 7). Toboggans and bigger sleds can rest atop raised platforms, ceiling joists, or collar beams.

Short steps from ski locker to car

Packing up for skiing is simple when the ski equipment is behind double doors in the carport. Skis, poles, and a ski rack rest on dowels in this long, shallow closet. Boots go on the floor. Architects: The Hastings Group.

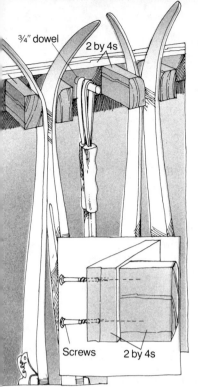

³⁄₄" dowel 2 by 4s

Screws 2 by 4s

Block-and-peg ski rack

Because skis conveniently curve at the tips, they'll hang from many kinds of blocks or runners spaced 1¼ inches or so apart. This simple and effective ski rack uses short blocks cut from a 2 by 4 of oak, pine, fir, or redwood. The blocks are glued and screwed to a longer 2 by 4 backing piece. Ski poles hang on adjacent recessed dowels. To add a finishing touch, and to protect skis from scratches, round off and sand smooth the inside top corner of each block. Finish the rack with penetrating resin or polyurethane varnish.

Overhead joist

Making the most of joists and beams

Open ceiling joists or collar beams supply a ready-to-use storage spot for sleds, saucers, and other outdoor equipment: simply rest the runners across a couple of joists. Another idea is to hang snowshoes and skates from nails, spikes, pegs, or hooks sunk into the joists.

Wire screen

1 by 3s

Drying out that soggy gear

When you get home from the slopes or the pond, you head for the warmth of the fire...but where do you put your cold, damp ski boots, skates, snowshoes, gloves, and socks?

These drying and storage shelves, adjacent to the water heater for extra drying power, are built from wire screen sandwiched by two 1 by 3 frames; the screens allow air to circulate and moisture to drip. For even quicker drying, run copper tubing—heated by the water heater— underneath each shelf.

Guard Against Storage Hazards

Open boxes spilling over with useless papers, a rickety ladder propped in a corner, carelessly placed sharp tools — these hazards deserve attention. If you're setting your storage in order, make room for safety, too.

Garages, attics, and basements are very susceptible to accident and fire. To prevent storage disasters, your first jobs are to sort, organize, and clean. Discard old paint cans, broken toys, and other unneeded items.

Following are some specific pointers and suggestions to help you with your task. For more safety guidelines, contact fire, health, and other appropriate officials.

Organize your workshop

A clean workshop is a safe workshop. Make it a habit to frequently discard wood scraps and vacuum up sawdust, especially behind panels, boxes, and equipment where highly flammable sawdust collects.

Power tools present a host of dangers. Power tools and lighting should be on separate circuits; a tool circuit should be at least 20 amps to prevent overload. Grounded (three-prong) outlets are a necessity. Also, don't use power tools in damp conditions. A master switch controlled by a key is a wise precaution. To guard against shock, purchase double-insulated power tools.

Make sure that your workshop has sufficient lighting (see page 66) and that the floor is clear of items that could cause a fall.

Guard garden supplies

Your garage or garden shed makes a perfect secret place for little ones playing hide-and-seek. Children — yours or your neighbor's — can easily get into toxic garden supplies or play with sharp tools if these items aren't properly stored.

Place dangerous tools and poisons well out of children's reach. Hang sharp tools high on walls with strong hooks; make sure they won't fall. Tools can also be stored, along with toxic substances, in drawers and cabinets that have plastic "childproof" latches (see drawing below left) or metal locks. Do not store poisons under utility sinks, on the ground between wall studs, or near bulk food supplies. Remember, pets should be protected from these dangers, too.

Ladders and staircases: watch your step

Ladders and staircases should be adequate for the loads you'll be carrying up and down them, and should always be in good condition. Never block a ladder or staircase with boxes or overflow storage.

Position a ladder so that its base is offset from the perpendicular by 1/4 of its length (the foot of a 20-foot ladder, for example, should be 5 feet from the point directly beneath the top of the ladder). Fold-down ladders usually aren't intended for heavy use; buy one with minimum bounce.

Handrails on staircases should be solidly secured, and the steps clear and well lighted, with light switches at the top and bottom. A minimum of 6½ feet of headroom all the way up is often required by code.

Be cautious with heating equipment

Make sure that combustibles are not positioned near heating equipment such as a furnace, water heater, heating ducts, or a chimney.

Store ashes in a metal container; don't place ashes in cardboard boxes or in a place where a breeze can stir up embers.

It's wise to have a professional inspect and clean your heating equipment every year. Do not leave portable heaters unattended, or place them where they can be tipped over.

Avoid electrical problems

Plugging too many tools or appliances into an extension cord is hazardous because the cord's insulation can ignite. Generally, do not rely heavily on extension cords. You can start a fire by stringing extension cords

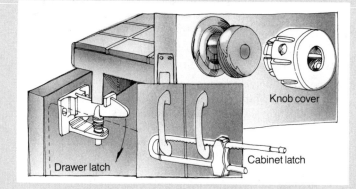

Knob cover

Drawer latch

Cabinet latch

under rugs, tying them to nails, or using extra-long cords of insufficient gauge. Periodically inspect extension cords for cracks, fraying, and broken plugs.

Check with an electrician to make sure that your circuits aren't overloaded; you may need to install additional circuits in your basement or garage workshop, or in your attic for lighting.

Isolate flammable liquids

Storing flammable liquids is a risky practice. Gasoline for lawnmowers and other equipment should be stored in a safety can (see drawing below) with a spring closure valve, vapor vent, pouring spout, and the label of a testing laboratory. Paint, solvent, rubber cement, and other flammable substances should be stored in metal cans with tight-fitting lids in a well-ventilated area far away from heat sources. Never store flammable liquids in glass, plastic, or makeshift containers.

It's a good idea to place correctly containered liquids in a metal cabinet. Do not store them in the house; the vapors that escape from cans are often dangerous. Rags that have soaked up flammable substances should also be kept in metal containers with tight-fitting lids away from heat sources. Better yet, throw them away.

Be sure to clean up any oil drippings.

Pouring spout
Testing lab label
Spring closure valve
Vapor vent

Install lifesaving devices

Smoke and heat detectors, automatic sprinklers, fire extinguishers, and modifications of attic fans can make your storage areas much safer. Other safety measures include solid-core doors (which slow the spread of fire) leading from a carport or garage into living space, and fire-retardant material covering insulation.

Smoke and heat detectors set off an alarm to alert people to danger, giving them time to escape. Smoke detectors alone, when properly placed, installed, and maintained, offer the minimum level of safety recommended by the National Fire Protection Association. Used in conjunction with a smoke detector, a home heat detector is particularly useful in an attached garage, attic, or basement. Heat detectors react when the air reaches a certain temperature, usually 135° F.

An automatic sprinkler system, typically seen in public buildings, is used with a smoke detector or other automatic alarm. A small sprinkler system provides protection in the vulnerable areas of your home: the garage, attic, and basement.

Sprinklers are designed to slow the development and spread of fire. A drawback of a sprinkler system, of course, is that water might damage valuables.

Fire extinguishers. Fire emergencies require quick action. Keep a multipurpose chemical fire extinguisher (see drawing) in or near your garage, attic, or basement. Make sure that the extinguisher carries the UL label of approval and is inspected yearly.

The only times you should try to put out a fire by yourself are when you're near the fire when it begins, or when you discover the fire in its early stages. And, of course, you must know how to use an extinguisher. Don't be overly ambitious in the face of fire; your personal safety comes first.

An attic fan can be a lethal instrument if a fire starts anywhere in your house while the fan is in operation. Air currents speed combustion, and can turn a small fire into a raging one in a few seconds. To eliminate this hazard, fit the louvered shutters on fans with fusible links, and equip fan power circuits with an automatic cut-off switch activated by a fire detection system.

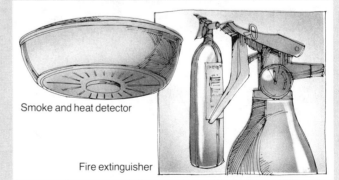

Smoke and heat detector

Fire extinguisher

Trailers, RVs & Boats

Great fun on the go, a sizeable challenge back home

Recreational vehicles, camper trailers, and boats on trailers are difficult to hide. To make matters more complex, many local ordinances demand that all trailers and RVs be off the street and out of sight. Your storage options include the back or side yard behind a fence, the garage (if possible), an independent structure, or an extension of the house or garage. (Before building a structure, check with local building officials.)

The big problem with most RVs is their height. The average garage door opening is 7 feet high; RVs demand clearance of up to 10 feet. Your boat trailer or camper trailer may fit inside a standard garage if you're willing to steal space from the family car.

Smaller boats without trailers can hang on a wall or overhead (see page 45). Larger boats share the same drawbacks as RVs and trailers.

Outboard motors for boats should be stored upright and off the floor, in a dry, ventilated garage, basement, or shed. Collar beams or ceiling joists are excellent for storing masts and booms.

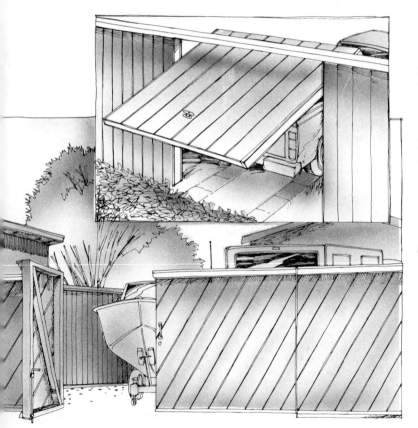

Invisible gates for sleek street view

To conceal a boat or camper trailer in a wide side yard, construct a special access gate that blends with the surroundings and presents only a smooth, continuous fence line when viewed from the street.

For your gate or set of gates, use overhead door hardware with a heavy-duty gate frame if your trailer isn't too high, lightweight gates that lift out of place, or standard hinged gates. The gate siding should match the adjoining fence exactly.

Don't ruin your camouflage with a paved driveway at the access area. Most lawns can handle occasional traffic; plant a sturdy ground cover, if necessary. For extra lawn protection when you need to move your trailer, lay down runners made from old plywood sheets.

Custom garage—costly but most protective

Though expensive, a new structure is the most protective way to house your RV, camper trailer, or boat. Shown here is an unobtrusive, flat-topped garage built against a back fence—the siding and doors match the fence materials, and the structure doesn't rise above the neighborhood fence line. Inside there's electrical power, as well as a workbench and room for water-skis and boat accessories.

Another option for a boat or trailer is a garage or house extension (see page 67) with large double doors for access, and storage space behind and above.

Waterside garages: a gift of height

The divided garage complex in this home has something most garages don't—height. That's what the owner had in mind when designing it. The added height in the garages provides the necessary space for parking a trailer, RV, or boat.

Workshop Basics

Consider safety first, then organize for project efficiency

The four major components of an efficient home workshop are the workbench, storage units, proper lighting, and adequate electrical wiring and outlets. (For a discussion of lighting and wiring considerations, see pages 48–49 and 66.)

The focus of your workshop should be a large, stable workbench. Many kinds are available premade, or you can make your own from a 2 by 4 frame and plywood or hardboard top. The area beneath a workbench is ideal for drawers, cabinets, boxes, and shelves.

Storage units and stationary power tools should be ordered in a way that reflects the sequence of a typical project. Similar tools and materials should be grouped together so that you can find them easily. Large power tools mounted on casters can be rolled out from a storage closet or cabinet, or away from a wall, then back again when the work is done. Wall cabinets are best for portable power tools because they protect the blades and working parts from damage and keep children from making dangerous mischief.

Besides tools and projects in progress, you'll want to store materials: leftover lumber, metal scraps, or bulk lumber from a special sale. Leftovers can be stored in a rolling box with a hinged top. Shelf brackets fastened to every other wall stud will handle light lumber. For heavier loads, assemble "ladder racks," like the ones used at lumberyards, from 2 by 4s and lag screws. Tough fiber storage tubes help pigeonhole and protect lengths of pipe or moldings. And if you're pressed for space, look to the rafters or ceiling joists.

Plywood shelves hold plenty

Good planning takes the spotlight in this woodworker's den. Graduated shelves on sturdy brackets keep lengthy timbers out of the way. When it's time to cut them down to size with the table saw, an outside door is opened to make room for any wood overhang. Lights fitted on overhead tracks illuminate the workbench and table saw; heat lamps help dry lamination projects. Architect: J. Alexander Riley.

Pristine platform workshop

Elevated on a 4½-inch-high concrete slab at the rear of the garage, this workshop makes efficient use of walls and floor space. Hand tools on the pegboard panels are conveniently within reach. Mounted on the left wall is a cabinet with small drawers for organizing nails, screws, hooks, and other supplies. A wall-mounted strip with outlets every 15 inches provides electricity for power tools on casters. The outlets are controlled by a key-operated switch, keeping youngsters from playing with the equipment. Architect: R. Gary Allan.

Workshop Hand Tools & Supplies

Maintaining order for a miscellany of small items

Hammers, paint cans, motor oil, nails, picture hooks, electrical fuses, extension cords: home maintenance supplies get out of hand fast without neat organization. And a home workshop can also mean woodworking, crafts, art, or darkroom supplies to store. What you need are storage containers and units that corral easily lost small items in specific, accessible places. The ideal workshop should combine both open and closed storage.

Hand tools are among the most bothersome workshop storables. The popular pegboard and hanger system (see pages 7 and 53) is best suited for visible, hands-on storage. You can also buy individual wall racks for small tools like screwdrivers and pliers.

Though less accessible, closed units protect tools from rust and dust. One space-saving closed unit is a shallow cabinet with sturdy double doors: line the cabinet back and both doors with tools.

Less-often-used storables, such as paint, brake fluid, and turpentine, can go on shelves installed high on the wall or suspended overhead or between ceiling joists. Graduate your shelf depth and spacing to fit the containers—gallons, quarts, and pints—and make sure that the labels are visible.

Drawers—plenty of them—are a blessing to any workshop owner. Build them into your work counters or an open frame, or recycle old bedroom dressers or kitchen units.

Dream home for fasteners

Fasteners of every size, type, and description can easily be spotted inside carefully labeled bins. Hinged doors in the top cabinet unit flip up for access, down for protection and neat appearance. The base cabinet is headquarters for painting supplies, and on the countertop are parts drawers—for even more fasteners.

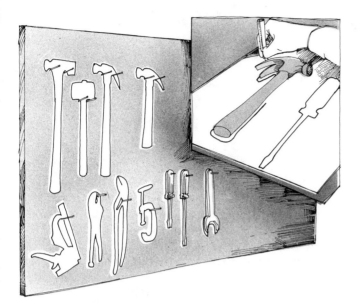

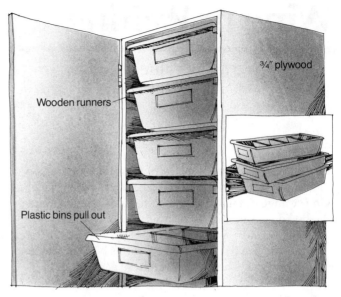

Instant guide to what goes where

It's no small task to keep hand tools in order and accounted for, especially when several family members share the same workshop. These simple silhouettes will help.

The simplest way to make silhouettes is to hang your tools in the ideal order, then outline each one with a broad-tipped indelible felt pen. Or lay each tool on heavy white paper and trace its outline. Carefully cut out each silhouette and glue it to the wall as shown. The glued-on silhouettes will last longer if you coat the entire board with clear sealer.

Slide-out supply bins

These sturdy plastic bins—purchased from office, restaurant, or school suppliers—are just right for home maintenance or crafts supplies. Build a plywood frame, then attach pairs of small wooden runners to both side walls as shown. Bins slide or lift out for easy access. For extra protection or just to be fancy, add a hinged door to the entire unit.

Cutlery trays, though less rugged, also make serviceable drawers or fine workshop drawer inserts.

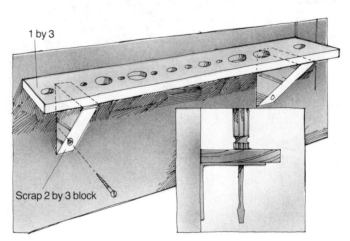

Natty solutions for nuts, bolts, nails

Jars, empty coffee cans, and cigar boxes can help save your workshop from chaos. House these containers on narrow shelves lipped with 1 by 2 trim. Jars for nails, nuts, and other items unscrew from their own lids, which are fastened to the bottoms of the lipped shelves.

Between-stud shelves with 1 by 4 or 1 by 6 strips across the fronts are also ideal for small storage.

Quick-reach tool rack

One simple way to keep small hand tools such as screwdrivers, files, or chisels instantly accessible is to build a tool rack at the rear of your workbench. Drill holes through a length of 1 by 3, large enough for each tool's shank to pass through, but too small for the handle. Attach your rack to the wall with L-braces or triangular blocks made from scraps of 2 by 4.

Wine in Waiting

Laying aside a few valued bottles—or aging by the case

If you're serious about your wines, you'll soon want an organized, stable environment (see pages 58–59 for wine storage details) for your collection. Racks or bins are the key to organizing your wines.

Will you store a few bottles for ready consumption or a by-the-case collection that requires bottle aging? For relatively few bottles, commercial accordion or cubbyhole racks are commonly available at department stores and at some wine shops. Diamond-shaped or triangular bins are traditional for long-term storage (see photo, page 59); the typical bin has a capacity of one to one and a half cases. Wine bottles of any size up to a magnum (2 quarts) may be stored on cabinet shelves or open shelves 14 inches deep.

When it comes to designing your own racks, remember two things: racks must be sturdy (one case of wine weighs about 40 pounds), and bottles should be stored on their sides to keep corks moist.

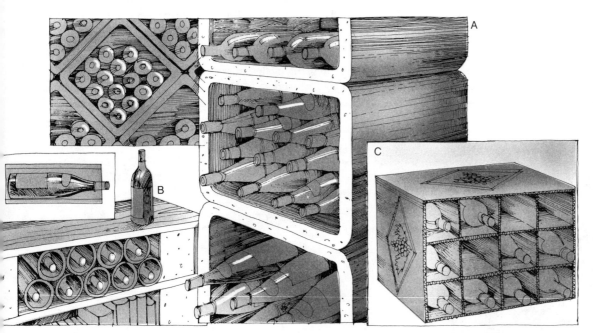

Vintner's classics, easy to re-create

Whether you want storage for a modest supply or a lavish one, these simple ideas may be all you need. Rectangular chimney tiles (A) handle a case or more apiece, but are relatively fragile in larger sizes and shouldn't be stacked too high; round drainpipe tiles or mailing tubes (B) pigeon-hole individual bottles. Of course, the simplest solution for short-term storage is to turn a divided cardboard wine box on its side (C).

Each slot stacks a case

This stylish vertical slot system is fashioned from vertical 1 by 10s faced with 1 by 3s shaped at the top so that bottles slide up and out. The platform on top displays the contents—up to one case—of each slot below. Make the basic unit 4 feet high; the number of slots is up to you.
Architect: Ron Bogley.

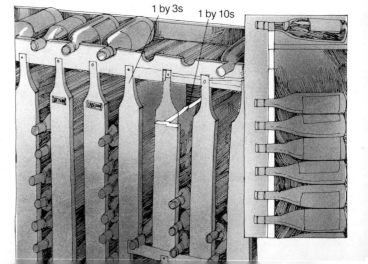

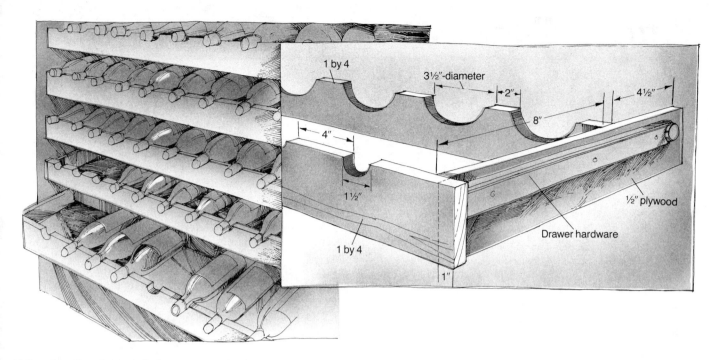

Labels on upper diagram: 1 by 4; 3½"-diameter; 2"; 4½"; 8"; 4"; 1½"; ½" plywood; Drawer hardware; 1 by 4; 1"

Wine by the drawerful

This handy rack is like a chest of open drawers for wine. To build it, first shape front and rear rails as shown, then connect them with plywood side strips. Mount your new drawers (they shouldn't be more than about 3 feet wide) inside a frame on heavy-duty drawer hardware. The drawers shown are 14 inches deep. Fasten your frame to a wall or to the ceiling for stability. Design: John Hamilton, George Kelce.

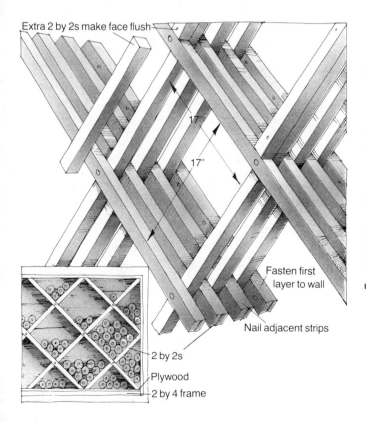

Labels on lower diagram: Extra 2 by 2s make face flush; 17"; 17"; Fasten first layer to wall; Nail adjacent strips; 2 by 2s; Plywood; 2 by 4 frame

For copious collecting

A large-capacity, diamond-shaped bin system can be built by crisscrossing successive layers of 2 by 2 strips. Rip the 2 by 2s from fir 2 by 4s; seal, stain, and varnish; then assemble. Fasten parallel 2 by 2s to the wall at a 45° angle, as shown (use masonry nails for masonry walls, screws for wood stud walls); then nail on successive layers, each one perpendicular to the last. Eight layers of 2 by 2s provide bins approximately 12 inches deep. To provide additional support for your system, and to keep wines off a damp or dusty floor, position your bins atop a base of 2 by 4s and plywood, as shown.

Your bin system might stretch from wall to wall and from floor to ceiling, but it can be as modest as you like. For a finished look in a smaller unit, enclose the bins within plywood or fir sides and top. The bin size shown holds two cases. Architect: Neil M. Wright.

Wine Cellars for Vintage Care

Why create a wine cellar? For one thing, you'll always have a special bottle on hand when friends drop by. But perhaps more important, by purchasing young wines or sale wines in bulk, then letting them mature in your own cellar, you'll save the appreciable markup that dealers tack on for each year that wines age on *their* shelves. Moreover, many fine wines disappear from the market long before they're mature. A wine cellar or storage area can rapidly save you more money than it cost to build.

Where does a wine cellar go? An attractively finished basement is ideal both for a booming collection and for candlelight tasting parties. But there are other spots—a crawl space (see page 79), a garage corner, an outdoor shed, even an excavated hillside "cave."

Constructing a smaller wine cellar room within a basement or other larger space normally entails building walls, insulating walls and ceiling (see drawing, page 26), then adding racks or bins for wine. A vacant closet or even some unused cabinets form ready-made cellars for small collections.

Regardless of your cellar's size or location, remember four factors for successful wine storage: temperature stability, peace and quiet, absence of light, and bottle positioning.

Temperature: keep it cool and stable

For the optimum aging of wine, it's best to keep your cellar between 50° and 60°F/10° and 16°C; 58°F/14°C is generally regarded as ideal. Some experts, however, wouldn't pale at the idea of storing wines at room temperature — 65° to 70°F/18° to 21°C. Temperature *stability* is more critical than precise temperature: wine can tolerate slow temperature changes over a period of days, but rapid or extreme fluctuations will cause damage.

Insulation is the key to temperature stability. Masonry—the building material for most basements—insulates well. Earth is an excellent natural insulator, which is why so many wine cellars are built below ground level. You don't have a basement? Search the house for an area that stays naturally cool (the north side of the house is shadiest) or that can be vented to a naturally cool crawl space or outside area.

Your cellar should not be near the furnace, heating ducts, or water heater. Insulating the walls heavily (the

more the better) will stabilize temperatures. And don't forget the door — it should be solid-core with double weatherstripping. In cool climates, you can leave cool (usually north or east) basement walls uninsulated. Where it's warm, you might choose a power fan or air conditioning unit with an automatic thermostat to keep the wine cool. Though it does consume energy, an air conditioner might be needed only two to three months a year if the cellar is well insulated, and it needn't be overly powerful. Cellar humidity, although not critical, is best around 50 percent. If your cellar is too damp, the labels may fall off your bottles — resulting in a real guessing game.

Peace and quiet

The conditions required for storing wines may sound like a sickroom atmosphere, but wine should not be disturbed. Protect it from sources of vibration such as stairways, washers, and dryers. Sturdy wine racks will help (see pages 56–57); in earthquake country, bolt your racks to fixed walls.

Shut out the light

Direct sunlight and other sources of ultraviolet light may harm wines (specifically, the yeast organisms still alive within the bottle), so make your cellar lightproof. But don't forget good artificial light for those times when you're hunting for that special bottle or hosting a wine-tasting party.

Keep bottles on their sides

Efficient wine racks are the key to organizing your cellar space. For specifics on racks, see pages 56–57. A genuine cork is the traditional sign that a bottle of wine deserves special care. The cork breathes slightly, so it must be kept moist by the wine inside to prevent air or airborne organisms from entering and spoiling the wine.

Store bottles on their sides or at a slight tilt from the horizontal, with necks toward you for easy access. To help sort out the Beaujolais from the Zinfandel, hang small labels around the necks, or label each slot in your rack. Keep a complete log of all your wines and their locations.

A simple corner cellar

Wooden grid panels, fore and aft, allow prize wines to rest at their preferred angle. Counter is handy for uncorking bottles and pouring wine. Architect: Kenneth Lim.

Elegant enough for entertaining

This wine cellar is much more than a wine storage room—the owners enjoy their converted crawl space so much that they have dinner parties here. From the table, guests can admire the triangular wine bins, each of which holds about a case of wine. A serving alcove in the wall opposite the bins is fitted with a rack for wine glasses. The brick floor and rough redwood paneling add to the atmosphere and help insulate the cellar. Design: Jean Chappell.

Garages,
Attics &
Basements

Turning troublesome spaces into work-for-you places

Space below the basement stairs *is fitted with shelves and hooks; floor space is open for bulky items.*

Closet within a closet *takes advantage of normally wasted space along attic eaves. The small access door opens from the master bedroom closet. Architect: James Jessup.*

Garage corner *lends plenty of wall space for bicycles, hand tools, and camping gear. The cutaway workbench with shelves underneath is a bonus. Architect: Wendell H. Lovett.*

Garages

Maximizing storage, yet leaving space for the car

A loft for lightweight items, *simple racks for tools, and roomy utility shelves help organize this garage. All of these features stretch storage space even when the car's inside. The tool rack is made from 1 by 4 rails fastened to studs. For loft-building help, see page 65. Design: Steve Wolgemuth.*

You can't find your best pair of hedge clippers. Ah!—you spy them hanging on a nail in the corner of what has become a jungle—the garage. Up, down, and around you go, clearing a path to the corner. As you balance among a garden rake, birdcage, mattress frame, and broken lawn chair, reaching for the clippers, you stumble and fall onto a pile of laundry next to the washing machine. The clippers are still in the corner.

Clearly, you're out of storage space in your garage or carport, and it's time to do something about it. Consider organizing your belongings, improving your present storage facilities and adding new ones, or extending the building.

As you tackle your garage storage problems, think "clean up and look up"—this can be your byword for discovering and using your garage's storage potential. A thorough cleanup alone can drastically increase your garage's capacity. And once your belongings are sorted through, you'll be able to make better use of existing and added storage units such as shelves, drawers, pegboards, and roll-outs.

But don't forget to look up. Overhead storage —cabinets, platforms, lofts, and ledges—can be used to tame your garage jungle and create room for a much needed laundry center, workshop, or potting table. Overhead storage is also feasible in carports, which call for secure, weatherproof storage units.

If you're already organized, this section will show you how to improve your garage—and the time you spend in it—with better heating, lighting, ventilation, and other amenities. And if you can't possibly fit in another paint can or tricycle, you'll find some ideas here on how to increase storage space by extending the garage itself.

Your garage's or carport's storage potential

With building costs multiplying as quickly as your storage inventory, you may well turn to your existing garage or carport with fresh hopes. Its length and width determine the structure's basic amount of available space, of course, but other factors count, too. Here are some questions to consider: How high is the roof? Is it flat or peaked? How large is your car? Does it need year-round protection?

Garage dimensions. Garages are nominally termed "one-car," "two-car," and "three-car." The size of a one-car garage begins at about 10 feet by 20 feet—small, but you can probably squeeze some good storage space out of it. You're in luck if your one-car garage has a peaked roof. Two-car spaces run upward from 18½ feet by 20 feet; 25 feet square is ideal. If you have a three-car space, you have a head start on storage.

Garage and carport types. The design of your garage or carport affects its storage potential. Garage walls are usually built from wood framing and sheathing, cement blocks, or prefabricated metal panels. Building materials have little influence on storage capacity, but it's easier to attach storage units to wood frame walls than to masonry or metal. Wood frame walls also allow shallow storage between studs.

A carport's open structure is a different story. Because carport storage is more exposed to weather and theft, you'll want to limit storage of valuables to lockable weatherproof units; install them either along the carport's perimeter or overhead.

Gable and hip roofs (see drawing below) are tops for storage. Shed-roof structures also provide some overhead space between the rafters and ceiling line. In a flat-roofed garage, you're limited to the space between the top of your head or vehicle and the ceiling.

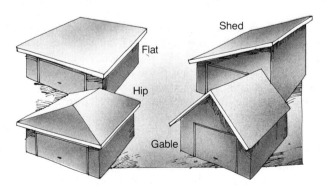

Subcompacts and limousines. The sizes of your automobiles directly affect the available floor space in a garage or carport. Fortunately for the storage-needy, average car dimensions have been shrinking (see drawing at right above for sample dimensions). Adapt

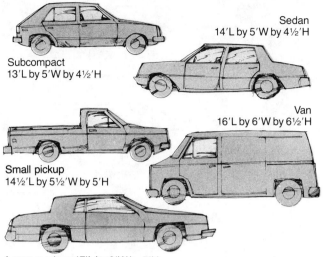

Subcompact
13'L by 5'W by 4½'H

Sedan
14'L by 5'W by 4½'H

Van
16'L by 6'W by 6½'H

Small pickup
14½'L by 5½'W by 5'H

Luxury sedan   17'L by 6'W by 5'H

your storage plans to the size of your vehicle or vehicles, but keep in mind that some day you might want to sell your home to a family with two vans.

Clearance. In your garage or carport, clearance is the space needed around the car when the car is parked inside; it affects how much room you'll have to work with when planning where to put storage units, appliances, and worktables.

See the drawing below for minimum clearance recommendations around typical vehicles. To calculate how much storage space you have to work with, drive your vehicle or vehicles into place. Then measure the distance from each vehicle to the ceiling, walls, rafters, and other obstructions. Subtract the recommended clearance figures, and you have the bottom line—the real storage potential.

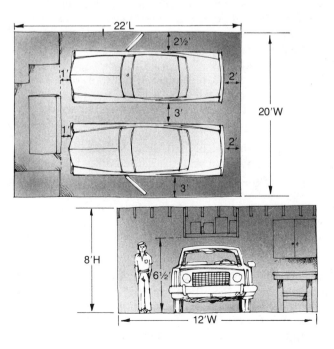

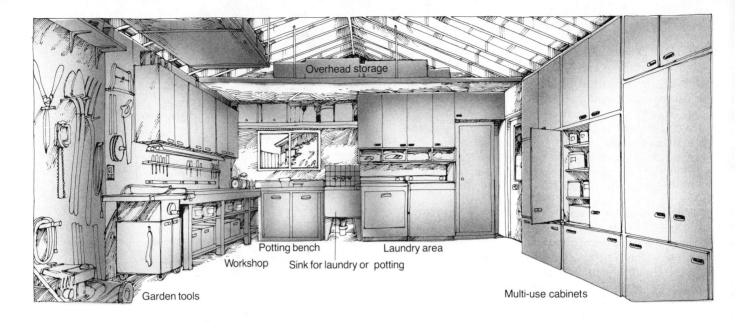

Overhead storage

Potting bench

Workshop

Sink for laundry or potting

Laundry area

Garden tools

Multi-use cabinets

The multi-use garage and carport

After you've assessed your usable storage space, take stock of what you need to store. Do you want to make room for that laundry center, workshop, or potting bench? Efficient overall planning, plus storage units especially designed for your garage or carport, will open up more space than you might imagine.

Coordinating your garage layout

The keys to an efficient garage layout are 1) using all available space, leaving minimum clearances next to, behind, and above vehicles; and 2) grouping items that go together—gardening supplies, for example.

Because most storage problems stem from a lack of floor space, you'll do well to raise storage units above the ground whenever possible. You can hang them high on a wall or suspend them from the joists or rafters. Or you can build an "upstairs" loft.

The items you use most often should, of course, be close at hand. Awkward spots and places that are inaccessible when the car is inside (such as rafter space) are best for seasonal or long-term storage.

Plan hanging shelves or wall-mounted cabinets around the contour of your car's hood and roof (see clearance diagram, preceding page). To ensure safe parking, attach a tennis ball to a cord with a fishhook or eyescrew, and hang the ball so that it will nudge your windshield when the car is properly parked; or fasten a length of 4 by 4 to the garage slab to "curb" the front wheels when the car is in place.

Some garage work areas to consider include these: a laundry center with sink and cabinets (see pages 38–39); a home workshop, with places for hand and power tools (pages 52–55); a house maintenance center for paint brushes, spare plumbing and electrical parts,

brooms, solvents, and cleaners; a potting center with workbench, mounted cabinets, and tilt-out bins; a garden maintenance area where you can gather such tools as the lawn mower, rake, clippers, and weeders; and a mudroom and closet for boots, rain gear, and other outdoor or seasonal clothes (see pages 20–23).

Position such areas for convenience and good working conditions. An outdoor maintenance area, for example, should be handy to the garden or yard.

Storage units for the garage

Here's a brief guide to storage units particularly suited for the garage (see drawing on facing page).

Between-stud shelves. Most garage walls are of wood frame construction; the vertical studs are spaced 16 or 24 inches apart, center to center. The shallow, uniform area between studs is ideal for storing miscellaneous small items like nail jars, engine oil, and paint cans.

Open shelves. Build freestanding frames for shelves or hang shelf units (those with backs) from the wall. You can also use adjustable tracks and brackets, L-braces, individual brackets, or continuous brackets attached to studs to hold up shelves. If your garage walls are of brick or concrete block, back shelves against the wall, hang them from ceiling joists, or use special masonry fasteners (see pages 78–79 for types and installation tips).

Cabinets, drawers, and closets. Enclosed units keep dust and moisture out, and help to organize easily lost small items. Large tools, lawn mowers, and cleaning supplies fit into vertical closets. Recycled cabinets from a remodeled kitchen are perfect for the garage. Securely locked, enclosed units keep children safe from garden poisons and sharp tools, and guard against theft. Sliding doors, roll-down window shades, or tilt-out bins make large units more accessible in tight places. For more on cabinets, see page 10.

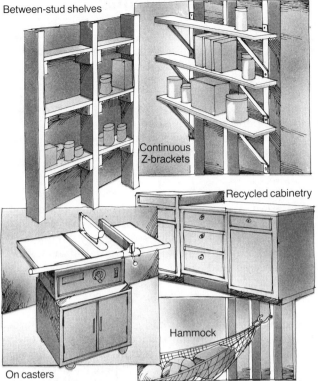

Between-stud shelves

Continuous
Z-brackets

Recycled cabinetry

Hammock

On casters

Racks and pegs. Most versatile for hanging storage is the pegboard hanger system shown on page 7. Oversize carpenter's nails and spikes, or dowels set into wall studs, can hold garden chairs—even ladders. Commercially manufactured racks, whether of heavy-duty metal or vinyl-coated wire, are versatile but more costly.

Roll-outs. One way to fit storage units, workbenches, or equipment into a tight garage is to mount them on heavy-duty casters. Store them close to the wall, then roll them out onto the main floor when the car is out.

Overhead storage units. Even in flat-roofed garages, overhead joists—the horizontal cousins of wall studs—form cubbyholes that are great for small storage, especially for seasonal or infrequently used items. To provide easy overhead "shelving," nail boards across joist bottoms (use heavy nails). A nylon or canvas hammock draped above head level can be used to store lightweight items such as seasonal sports equipment and winter blankets.

Overhead platforms

Often the most neglected storage space throughout a house is the area above your head. Garages with gable, hip, or shed roofs are ideal for anything from a perimeter ledge (page 41) to a finished upstairs room.

When putting overhead garage space to work, remember to leave adequate clearance for the garage door to operate smoothly—and for you and your family to move freely about the garage. In general, any

loft or other overhead structure that you'll be walking under should be at least 6½ feet above the ground.

Building a loft. An overhead loft is an effective means to increasing storage space—especially in a cramped one-car garage—and it's comparatively straightforward for you and a helper to build. To construct the simplest type of loft, take advantage of existing ceiling joists, adding more joists as necessary. Lay a ½ or ⅝-inch plywood "floor" on top of the joists (use ⅝-inch sheets if you're going to be using the loft for heavy storage).

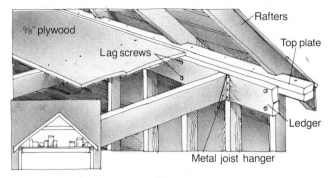

⅝" plywood

Rafters

Lag screws

Top plate

Ledger

Metal joist hanger

When planning a garage loft, inspect the size and condition of the existing joists. High-quality 2 by 6s should be strong enough to support the weight of ordinary storage. But if you plan to walk on the surface or store heavy furniture in the loft, or if the joists must span more than 12 feet, they should be stouter than 2 by 6s. Diagonal 1 by 4 braces running between joists and overhead rafters provide extra support. Ask your local building department about requirements in your area. Joists should be spaced on 16-inch centers for heavy storage.

If you have to add ceiling joists, remember that ideally they should sit on opposing top plates. If the top plates are inaccessible, bolt ledger strips to the wall studs, attach metal joist hangers, and use these to support the joists.

With a peaked roof framed by trusses (see drawing on page 70) or low collar beams, install smaller plywood platforms in the spaces between consecutive trusses (commonly 24 inches) or beams; support the platforms with 2 by 4 cleats nailed to the sides of the trusses.

Access. To gain access to your new loft, use a sturdy stepladder or utility ladder. For a large loft space, see page 73 for information on building stairs and other kinds of access. If you plan to haul bulky, heavy items up and down, a narrow ladder is not only exasperating, but also dangerous.

Pulley system. You might consider a suspended plywood platform operated with pulleys (see page 41) for garage storage. Here's another option: bend 1-inch-wide iron straps so that they extend 3 inches under the platform on each side, and screw them to the bottom and sides. Attach cable or rope to the strap ends. This kind of unit should be used for lightweight storage only.

Carport storage ideas

The two major shortcomings of carport storage are exposure to weather and lack of security; the most common solution to both is to install enclosed cabinets. Build units from exterior-grade ¾-inch plywood, and finish them with tough exterior enamel or polyurethane. (See page 10 for more details on cabinets.) Build units with bases that raise them several inches above the floor; either waterproof the bases or build them with pressure-treated lumber. For greater security, use good locks and hasps (see page 10) and inside-mounted hinges.

The number one spot for carport storage units is between the roof support posts. Attach units to the floor slab, suspend them from overhead beams, or add intermediate vertical framing to hold them up. A long cabinet might have separate doored compartments—one shelved, one with drawers, and one without interior divisions. Units that have doors that slide or that open to the outside leave more clearance inside the carport (see drawing on page 63 for minimum clearances).

If your carport has a pitched gable or hip roof, consider an overhead storage area (see page 65). Lockable plywood chests bolted to a loft "floor," joists, or ledger strips can be used to store valuables (see drawing below).

A small room—perhaps 6 feet by 8 feet—added to the rear of the carport and equipped with windows, electrical outlets, and a small heater, makes a protected "mini-workshop," laundry, or crafts studio. You can fit such a room with shelves, pegboard, and other open storage standbys.

Garage improvements

If your garage (or carport) is to be used for more than parking, it may require specific improvements to ensure that it's safe, comfortable for working, weathertight, and up to code. Consider these possibilities:

Ventilation. To prevent the buildup of moisture, auto exhaust, paint fumes, or shop dust in a closed garage, open ventilation is a necessity. As a rule, there should be 1 square foot of open vent space per 150 square feet of floor area. A laundry must have its own vent system.

Insulation. You might choose to insulate your garage for either of two reasons: 1) to prevent swings in temperature that might damage storage; or 2) to make a heated garage more energy efficient. Put insulation between wall studs and rafters. Choose fiberglass batts, blankets, or rigid board insulation with a vapor barrier, or add a plastic barrier (see pages 70–71).

Lighting. Ideally, you should mix natural and artificial light. To obtain more natural light, install windows and skylights, or replace a large section of a wall, or even the garage door, with translucent panels. Carports are often roofed with rippled plastic sheeting that lets in muted light. By placing garage windows high, you'll save wall space for storage.

Overhead fluorescent shop units are the most efficient for general artificial lighting; one 4-foot double-tube shop unit lights up about 40 square feet. Place individual, adjustable spotlights—incandescent or fluorescent—where direct lighting is needed. Paint the garage walls and ceiling, as well as pegboard storage panels, white to amplify light by reflection.

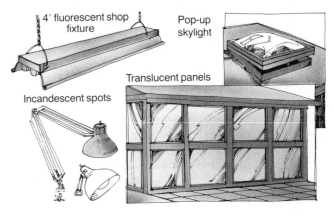

4' fluorescent shop fixture

Pop-up skylight

Translucent panels

Incandescent spots

Wiring. Power tools and garage lighting should be on different circuits; a tool or laundry circuit should be at least 20 amps. Install as many circuits as possible to prevent an overload. A laundry, a workshop, or an electric heater may require up to 240 volts.

Several grounded (three-prong) electrical outlets are a necessity, and continuous power strips are a great convenience. You can run wires either underground or overhead from a power source to a detached garage.

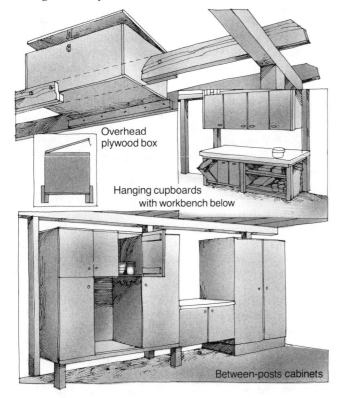

Overhead plywood box

Hanging cupboards with workbench below

Between-posts cabinets

Plumbing. Laundries, photo darkrooms, garden center sinks, hose spigots, and mudrooms may require plumbing improvements. Extending plumbing to a detached garage can be a problem. Remember that outdoor pipes must be placed below the frost line (check local codes), and facilities that require plumbing must be higher than the drainage system. In freezing climates, plumbing systems for unheated garages or carports should be equipped with shutoff valves.

Floors. Concrete slab floors are standard. If you want to use your garage for work or play during the day and for car storage at night, you can protect the floor from oil drippings by laying down a 10-mil layer of polyethylene sheeting. For a more finished look, you might consider vinyl-asbestos tiles; some types take wear and tear from cars surprisingly well.

To insulate and dress up a drab slab, simply cover the floor with straw mats or colorful rugs. You can also paint the slab with special concrete paint, or lay vinyl-asbestos or asphalt tiles in adhesive over the concrete (waterproof it first). If you want to use a covering that requires a wooden base, you can build up such a base over the waterproofed concrete (see pages 78–79 for details). A separate work area within your garage or carport might warrant such treatment.

Heating. Insulation and a built-up subfloor in the work area will help reduce heat loss. To provide heat, you have three options: 1) extend ducts from your central heating system to the garage (not feasible with detached garages); 2) install a separate forced-air unit in the garage (illegal in some areas); or 3) set up a built-in or portable room heater—probably your best choice.

The four types of room heaters are these: electric (baseboard, portable, or quartz type); kerosene; oil or gas wall heaters (designed to fit between wall studs); and woodstoves. Neither a kerosene heater nor a woodstove requires any power hookup, but both need ventilation; a woodstove also requires special fittings and flashing.

Room heaters operate either by convection (they heat the air in a room) or by radiation (they heat objects first). Radiation is most effective in a small area. In general, wall-mounted units are more efficient, but a portable unit can go where you go.

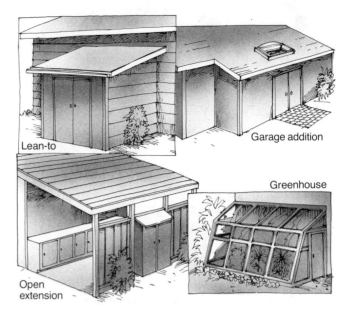

Lean-to

Garage addition

Greenhouse

Open extension

Garage extensions

You've tried all the possibilities, but you just can't fit all your sports gear, garden tools, and lumber into the garage. Before you build a new structure—shed, carport, or garage—consider a simpler garage extension.

Extension types. An extension represents a smaller investment in both time and money than a new structure, and takes less space. Among your options (see drawing above): a roof extension for sheltering a car, boat, or RV—or for storage and work space in milder climates; a lean-to with outside access; a glass greenhouse version of the lean-to (consider a prefabricated unit); or a garage addition. If you're ambitious, you can also convert a one-car to a two-car garage.

Building tips. An extension borrows the garage's framework for part of its structural support. A lean-to is essentially three walls and a roof—the fourth wall is the garage. More elaborate additions entail cutting a door between the garage and an added room, or "punching out" an entire wall. In such cases, be sure to preserve adequate structural supports (headers) for the remaining garage framework. When any structural alterations are required, consult a contractor or architect for recommendations, and have your plans checked out by local building inspectors. Building codes may place limits on extension materials, height, setback from the property line, and foundation type.

Normally, an extension is built over a poured concrete slab that has been tied into the garage slab. However, a more solid foundation, extending below the frost line, may be required in severe climates. Your new extension must be weathertight: provide a sound roof and install flashing where the extension adjoins the old garage roof or siding. Select a design, materials, and colors that match or complement your garage and house.

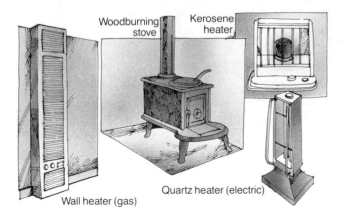

Woodburning stove

Kerosene heater

Quartz heater (electric)

Wall heater (gas)

Attics

Taking the mystery out of access, sloping walls, air vents, and floors

An attic is like a treasure chest—it's usually filled with a few treasures, some disappointments, and a little mystery. Grandfather's steamer trunk, your summer camping gear, and holiday decorations are your treasures. But how do you take the mystery out of storing—and finding—prize possessions within that oddly shaped space?

Attics are scarce in modern housing, particularly in the West. If you grew up with an attic or recently acquired an older or custom home with an attic, you'll welcome solutions to the storage problems posed by attics. These pages offer ways to create a great storage area that's warm, dry, accessible, and even pleasant to visit.

Even if you don't have a formal attic, you may still have a low crawl space above the ceiling that you can convert into a handy storage area.

These are the biggest problems confronting those who wish to make good use of attic space: the awkwardness of sloping walls, sharp roof peaks, and unfinished floors; temperature fluctuations—stifling heat in the summer and icy air in the winter; dampness and humidity from roof leaks and improper air circulation; and insufficient access from below. The following sections treat these problems individually. Overcoming them is something many homeowners can do themselves; refer to the *Sunset* book *Basic Carpentry Illustrated*.

Anatomy of an attic. *The classic attic triangle is shaped by opposing roof rafters rising to a ridge board at the peak, and by floor joists—which double as ceiling joists downstairs—that span the outer house walls. Collar beams sometimes brace opposing rafters, or are added as ceiling supports. Plywood sheets or "1-by" strip boards laid atop the joists serve as flooring. In addition to the open floor space, use these three key storage areas: along the sloping walls, against the gable walls, and along the ridge line.*

An attic overview

An attic's shape—and its capacity for storage—depend on how steeply the roof is pitched (attic height) and on the house's dimensions (floor space). Steep roofs make the best attics, flat roofs none at all. For a living space, a room should normally have a 7½-foot ceiling over at least one-half of the available floor space. For storage, though, you can use whatever space is accessible. Even a minimal crawl space, common in newer homes, has usable storage space.

Organizing your attic

Familiarize yourself with the attic vocabulary explained in the drawing on the facing page. Then add two more terms: *organization* and *accessibility*.

An attic's layout needn't be stylish or fancy, but it should be orderly. The goal is to organize the attic so that you can easily find everything. Arrange related objects in one place, and store those you use often where they're easy to reach. To save a lot of teeth-gnashing, label covered items and boxes with permanent ink on white tape for identification, and keep an inventory of everything in the attic.

Those small, fragile keepsakes requiring extra protection from moisture, dust, and insects should be carefully packed in sturdy boxes and sealed; cover furniture with mattress pads and wrap with polyethylene.

Fitting storage to the attic

An attic's configuration is usually a challenge for orderly storage. How do you deal with sloping walls, corners you have to crawl into, triangular gable walls, and the high but narrow ridge line overhead? Here are some tested ideas; see pages 6–11, too, for general information on storage units.

Sloping walls. You can either shape storage units to conform to eave spaces or give up on the eaves and build vertical units. A 4-foot-high knee wall unit with cabinet doors, recessed drawers, or even a curtain across the front is an efficient way to use eave space (see drawing below). Knee wall units should not be deeper than your reach, unless they're large enough to be walk-ins.

Simpler solutions? Shelves hung with rope or chain, or items hanging from a closet rod, use the force of gravity to square off attic space. Or between adjacent rafters, horizontal 1 by 12s create another version of "between-stud" shelves for out-of-the-way storage.

Gable walls are good spots for a combination closet to store seasonal clothes, toys, and sporting goods. Shelves are easy to fit on a gable wall: install track and bracket hardware for shelves (see drawing below), or place shelves or cabinets along the base of the wall.

Articles that would be damaged by extremes of heat or cold (artwork, for example) shouldn't be stored against a gable wall unless it's insulated. This is particularly true if the gable wall is on the north side of the house or if it's exposed to direct sun for substantial periods. Also, be sure not to block any vents in the wall (page 71).

Along the ridge line. Cut off the triangular peak with rope-hung or chain-hung shelves (accessible from the sides), or hang storage from long nails, hooks, and pegs fixed high on the rafters. A closet rod or simply a long 1 by 2 fastened to opposing rafters will support garment bags full of seasonal clothes. If there's a ridge vent (page 71), don't block it.

To form an "attic within an attic"—a scaled-down version of the loft platform on page 65—place boards or plywood between existing collar beams or between beams you've added yourself. Such a platform should be used for lightweight storage only.

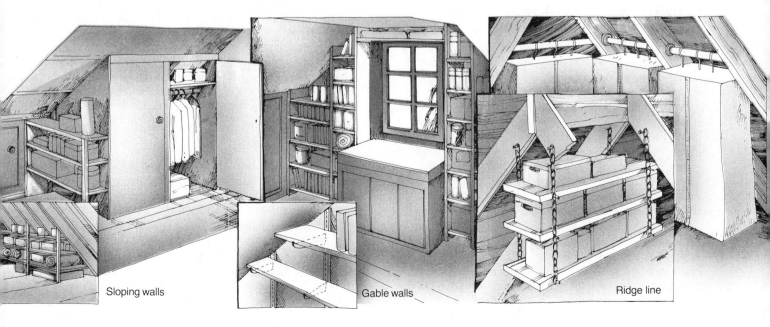

Sloping walls Gable walls Ridge line

Cramped quarters. Many newer homes, particularly in the West and South, were built with relatively flat roofs that leave only a minimal attic or a crawl space. Usually, even a crawl space has some usable storage in the middle and at the gable ends. You can at least lay down plywood around the access hatch. If you can reach the gables easily, build storage cupboards and a catwalk (page 72) leading from the hatch.

Truss framing presents an obstacle to increased attic use; the trusses integrate rafters, collar beams, and sometimes ceiling joists into single framing members, usually spaced 24 inches apart. Trusses may not be removed or cut into, so storage must be built around or between them. Access will often be a trial, as you have to crawl through the spaces within trusses. But don't give up—lay down plywood (see below) and make the most of the space.

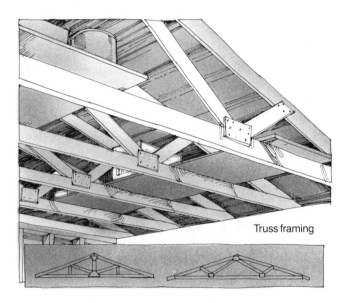

Truss framing

Solving attic problems

Attics revive that old cliché "Out of sight, out of mind." Often you won't notice an attic's problems until you open up the space for storables that demand dry, stable conditions.

Your major enemies are swings in temperature and moisture. If the space is improperly vented or insulated, an attic's temperature might soar to 150° in August, then plunge below freezing in January. Moisture enters the picture as humidity from downstairs condenses on cold attic walls, or—more trying—through a roof leak (for information on making repairs, see the *Sunset* book *Roofing & Siding*).

To eliminate swings in temperature, install insulation between the roof rafters and along gable walls. Add a vapor barrier to prevent humid house air from condensing inside the attic. To improve ventilation, consider adding gable vents, soffit vents, ridge vents, turbine vents, and fans.

Attic insulation—the "balancer"

Insulation slows the transfer of heat from one space to another through a solid surface—wall, roof, or floor. Attic insulation is a "balancer"—it prevents warm air from escaping through the roof in winter, and slows down the accumulation of heat from outside in summer. An "R-rating" is given to all standard building materials—the higher the number, the more effective the insulation.

How much insulation does your attic need? Climate and personal choice are factors: check with the building department for the optimum R-rating where you live.

Where does it go? To make an attic suitable for storage or living space, insulation should be placed between the roof rafters and used to line gable walls—not incorporated into the attic floor as is common. You could insulate behind knee walls—ending the storage space there—instead of the lowest rafters. If your attic floor, or the ceiling below, is already insulated, so much the better; such insulation slows down humidity and heat exchange and deadens sound.

Insulation types. In unfinished attics the most common types of insulation are blankets or batts of spun fiberglass or rock wool, and lightweight rigid boards of compressed fiberglass, polystyrene, or urethane. Blankets and batts are sized to fit common framing gaps of 22½ inches and 14½ inches. Panels are available in the following sizes: 4 feet by 8 feet, 4 feet by 4 feet, and 2 feet by 8 feet. Different thicknesses have different R-ratings. Blankets are easier to install, but boards have a higher R-rating per inch of thickness. Some codes require that insulation be covered with ½-inch gypsum wallboard or a layer of another fire-retardant material.

Vapor barriers. It's necessary in all but the driest climates to install a vapor barrier to prevent humid house air from condensing inside attic walls and roof materials. Blankets and batts are commonly sold with a vapor barrier of foil or kraft paper; if your insulation doesn't have this protection, cover it with polyethylene sheeting (at least 2 mils thick), foil-backed wallboard, or asphalt-covered building paper. Normally, vapor barriers should face in toward the attic.

Attic ventilation

For a simple solution to heat buildup in summer, and humidity and condensation in the winter, try good ventilation. *Natural ventilation* takes advantage of thermal air movement and wind pressure; *power ventilation* uses an electric fan to push or draw hot air up and out of the attic through vents near the ridge line.

The key to proper ventilation is the placement of the vents. The lower drawing on the facing page illustrates the various options for placing vents—but you won't need all those vents. You'll need about 1 square foot of

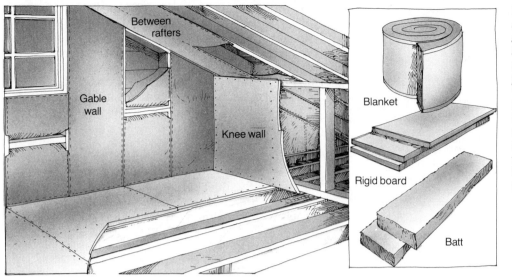

Insulate the shell. *If you're developing attic storage or workspace, provide attic insulation between rafters and inside gable walls. Check your building department for the optimum local "R-rating," then choose from blankets, batts, or rigid boards. Buy insulation with an attached vapor barrier, or add polyethylene sheeting—2-mil or thicker. (The vapor barrier faces inside.) Cover insulation with fire-retardant wallboard or paneling.*

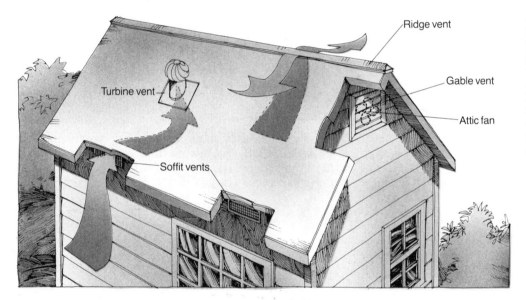

Attic ventilation. *Natural air movement is the key to attic vent placement. Cooler air enters low, pushing rising hot air out the top. Low soffit vents coupled with ridge or gable vents are standard. For problem cases, an electric fan in a downwind gable expels hot air quickly. Slotted turbine vents set up a natural vacuum when the wind blows.*

open vent space (don't count screens or slats) per 150 square feet of floor area.

Gable vents are set in the gable walls, as close to the ridge line as possible. They're usually installed in pairs: one facing into the prevailing wind, the other downwind. A breeze entering one vent pushes hot attic air out the other. Gable vents are often combined with soffit vents. To prevent icy winds from blowing through your attic, close or cover a windward vent during the winter.

Soffit (eave) vents are openings at the attic floor level, below the rafter overhang, that bring cool air into the attic. This air is drawn up by warm-air convection, which forces hot air out vents near the ridge line.

Ridge vents are very efficient, but they're troublesome to install. They release hot air from the roof peak, and

because they're two-sided, they'll always vent in the downwind direction. Ridge vents require extensive complementary soffit venting below for good results.

Turbine vents. When the wind is blowing, the slotted ball atop the vent rotates freely, creating a vacuum that draws attic air up and out. The vent remains open when the wind doesn't blow.

Electric attic fans are powerful tools for pushing hot air out of an attic. A fan is inserted into a cutout in the gable wall, then wired; it's usually paired with an opening in the attic floor that draws air from the house below. Some fans are equipped with a thermostat that conveniently monitors their operation. The disadvantages of electric fans—aside from the effort it takes to install them—are that they consume energy and make noise; some fire codes prohibit their use (see page 49).

Upgrading your attic

If your attic is properly insulated and ventilated, you're ready to attend to three other big considerations: your attic's floor, lighting, and accessibility.

The attic floor

Is your attic floor ready for storage or heavy traffic? If the floor joists are exposed, the answer is a loud "no." *Don't* walk or place storage in the areas between joists—that's your downstairs ceiling, not intended to support weight. For flooring, you can choose between an attic "catwalk" and a finished floor.

A catwalk is a narrow weight-bearing surface extending the length of the attic and possibly to areas under the eaves. With a catwalk you can gain access to the whole attic area without balancing on joists or installing a complete floor.

A catwalk—or a portion of one—is usually built of plywood laid right on top of the joists. Be sure the joists are strong enough—see "A new attic floor," below. Standard plywood sheets 5/8-inch thick are usually adequate, provided you can fit the large (4 feet by 8 feet) sheets up into the attic. If you can't fit standard plywood sheets through the hatch, the stairway, or a dormer opening, cut the sheets down to a manageable size or use strip lumber (1 by 6s should be adequate).

A new attic floor. Attic floor joists, which are of course also the ceiling joists for downstairs, may not be built to support the weight of human traffic, heavy storage,

or furniture. Your first task is to inspect the joists. Check two things: the spacing of the joists—which should be 16 inches center to center (or 24 inches if the joists are stout enough); and the joist dimensions—joists should be at least 2 by 8s for heavy use, even more stout for long spans. Check with building department officials for requirements in your area.

See the drawing below for details about installing new joists, if necessary, and laying a floor. About floors: for simple utility and strength, 5/8-inch or 3/4-inch plywood is the best choice. Plywood is easy to lay, adds rigidity and strength to the floor structure, and is usually squeakproof. Top-grade plywood isn't necessary for attic floors. However, special subfloor panels with tongue-and-groove edges are stronger than standard plywood, though they cost more.

Lighting

Light fixtures don't have to be fancy in the attic, but they should provide illumination where it's most needed. Well-placed electric lights can save you a lot of anguish when you're looking for small items under the eaves or atop a ridge line shelf. One main attic light should be operable from a switch below; individual lights can be turned on by switches or pullchains as you move about the attic.

Attic access

Is your attic readily accessible? How do you plan to use it? If it's for light or seasonal storage only—especially in minimal crawl spaces—a trap door and folding ladder will probably be adequate. Heavier storage requires

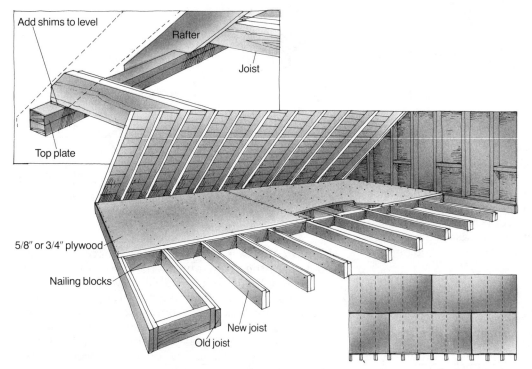

Labels: Add shims to level · Rafter · Joist · Top plate · 5/8" or 3/4" plywood · Nailing blocks · New joist · Old joist

Laying a floor. *If your present joists aren't up to the task of supporting stored items, you'll have to add new ones. Lay new joists next to old ones (if the original spacing is correct); nail the new joists to the old and to the top plate or bearing wall at each end. To level the new joists, slip small wood blocks or shims beneath them as necessary.*

Then it's on to the plywood floor. Lay the sheets lengthwise across the joists; panel ends should meet midway over a joist for solid support. Stagger rows so that no two adjacent joints line up. Adding nailing blocks between joists or installing tongue-and-groove plywood strengthens edges.

a sturdy ladder or stairs, as well as a larger opening for lugging mattresses, dressers, and chairs up and in. If you'll be using the space frequently, you'll almost certainly want a fixed stairway.

Stairs or ladders adjoining a wall will be sturdier, safer, and less obtrusive than those placed further out in a room. Remember, though, that stairways are often required by code to have a minimum of 6½ feet of headroom, so a stair opening in the attic can't be tucked under the eaves.

The access opening. Here are the three rules for an attic opening: 1) the opening must be large enough for you and your storage to fit through without undue gymnastics; 2) you should have sufficient overhead clearance when you step up into the attic; and 3) the ladder or stairway should not interfere with traffic patterns or take up too much space below.

A door-size opening will admit most large storage. Width is the critical dimension, though. Homeowners with limited crawl spaces can make do with a push-up hatch smaller than door size.

Look for ways to provide attic access from out-of-the-way spots. If your garage is attached, you may be able to get into the attic from the garage. You could also remove the ceiling from a large closet, install a ladder, and convert a crawl space above into a "storage loft."

Ladders—fixed and fold-down. Fixed ladders and fold-down stairs are best for occasional traffic and light storage. Fold-down stairs, available from building suppliers or well-stocked hardware stores, swing up into the ceiling to close, leaving open floor space below; they also demand little clearance above. Their disadvantages: they usually provide no hand support and they lack stability. Look for a ladder with minimal bounce at the hinges.

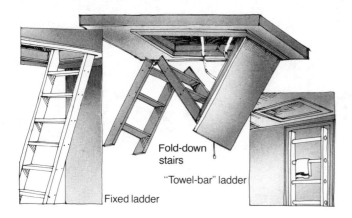

Fold-down stairs

"Towel-bar" ladder

Fixed ladder

Fixed ladders are more stable, especially when fastened to a wall. They range from traditional structures to door-mounted rungs that double as towel bars (see drawing above). In general, the heavier the intended use, the more sturdy the ladder should be. A ladder's biggest drawback is its steepness; it's difficult to climb up and down with full hands.

Planning your staircase. A well-crafted main staircase is a carpenter's showpiece, demanding the same attention to detail as fine cabinetry. But, an unadorned flight of attic utility stairs is much easier to build than it may look, and it doesn't require fancy materials or many tools. The key is in the planning.

First, consider your available space and the total rise and total run to be covered; then choose your basic stair type and dimensions accordingly. The three basic types, as shown below, are straight-run, "L"-type, and "U"-type. Straight-run stairs are the easiest and cheapest to build; L and U-types are better in tight spaces and for avoiding obstructions. Spiral or "winder" stairs, a fourth type, take up even less space, but they're awkward and dangerous for transporting storage goods up and down; some local codes ban their use altogether.

A typical stair assembly consists of stringers, risers, treads, and railings. Design factors, which are commonly subject to building codes, include riser height, tread depth, stair angle, and stair width. The drawing below illustrates the major elements. Check local codes for specific requirements in your area.

Stairways may be open or closed, or a combination of the two. Open sides should be equipped with handrails above vertical banisters or a solid side guard. On a closed side, a rail can be wall-mounted with metal brackets. Manufactured assemblies are common, but a 2 by 4 rail and supports are sufficient.

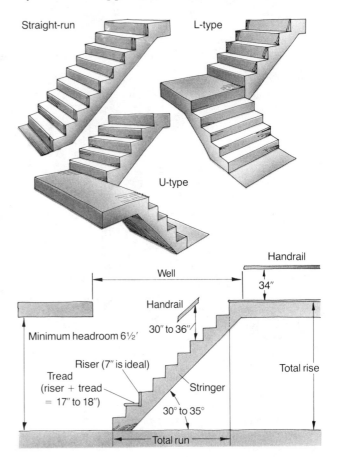

Straight-run

L-type

U-type

Handrail

Well

34"

Handrail

30" to 36"

Minimum headroom 6½'

Riser (7" is ideal)

Tread (riser + tread = 17" to 18")

Stringer

Total rise

30° to 35°

Total run

Basements

Getting on top of what's down under: ideas for dry storage

Like the Rock of Gibraltar, a basement should be an impregnable fortress, impervious to weather, water, and rodents. If your fortress is crumbling under the attack of any or all of these enemies, you're probably wondering how to guard your storage.

In the following pages, we show you how to solve moisture problems, whether from sweating pipes or outright leaks, and how to control basement temperatures by using insulation, heating, and air conditioning. Darkness—another common basement foe—can be overcome by the addition of new lights (the *Sunset* book *Basic Home Wiring Illustrated* tells how).

Depending on your needs, it may not be necessary to improve your entire basement. Instead, consider sectioning off an area with easy access and focus your best efforts there.

All kinds of storage units—closets, cabinets, shelves, and racks—have a place in the basement. You can use masonry fasteners to attach these and other accessories to brick and concrete walls. You may also want to install a combination of such units beneath the stairs.

Even if you don't have a basement, you might have a crawl space between the floor joists and the ground below. There are lots of possibilities—including further excavation—for utilizing this area.

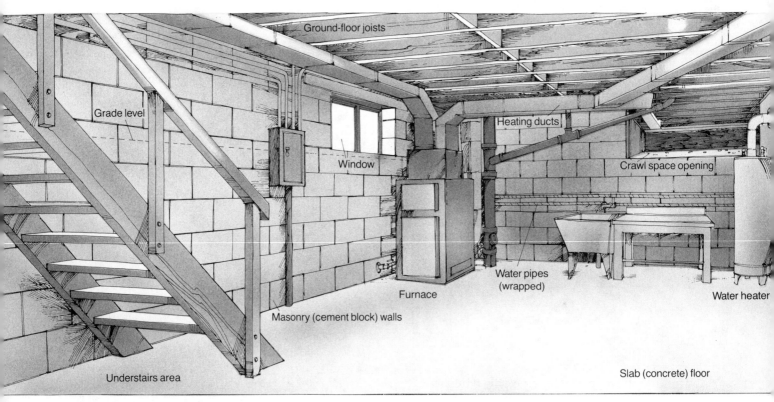

The view down under. *A full basement extends underneath an entire house, and reaches from the slab level to the first floor joists above. Foundation walls—commonly poured concrete or masonry blocks—form the perimeter. Basements are prone to seepage, condensation, and temperature problems, but once these are controlled, basement space is great for storage. Prime storage spots include along the walls, between overhead floor joists, and beneath stairs.*

A basement overview

A basement, loosely defined, is the area between the base of a house's foundation and the floor joists that support the living space above. In the case of a "full" basement, the concrete slab and foundation walls form an enclosed, defined room—but one usually left unimproved by the builders. A full basement has sufficient headroom for a livable space, usually 7½ feet.

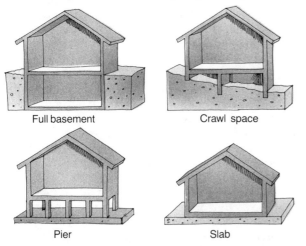

Full basement

Crawl space

Pier

Slab

In many newer homes, the foundation is made shallow to save money and labor, and perhaps to avoid problems with the underground water table. In such cases, only a minimal foundation wall extends above the footings, so basement space is greatly reduced. This kind of mini-basement, or *crawl space,* can still be very useful for storage (see page 79). Split level homes often have both a full basement and crawl space.

Exceptions to the usual basement scheme are pier and slab foundations (see drawing above). Slab foundations are unusable for storage. Pier foundations af-

ford some space, but it's open to the elements, insects, and animals—as well as theft. Hardy storables such as firewood would be fine here; for other types of storage in a pier foundation, use enclosed, lockable units (see "Carport storage ideas," page 66).

Simple basement storage solutions

What kind of storage can you create in your basement without going to very much trouble and expense? If you're lucky enough to have only minor moisture and pest problems, note the precautions that follow.

The structure of your basement may offer ready-to-use storage space: look underneath the stairs, overhead, and around and between ducts. With masonry fasteners you can attach shelves, hooks, and hangers to concrete or brick basement walls.

Moistureproof storage. Waterproofing or dehumidifying may be more expensive than it's worth if the moisture problem is minor and your storage hardy. For damp, unimproved basements, choose metal storage units instead of wood—metal won't swell and warp (though it might rust). Don't pile up containers—let air circulate around them. And don't install closets and cabinets on the floor or against an uninsulated masonry wall; instead, raise them 3 to 4 inches off the ground on a treated wooden base, and fur them out (see page 78) from the wall at least an inch. Heavy polyethylene sheeting placed below and behind storage is an added protection (see drawing below left).

If your basement is subject to occasional flooding or standing water, consider placing loose items on a makeshift raft to float through any unexpected deluge.

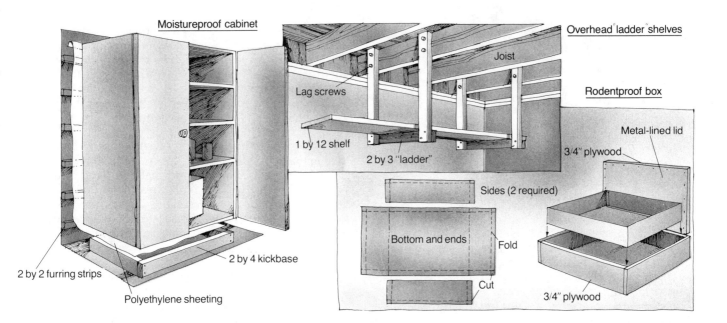

Moistureproof cabinet

Overhead "ladder" shelves

Lag screws

Joist

Rodentproof box

1 by 12 shelf

2 by 3 "ladder"

Metal-lined lid

3/4" plywood

Sides (2 required)

Bottom and ends

Fold

Cut

2 by 2 furring strips

2 by 4 kickbase

Polyethylene sheeting

3/4" plywood

Rodentproof storage. A basement with a dirt floor is a rat's delight. A good cement wall-and-slab foundation certainly helps keep rats and mice at bay. Most rodents enter through rotted sheathing (just above the foundation wall), dilapidated vent screens, and vent pipes; check these regularly. Metal containers, taped shut, or plywood boxes lined with sheet metal (see drawing on page 75) will keep rodents away from stored items.

Ideas for overhead storage. An unfinished basement is "roofed" with the floor joists and subfloor materials of the rooms above. The spaces between exposed joists, and the clearance between your head and the joists, are excellent for storing small goods. Pick spots that are free of girders, ducts, and wiring.

Nail plywood or boards across several joists to create overhead shelves; two strips in line make a rack. Shelves suspended with rope or chain or "ladder shelves" (see drawing on page 75) are easy to make.

Understairs storage. A frequently wasted space, the wedge-shaped area under stairs offers the space-conscious homeowner a place to build tailored shelves, roll-out bins, cupboards, or a closet. Straight-run stairs offer access from one or both sides; L or U-type stairs may provide several individual cubbyholes.

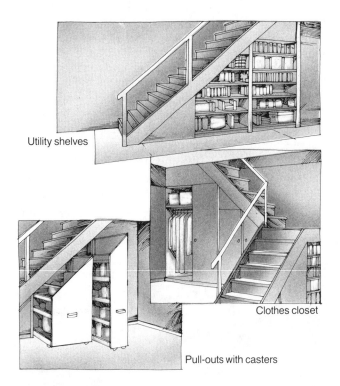

Utility shelves

Clothes closet

Pull-outs with casters

Attaching storage units to walls. If you've solved the moisture problem, basement walls are prime spots for shelving, pegboards, and hanging cabinets (see pages 6–11). It's easy if you have wood stud walls inside the foundation wall, because the units can be attached with standard woodscrews, nails, or lag screws. If you're fastening directly to masonry, see page 79.

Dealing with moisture and temperature

Here's a game plan for beating moisture buildup and temperature fluctuations, the major opponents of basement storage.

Moisture buildup

Correct diagnosis is the key to solving basement moisture problems, which range from the subtle drip of condensation to a running stream. Where does the water come from and how does it get in?

Most basement moisture problems are the result of improper drainage away from the house and foundation. When water builds up near the foundation, hydrostatic pressure eventually drives it to seep through or actually crack masonry walls or floors. Your best course of action is to prevent moisture buildup at the source. These are the most common culprits:
- *Clogged gutters* that concentrate water and cause overflow near the house walls.
- *Downspouts* that aren't connected to drainpipes or tiles to lead water away from the house.
- *Improper grading*—less than 1 inch of drop for each of the first 10 feet away from the house.
- *Flowerbeds* that pool and store water.
- *Window wells* around basement windows that lack drainage or proper caulking or weatherstripping.

· If you can actually *see* water leaking through your basement wall, you'll probably have to stem the flow of water at its source; see the preceding list and the drawing above right for pointers. The alternative is waterproofing the wall itself from the outside—a messy and costly job.

A serious flow of moisture can't simply be plugged up from inside the basement, but many minor ones can. Here's how:

Stopping seepage. Masonry sealers, primarily of Portland cement, chemical combinations, or both, are designed to stop seepage. Follow the manufacturer's instructions closely; most require a clean wall and two coats. The powder types, less convenient than the liquids, can be applied to a wet wall—which is, alas, often what you'll have to work with.

Stopping minor leaks. Common sites of leaks are between masonry blocks, in stress cracks, and where the foundation wall meets the floor slab. Portland cement—or heavy-duty patching mixtures containing Portland cement—can be pressed into a crack after it's been enlarged with a cold chisel. Again, follow the instructions provided by the manufacturer. Some compounds are formulated for use on active leaks.

Condensation occurs when humid interior air meets a colder surface—an outside wall or cold-water pipe. Sweating pipes are one tipoff; wrap them with insulating tape or special jackets and a vapor barrier. To test

Stopping the flow. *Basement water buildup can usually be traced to familiar outside problems.*

Be sure that gutters are adequate and in good condition. Downspout flow should be steered at least 10 feet from the house to drain or dry properly; provide drainage for window wells, too.

Flowerbeds that pool water next to the house should be moved, or at least sloped for a distance of 6 to 8 feet to hasten runoff; for proper grading in general, provide a drop of at least 1 inch for each of the first 10 feet away from the house.

Clogged gutter

Downspout flow

Window well

Flowerbeds

Improper grading

whether your problem is condensation or seepage, tightly tape a square of thin metal or aluminum foil to the foundation wall, and leave it for a few days. If moisture builds up on the wall side of the foil, it's seepage; on the basement side, condensation.

Insulating basement walls (page 78) will eliminate most condensation problems. Even opening a window helps. If the problem persists, the answer is often an electric dehumidifier. To be effective, a dehumidifier usually requires an air temperature of at least 60°.

The water table blues. At some level below the ground lurks the water table. Its depth varies with the topography, season, and soil, among other factors. An excavated basement may suddenly "fall" below the water table after a heavy rain, causing floor seepage or actual flooding. To find out if you're getting seepage from below, tape a small square of plastic to the basement floor. If the floor beneath the plastic is wet after a few days, seepage is occurring.

Water table problems are difficult to remedy. If the problem is slight, you can waterproof the floor and build a new floor above it (see pages 78–79), or simply elevate your storage units. If the problem is more severe, either embed perforated drain pipe around the perimeter of the floor (a laborious project) or install an automatic sump pump to at least handle flooding.

Temperature: the ups and downs

Ideally, most of your basement should be warm and dry, but you may want to plan some cooler space for a wine cellar—and if you're a gardener, you may be wishing for cool and even humid storage for root crops. Wall off a separate, insulated area—large or small—adjacent to an outside wall for your cold storage. Then heat the remaining basement space.

Cooling. Basically, you have two cooling options: natural and mechanical. Natural cooling takes advantage of outside air and ground temperatures to cool the air, and an insulated space to maintain the coolness. Construct a simple room on the basement's north or east side; insulate the new inside walls (see page 78 for tips on building and insulating walls) and the ceiling above the room to confine the cold air and to prevent warm air from entering. Vent the space to the outside (see food storage on pages 26–27, for details). A natural cooling system might involve a manually controlled vent with a thermostat you must regulate.

For food or wine storage, you may need a more reliable mechanical cooling system. Mechanical units include thermostat-controlled vent fans, window air conditioners, or even an old refrigerator (its door removed) recessed into an inside wall (otherwise, heat from coils would dilute the cooling effect). If the outside air temperature is above 40° for a significant part of the food storing season, or if you want to create a wine cellar in a climate with temperatures commonly above 60°, investigate mechanical means for cooling your basement.

Heating. Your basement or crawl space may already be heated—at least indirectly—by your house's central heating system. If not, check the system's capacity, and if possible run new ducts to the basement space. If you don't have a central heating system, consider an independent source of heat: a gas, electric, or kerosene heater, portable or built-in. See page 67 for more information.

Basic basement improvements

After you've conquered any moisture problems your basement might have, you can move on to other improvements that will make it weathertight for storage or multipurpose use—like a garage, a basement often doubles as a workshop, crafts studio, or laundry room. You'll find here the basic techniques for insulating and "furring out" masonry walls, and for building a subfloor. For more improvement ideas, see "Garages," especially pages 66–67.

Beefing up basement walls

Two basic ways to build up masonry walls (see drawing below) are with furring strips or standard 2 by 4 framing. Furring strips—2 by 2s or 1 by 3s—are attached directly to masonry walls with paneling adhesive, or with hammer or gun-driven masonry nails (see facing page). Walls built from 2 by 4s "float" in front of masonry walls—or can be positioned anywhere within the basement. They provide a better "dead" space for condensation control, as well as extra room for thicker insulation and for wiring. They are, however, more expensive and complicated to build than furring-strip walls. (See the drawing below for examples of both types.)

Types of insulation commonly used on basement walls include rigid polystyrene boards, fiberglass blankets, and fiberglass batts. If the insulation you choose doesn't include a vapor barrier (pages 70–71), add a complete layer of polyethylene (at least 2 mils thick) over the studs and insulation. Rigid board insulation and the vapor barriers on fiberglass types are flammable and should be covered with ½-inch gypsum wallboard or another fire-retardant material.

The soil itself is a good insulator. It's usually not necessary to insulate more than 2 feet below grade in many areas or below the frost line in others; check with your local building department.

High and dry basement floors

If you can't cure your cold, leaky basement floor, build another one above it (see drawing on facing page).

For the best results in problem cases, first cover the old slab with asphalt. Be sure to plug any floor drains. Floor framing of 1 by 4 sleepers (see drawing on facing page) is attached with masonry nails (see below right) to the slab. Add shims or wood blocks below the sleepers to level out a sloping or wavy floor. If your new floor is to be of plywood sheeting, be sure the sleepers are spaced on 16 or 24-inch centers. Insulation between sleepers is optional—it's not strictly necessary when the slab is below grade.

With the sleepers in place, spread 4-mil polyethylene sheeting (for a vapor barrier) over their tops, overlapping and taping all edges together. Next, add another layer of 1 by 4s above the first, "sandwiching" the sheeting. Then lay your subflooring— plywood or "1-by" floor boards (see page 72).

A simpler flooring job, if your slab is dry and level, entails brushing on a chemical sealer, then laying tiles —asphalt or vinyl-asbestos—directly on the slab.

Masonry fasteners

Fastening storage units, brackets, and structural framing to masonry is a challenge. Fortunately, a good selection of tried-and-true hardware and techniques is available. The composition of the wall or floor you're working with and the type of fixture to be attached determine what kind of fasteners you should use. Some tips: always attach fasteners to solid masonry, not to the mortar between segments; cement block foundations, because of their hollow construction, require toggle bolts or very short plugs; and always wear

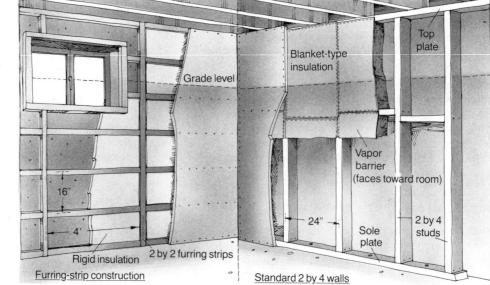

Two types of walls. *Furring-strip construction is less expensive and easier to build than standard 2 by 4 walls. The 2 by 4s provide better condensation control, though, and room for wiring and thicker insulation.*

Grade level

16"

4'

Rigid insulation

2 by 2 furring strips

Furring-strip construction

Top plate

Blanket-type insulation

Vapor barrier (faces toward room)

24"

Sole plate

2 by 4 studs

Standard 2 by 4 walls

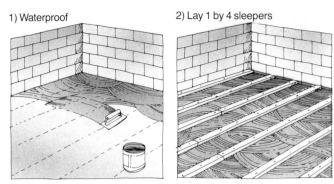

1) Waterproof

2) Lay 1 by 4 sleepers

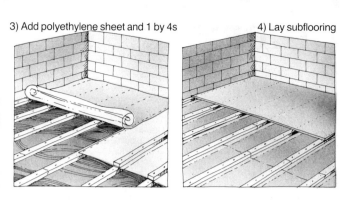

3) Add polyethylene sheet and 1 by 4s

4) Lay subflooring

Follow these four steps *to build a floor in your basement.*

safety glasses when drilling holes in masonry or driving masonry nails.

Expansion anchors include fiber and plastic plugs, and lead expansion shields and plugs. Use fiber or plastic plugs for lightweight installations, where you'd normally use woodscrews. Expansion shields, which secure lag bolts or machine screws, are for heavy jobs—hanging large shelf units or cabinets from walls, or anchoring the sole plate of a new wall to the floor.

All expansion anchors are installed in a similar manner. Drill a hole the diameter of, and slightly longer than, the plug in the wall or floor. Use either a star drill and hammer, or an electric drill equipped with a carbide-tipped bit. Tap the plug in. Insert the screw or bolt through the fixture to be attached, and drive it into the plug.

Masonry nails. Driven with a hammer or a .22-caliber cartridge-powered stud gun, masonry "cut" nails, pins, and studs are excellent where strength isn't critical, because they're simple to install. Use them for fastening furring strips to a masonry wall and for hanging lightweight brackets and accessories. Stud guns, commonly available for rent, can fire pins through a 2 by 4 sole plate into a concrete floor to anchor a wall.

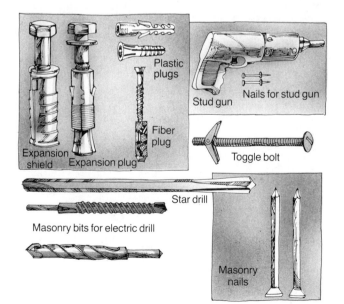

Plastic plugs

Stud gun

Nails for stud gun

Fiber plug

Expansion shield

Expansion plug

Toggle bolt

Star drill

Masonry bits for electric drill

Masonry nails

Toggle bolts. Hollow cement block foundation walls demand toggle bolts. Drill a hole in the wall just large enough for the wings (see drawing) to pass through when compressed. Thread the bolt through the fixture to be mounted, attach the wings, and slip the assembly through the hole. Once through, the wings will spring open, then pull up against the back of the wall when the bolt is tightened.

Crawl space improvements

Though you're desperate for storage space and lack a full basement, if you have a crawl space you may still be in luck. As long as you can negotiate at a crawl and sit up without bonking your head, the space is usable.

If your crawl space is less than 4½ feet deep—or in any case if it inspires feelings of claustrophobia—you'll need to enlarge it by excavating.

Access. If you need to provide entry to your crawl space from above, where is it convenient? An out-of-the-way kitchen pantry or a large hall closet, perhaps? A ladder or a steeply angled ladderlike set of stairs is your best route of descent. The door itself may be a simple trap or a larger double door.

Excavating can be messy as well as awkward, evoking memories of prison escape movies. For cement or asphalt surfaces, you'll need a pick, cement chisel, or jack. Excavate only the area you'll need, which could be as small as 3 feet deep and 5 feet square. Be careful that no water pipes or sewer lines are in the area—look over your house's plans before starting to dig.

If the water table rises above your excavation, you'll end up with a pool of water instead of a storage area. Check with the local building department for underground water levels in your area.

Flooring. A dirt floor can be left as is or covered with new cement, asphalt, sawdust, wood chips, pebbles, or plastic sheeting. A cement floor is framed with a wooden form, then poured using a shovel and wheelbarrow from above or inside (see the *Sunset* book *Basic Masonry Illustrated* for more detailed information). You can insert anchor bolts for stud frame walls in the cement while it's wet.

INDEX

COMBINED INDEX

A comprehensive index to all three volumes appears on the following pages. This is in addition to the individual book indexes which appear on page 80 of each title.

**KITCHEN
STORAGE**

**BEDROOM
& BATH
STORAGE**

**GARAGE, ATTIC
& BASEMENT
STORAGE**